What readers are saying about *Programming Groovy*

More than a tutorial on the Groovy language, *Programming Groovy* is an excellent resource for learning the advanced concepts of metaobject programming, unit testing with mocks, and DSLs. This is a must-have reference for any developer interested in learning to program dynamically.

► **Joe McTee**
Developer, JEKLsoft

Venkat does a fantastic job of presenting many of the advanced features of Groovy that make it so powerful. He is able to present those ideas in a way that developers will find very easy to internalize. This book will help Groovy developers take their kung fu to the next level. Great work, Venkat!

► **Jeff Brown**
Member, the Groovy and Grails development teams

At this point in my career, I am really tired of reading books that introduce languages. This volume was a pleasant breath of fresh air, however. Not only has Venkat successfully translated his engaging speaking style into a book, he has struck a good balance between introductory material and those aspects of Groovy that are new and exciting. Java developers will quickly grasp the relevant concepts without feeling like they are being insulted. Readers new to the platform will also be comfortable with the arc he presents.

► **Brian Sletten**
Zepheira, LLC

You simply won't find a more comprehensive resource for getting up to speed on Groovy metaprogramming.

► **Jason Rudolph**
Author, *Getting Started with Grails*

This book is an important step forward in mastering the language. Venkat takes the reader beyond simple keystrokes and syntax into the deep depths of "why?" Groovy brings a subtle sophistication to the Java platform that you didn't know was missing. Once you see those missing language features in action, you can't imagine how you ever programmed without them. As I read the book, I asked my own "why?" question over and over: "Why wasn't this book around when I was learning Groovy?" After you've read this book, it's difficult to look at programming on the Java platform the same way.

▶ **Scott Davis**
  Editor-in-Chief, aboutGroovy.com; author of *Groovy Recipes*

Venkat neatly dissects the Groovy language—a language that is far more than just "Java++"—in nice, edible chunks for the Groovy programmer to consume. If you're a Java programmer and you're trying to figure out why everybody is getting all excited about dynamic languages on top of the Java Virtual Machine, look no further than Venkat's book.

▶ **Ted Neward**
  Java/.NET/XML services, http://www.tedneward.com

Despite signs to the contrary, Java isn't dead—it's just evolving. Today's developer needs a dynamic language like Groovy in their toolkit, and Venkat does a tremendous job presenting this exciting new addition to the JVM. With all of his examples, you'll be up and running in no time!

▶ **Nathaniel T. Schutta**
  Author/Speaker/Teacher

I am always on the lookout for good books on the metaprogramming features of languages, and Groovy finally has one. Part 3 of Venkat's book is devoted entirely to Groovy's metaprogramming features. Sweet. I won't tell you which language to use, but if you are considering Groovy, read Part 3 of this book.

▶ **Stuart Halloway**
  CEO, Relevance, Inc.
  www.thinkrelevance.com

This is a very well-written guide to Groovy. It's an easy read, completely devoid of fluff, that will get you on the path to Groovy goodness right out of the gate.

▶ **David Geary**
Author, Clarity Training, Inc.

Venkat could make rocket science sound easy. He definitely makes Groovy for Java developers sound easy.

▶ **Erik Weibust**
Senior Architect, Credera

Programming Groovy

Dynamic Productivity for the Java Developer

Programming Groovy

Dynamic Productivity for the Java Developer

Venkat Subramaniam

The Pragmatic Bookshelf
Raleigh, North Carolina   Dallas, Texas

Many of the designations used by manufacturers and sellers to distinguish their products are claimed as trademarks. Where those designations appear in this book, and The
Pragmatic Programmers, LLC was aware of a trademark claim, the designations have
been printed in initial capital letters or in all capitals. The Pragmatic Starter Kit, The
Pragmatic Programmer, Pragmatic Programming, Pragmatic Bookshelf and the linking *g*
device are trademarks of The Pragmatic Programmers, LLC.

Every precaution was taken in the preparation of this book. However, the publisher
assumes no responsibility for errors or omissions, or for damages that may result from
the use of information (including program listings) contained herein.

Our Pragmatic courses, workshops, and other products can help you and your team
create better software and have more fun. For more information, as well as the latest
Pragmatic titles, please visit us at

http://www.pragprog.com

ISBN-10: 1-934356-09-3

ISBN-13: 978-1-934356-09-8

Printed on acid-free paper with 50% recycled, 15% post-consumer content.

P1.0 printing, March 2008

Version: 2008-3-21

எவ்வ துறைவது உலகம் உலகத்தோடு
அவ்வ துறைவ தறிவு.
                                    திருக்குறள்—426

"As moves the world, to move in tune with

changing times and ways is wisdom"

— Thiruvalluvar, Poet and Philosopher, 31 B.C.

(Verse 426 from Thirukural, a collection of 1330 noble couplets)

Contents

Foreword

Back in 2003, when we started Groovy, our goal was to provide Java developers with an additional language to complement Java, a new Swiss Army knife to add to their tool belt. Java is a great language and a wonderful platform, but sometimes you need the agility and expressiveness of scripting languages or, even better, dynamic languages. We didn't want a new language that would be a paradigm shift for Java developers. Instead, Groovy was made to seamlessly integrate with Java in all possible ways while at the same time adding all the goodies you would expect from a dynamic language. The best of both worlds! You don't even have to wait for Java 7, 8, or 9 to get all the nuggets you'd want to have in your next programming language of choice: closures, properties, native syntax for lists, maps, and regular expressions. Everything is already there.

Over the course of time, Groovy has matured a lot and has become a very successful open source dynamic language used by tons of Java developers and by big companies that embed it in their applications servers or their mission-critical applications. Groovy lets you write more expressive unit tests and simplifies XML parsing or SQL data imports, and for your mundane tasks, there's a scripting solution perfectly integrated with your Java ecosystem. When you need to extend your application to customize it to your needs, you can also integrate Groovy at specific points by injecting Groovy scripts. Thanks to Groovy's malleable syntax, you can even create domain-specific languages fairly easily to represent business rules that even end users can author.

Now, step back a little. At first sight, despite the marketing taint of the previous paragraphs, it sounds great, and you probably see a few places where you'd definitely need to use such a versatile tool. But it's just something else you have to learn to be able to leverage it to its fullest extent, right? You're a Java developer, so do you fear it's going to be difficult to get the best out of it without wasting too much of your time and energy?

Fortunately, this book is right for you. Venkat will guide you through Groovy and its marvels. Without being a boring encyclopedia, this book covers a lot of ground. And in a matter of hours (well, in fact, just the time to read the book), you'll be up to speed, and you'll see how Groovy was made by Java developers for Java developers. You won't regret your journey, and you'll be able to keep this book on your desk for reference or for finding new creative ways to solve the problem of the day.

Guillaume Laforge (Groovy project manager)
February 5, 2008

Chapter 1

Introduction

As a busy Java developer, you're constantly looking for ways to be more productive, right? You're probably willing to take all the help you can get from the platform and tools available to you. When I wax poetic about the "strength of Java," I'm not talking about the language or its syntax. It's the Java platform that has become more capable and more performant. To reap the benefit of the platform and to tackle the inherent complexities of your applications, you need another tool—one with a dynamic and metaprogramming capabilities. Java—the language—has been flirting with that idea for a while and will support these features to various degrees in future versions. However, you don't have to wait for that day. You can build performant Java applications with all the dynamic capabilities today, right now, using Groovy.

1.1 Why Dynamic Languages?

Dynamic languages have the ability to extend a program at runtime, including changing the structure of objects, types, and behavior. Dynamic languages allow you to do things at runtime that static languages do at compile time; they allow you to execute program statements that were created on the fly at runtime.

For example, if you want to get the date five days from now, you can write this:

```
5.days.from.now
```

Yes, that's your friendly java.lang.Integer chirping dynamic behavior in Groovy, as you'll learn later in this book.

The flexibility offered by dynamic languages gives you the advantage of evolving your application as it executes. You are probably familiar with code generation and code generation tools. I consider code generation to be soooo 20th century. In fact, generated code is like an incessant itch on your back; if you keep scratching it, it turns into a sore. With dynamic languages, there are better ways. I prefer *code synthesis*, which is in-memory code creation at runtime. Dynamic languages make it easy to "synthesize code." The code is synthesized based on the flow of logic through your application and becomes active "just in time."

By carefully applying these capabilities of dynamic languages, you can be more productive as an application developer. This higher productivity means you can easily create higher levels of abstractions in shorter amounts of time. You can also use a smaller, yet more capable, set of developers to create applications. In addition, greater productivity means you can create parts of your application quickly and get feedback from your fellow developers, testers, domain experts, and customer representatives. And all this leads to greater agility.[1]

Dynamic languages have been around for a long time, so you may be asking, why is now a great time to get excited about them? I can answer that with four reasons:[2]

- Machine speed
- Availability
- Awareness of unit testing
- Killer applications

Let's discuss each of these reasons for getting excited about dynamic languages, starting with machine speed. Doing at runtime what other languages do at compile time first raises the concern of the speed of dynamic languages. Furthermore, interpreting code at runtime rather than simply executing compiled code adds to that concern. Fortunately, machine speed has consistently increased over the years—handhelds have more computing and memory power today than what large computers had decades ago. Tasks that were quite unimaginable using a

---

1. Tim O'Reilly observes the following about developing web applications: "Rather than being finished paintings, they are sketches, continually being redrawn in response to new data." He also makes the point that dynamic languages are better suited for these in "Why Scripting Languages Matter" (see Appendix A, on page 287).
2. A fifth reason is the ability to run dynamic languages on the JVM, but that came much later.

1980s processor are easy to achieve today. The performance concerns of dynamic languages are greatly eased because of processor speeds and other improvements in our field, including better just-in-time compilation techniques.

Now let's talk about availability. The Internet and active "public" community-based development have made recent dynamic languages easily accessible and available. Developers can now easily download languages and tools and play with them. They can even participate in community forums to influence the evolution of these languages.[3] This is leading to greater experimentation, learning, and adaptation of languages than in the past.

Now it's time to talk about the awareness of unit testing. Most dynamic languages are dynamically typed. The types are often inferred based on the context. There are no compilers to flag type-casting violations at compile time. Since quite a bit of code may be synthesized and your program can be extended at runtime, you can't simply rely upon coding-time verification alone. Writing code in dynamic languages requires a greater discipline from the testing point of view. Over the past few years, we've seen greater awareness among programmers (though not sufficiently greater adoption yet) in the area of testing in general and unit testing in particular. Most of the programmers who have taken advantage of these dynamic languages for commercial application development have also embraced testing and unit testing.[4]

Finally, let's discuss the fourth bullet point listed earlier. Many developers have in fact been using dynamic languages for decades. However, for the majority of the industry to be excited about them, we had to have killer applications—those compelling stories to share with your developers and managers. That tipping point, for Ruby in particular and for dynamic languages in general, came in the form of Rails ([TH05], [SH07], [Tat06]). Rails showed struggling web developers how they could quickly develop applications using the dynamic capabilities of Ruby. Along the same vein came Grails built using Groovy and Java, Django built using Python, and Lift built using Scala, to mention a few.

---

3. The Groovy users mailing list is very active, with constant discussions from passionate users expressing opinions, ideas, and criticisms on current and future features. Visit http://groovy.codehaus.org/Mailing+Lists and http://groovy.markmail.org if you don't believe me.
4. "Legacy code is simply code without tests." —Michael C. Feathers [Fea04]

These frameworks have caused enough stir in the development community to make the industry-wide adoption of dynamic languages a highly probable event in the near future.

I find that dynamic languages, along with metaprogramming capabilities, make simple things simpler and harder things manageable. You still have to deal with the inherent complexity of your application, but dynamic languages let you focus your effort where it's deserved. When I got into Java (after years of C++), features such as reflection, a good set of libraries, and evolving framework support made me productive. The JVM, to a certain extent, provided me with the ability to take advantage of metaprogramming. However, I had to use something in addition to Java to tap into that potential—heavyweight tools such as AspectJ. Like several other productive programmers, I found myself left with two options. The first option was to use the exceedingly complex and not-so-flexible Java along with heavyweight tools. The second option was to move on to using dynamic languages such as Ruby that are object-oriented and have metaprogramming capability built in (for instance, it takes only a couple of lines of code to do AOP in Ruby and Groovy). A few years ago, taking advantage of dynamic capabilities and metaprogramming and being productive at the same time meant leaving behind the Java platform. (After all, you use these features to be productive and can't let them slow you down, right?) That is not the case anymore. Languages such as Groovy and JRuby are dynamic and run on the JVM. They allow you to take full advantage of both the rich Java platform and dynamic language capabilities.

1.2 What's Groovy?

Groovy[5] is a lightweight, low-ceremony, dynamic, object-oriented language that runs on the JVM. Groovy is open sourced under Apache License, version 2.0. It derives strength from different languages such as Smalltalk, Python, and Ruby while retaining a syntax familiar to Java programmers. Groovy compiles into Java bytecode and extends the Java API and libraries. It runs on Java 1.4 or newer. For deployment, all you need is a Groovy JAR in addition to your regular Java stuff, and you're all set.

---

5. Merriam-Webster defines Groovy as "marvelous, wonderful, excellent, hip, trendy."

I like to define Groovy as "a language that has been reborn several times."[6] James Strachan and Bob McWhirter started it in 2003, and it was commissioned into Java Specification Request (JSR 241) in March 2004. Soon after, it was almost abandoned because of various difficulties and issues. Guillaume Laforge and Jeremy Rayner decided to rekindle the efforts and bring Groovy back to life. Their first effort was to fix bugs and stabilize the language features. The uncertainty lingered on for a while. I know a number of people (committers and users) who simply gave up on the language at one time. Finally, a group of smart and enthusiastic developers joined force with Guillaume and Jeremy, and a vibrant developer community emerged. JSR version 1 was announced in August 2005.

Groovy version 1.0 release was announced on January 2, 2007. It was encouraging to see that, well before it reached 1.0, Groovy was put to use on commercial projects in a handful of organizations in the United States and Europe. In fact, I've seen growing interest in Groovy in conferences and user groups around the world. Several organizations and developers are beginning to use Groovy at various levels on their projects, and I think the time is ripe for major Groovy adoption in the industry. Groovy version 1.5 was released on December 7, 2007.

Grails ([Roc06], [Rud07]),[7] built using Groovy and Java, is a dynamic web development framework based on "coding by convention." It allows you to quickly build web applications on the JVM using Groovy, Spring, Hibernate, and other Java frameworks.

1.3 Why Groovy?

As a Java programmer, you don't have to switch completely to a different language. Trust me, Groovy feels like the Java language you already know with but with a few augmentations.

There are dozens of scripting languages[8] that can run on the JVM, such as Groovy, JRuby, BeanShell, Scheme, Jaskell, Jython, JavaScript, etc. The list could go on and on. Your language choice should depend on a number of criteria: your needs, your preferences, your background, the projects you work with, your corporate technical environment, and so

---

6. See "A bit of Groovy history," a blog by Guillaume Laforge at http://glaforge.free.fr/weblog/index.php?itemid=99.
7. See Jason Rudolph's "Getting Started with Grails" in Appendix A, on page 287.
8. https://scripting.dev.java.net

on. In this section, I will discuss whether Groovy is the *right* language for you.

As a programmer, I am shameless about languages. I can comfortably program in about eight structured, object-oriented, and functional programming languages and can come dangerously close to writing code in a couple more. In any given year, I actively code in about two to three languages at least. So, if one thing, I am pretty unbiased when it comes to choosing a language—I will pick the one that works the best for a given situation. I am ready to change to another language with the ease of changing a shirt, if that is the right thing to do, that is.

Groovy is an attractive language for a number of reasons:

- It has a flat learning curve.

- It follows Java semantics.

- It bestows dynamic love.

- It extends the JDK.

I'll now expand on these reasons. First, you can take almost any Java code[9] and run it as Groovy. The significant advantage of this is a flat learning curve. You can start writing code in Groovy and, if you're stuck, simply switch gears and write the Java code you're familiar with. You can later refactor that code and make it groovier.

For example, Groovy understands the traditional for loop. So, you can write this:

```
// Java Style
for(int i = 0; i < 10; i++)
{
        //...
}
```

As you learn Groovy, you can change that to the following code or one of the other flavors for looping in Groovy (don't worry about the syntax right now; after all, you're just getting started, and very soon you'll be a pro at it):

```
10.times {
        //...
}
```

---

9. See Section 3.8, *Gotchas*, on page 55 for known problem areas.

Second, when programming in Groovy, you can expect almost everything you expect in Java. Groovy classes extend the same good old java.lang.Object—Groovy classes are Java classes. The OO paradigm and Java semantics are preserved, so when you write expressions and statements in Groovy, you already know what those mean to you as a Java programmer.

Here's a little example to show you that Groovy classes *are* Java classes:

Introduction/UseGroovyClass.groovy

```
println XmlParser.class
println XmlParser.class.superclass
```

If you run groovy UseGroovyClass, you'll get the following output:

```
class groovy.util.XmlParser
class java.lang.Object
```

Now let's talk about the third reason to love Groovy. Groovy is dynamic, and it is optionally typed. If you've enjoyed the benefits of other dynamic languages such as Smalltalk, Python, JavaScript, and Ruby, you can realize those in Groovy. If you had looked at Groovy 1.0 support for metaprogramming, it probably left you desiring for more. Groovy has come a long way since 1.0, and Groovy 1.5 has pretty decent metaprogramming capabilities.

For instance, if you want to add the method isPalindrome() to String—a method that tells whether a word spells the same forward and backward—you can add that easily with only a couple lines of code (again, don't try to figure out all the details of how this works right now; you have the rest of the book for that):

Introduction/Palindrome.groovy

```
String.metaClass.isPalindrome = {->
  delegate == delegate.reverse()
}

word = 'tattarrattat'
println "$word is a palindrome? ${word.isPalindrome()}"
word = 'Groovy'
println "$word is a palindrome? ${word.isPalindrome()}"
```

The following output shows how the previous code works:

```
tattarrattat is a palindrome? true
Groovy is a palindrome? false
```

Finally, as a Java programmer, you rely heavily on the JDK and the API to get your work done. These are still available in Groovy. In addition,

Groovy extends the JDK with convenience methods and closure support through the GDK. Here's a quick example of an extension in GDK to the java.util.ArrayList class:

```
lst = ['Groovy', 'is', 'hip']
println lst.join(' ')
println lst.getClass()
```

The output from the previous code confirms that you're still working with the JDK but that you used the Groovy-added join() method to concatenate the elements in the ArrayList:

```
Groovy is hip
class java.util.ArrayList
```

You can see how Groovy takes the Java you know and augments it. If your project team is familiar with Java, if they're using it for most of your organization's projects, and if you have a lot of Java code to integrate and work with, then you will find that Groovy is a nice path toward productivity gains.

1.4 What's in This Book?

This book is about programming using the Groovy language. I make no assumptions about your knowledge of Groovy or dynamic languages, although I do assume you are familiar with Java and the JDK. Throughout this book, I will walk you through the concepts of the Groovy language, presenting you with enough details and a number of examples to illustrate the concepts. My objective is for you to get proficient with Groovy by the time you put this book down, after reading a substantial portion of it, of course.

The rest of this book is organized as follows:

The book has has three parts: "Beginning Groovy," "Using Groovy," and "MOPping Groovy."

In the chapters in Part 1, "Beginning Groovy," I focus on the whys and whats of Groovy—those fundamentals that'll help you get comfortable with general programming in Groovy. Since I assume you're familiar with Java, I don't spend any time with programming basics, like what an if statement is or how to write it. Instead, I take you directly to the similarities of Groovy and Java and topics that are specific to Groovy.

In the chapters in Part 2, "Using Groovy," I focus on how to use Groovy for everyday coding—working with XML, accessing databases, and working with multiple Java/Groovy classes and scripts—so you can put Groovy to use right away for your day-to-day tasks. I also discuss the Groovy extensions and additions to the JDK so you can take advantage of both the power of Groovy and the JDK at the same time.

In the chapters in Part 3, "MOPping Groovy," I focus on the metaprogramming capabilities of Groovy. You'll see Groovy really shine in these chapters and learn how to take advantage of its dynamic nature. You'll start with the fundamentals of MetaObject Protocol (MOP), learn how to do aspect-oriented programming (AOP) such as operations in Groovy, and learn about dynamic method/property discovery and dispatching. Then you'll apply those right away to creating and using builders and domain-specific languages (DSLs). Unit testing is not only necessary in Groovy because of its dynamic nature, but it is also easier to do—you can use Groovy to unit test your Java and Groovy code, as you'll see in this part of the book.

Here's what's in each chapter:

Part 1: "Beginning Groovy"

In Chapter 2, *Getting Started*, on page 17, you'll download and install Groovy and take it for a test-drive right away using groovysh and groovy-Console. You'll also learn how to run Groovy without these tools—from the command line and within your IDEs.

In Chapter 3, *Groovy for the Java Eyes*, on page 25, you'll start with familiar Java code and refactor that to Groovy. After a quick tour of Groovy features that improve your everyday Java coding, you'll learn about Groovy's support for Java 5 features. Groovy follows Java semantics, except in places it does not—you'll also learn gotchas that'll help avoid surprises.

In Chapter 4, *Dynamic Typing*, on page 63, you'll see how Groovy's typing is similar and different from Java's typing, what Groovy really does with the type information you provide, and when to take advantage of dynamic typing vs. optional typing. You'll also learn how to take advantage of Groovy's dynamic typing, design by capability, and multi-methods.

In Chapter 5, *Using Closures*, on page 81, you'll learn all about the exciting Groovy feature called *closures*, including what they are, how they work, and when and how to use them.

In Chapter 6, *Working with Strings*, on page 101, you'll learn about Groovy strings, working with multiline strings, and Groovy's support for regular expressions.

In Chapter 7, *Working with Collections*, on page 115, you'll explore Groovy's support for Java collections—lists and maps. You'll learn various convenience methods on collections, and after this chapter, you'll never again want to use your collections the old way.

Part 2: "Using Groovy"

Groovy embraces and extends the JDK. You'll explore the GDK and learn the extensions to Object and other Java classes in Chapter 8, *Exploring the GDK*, on page 133.

Groovy has pretty good support for working with XML, including parsing and creating XML documents, as you'll see in Chapter 9, *Working with XML*, on page 147.

Chapter 10, *Working with Databases*, on page 157 presents Groovy's SQL support, which will make your database-related programming easy and fun. In this chapter, you'll learn about iterators, datasets, and how to perform regular database operations using simpler syntax and closures. I'll also show how to get data from Microsoft Excel documents.

One of the key strengths of Groovy is the integration with Java. In Chapter 11, *Working with Scripts and Classes*, on page 165, you'll learn ways to closely interact with multiple Groovy scripts, Groovy classes, and Java classes from within your Groovy and Java code.

Part 3: "MOPping Groovy"

Metaprogramming is one of the biggest benefits of dynamic languages and Groovy; it has the ability to inspect classes at runtime and dynamically dispatch method calls. You'll explore Groovy's support for metaprogramming in Chapter 12, *Exploring Meta-Object Protocol (MOP)*, on page 179, beginning with the fundamentals of how Groovy handles method calls to Groovy objects and Java objects.

Groovy allows you to perform AOP-like method interceptions using GroovyInterceptable and ExpandoMetaClass, as you'll see in Chapter 13, *Intercepting Methods Using MOP*, on page 189.

In Chapter 14, *MOP Method Injection and Synthesis*, on page 197, you'll dive into Groovy metaprogramming capabilities that allow you to inject and synthesize methods at runtime.

In Chapter 15, *MOPping Up*, on page 219, you will learn how to synthesize classes dynamically, how to use metaprogramming to delegate method calls, and how to choose between different metaprogramming techniques you've learned in the previous three chapters.

Unit testing is not a luxury or a "if-we-have-time" practice in Groovy. The dynamic nature of Groovy requires unit testing, and fortunately, at the same time, it facilitates writing tests and creating mock objects, as you'll learn in Chapter 16, *Unit Testing and Mocking*, on page 229. You will learn techniques that will help you use Groovy to unit test your Java code and Groovy code.

Groovy builders are specialized classes that help you build internal DSLs for a nested hierarchy. You can learn how to use them and to create your own builders in Chapter 17, *Groovy Builders*, on page 255.

You can apply Groovy's metaprogramming capabilities to build internal DSLs using the techniques you'll learn in Chapter 18, *Creating DSLs in Groovy*, on page 273. You'll start by learning about DSLs, including their characteristics, and quickly jump in to build them in Groovy.

Finally, Appendix A, on page 287 and Appendix B, on page 293, gather together all the references to web articles and books cited throughout this book.

1.5 Who Is This Book For?

This book is for developers working on the Java platform. It is better suited for programmers (and testers) who understand the Java language fairly well. Other developers who understand programming in other languages can use this book as well, but they should supplement it with books that provide them with an in-depth understanding of Java and the JDK.

Programmers who are somewhat familiar with Groovy can use this book to learn some tips and tricks of the language that they may not otherwise have the opportunity to explore. Finally, those already familiar with Groovy may find this book useful for training or coaching fellow developers in their organizations.

1.6 Acknowledgments

Writing a book is like writing a screenplay—a lot of things are added, changed, and deleted from the original manuscript. What you're holding in your hand is a work I started, but a number of people helped get it into its current form. If you find this book useful and interesting, it was a result of a collective effort. Any mistakes you find are my own—I take responsibility for those.

First, I thank Daniel Steinberg for editing this book. His command of the subject, attention to the detail, patience, and real-time response[10] were instrumental to the quality and record-time completion of this book. I call his edits "immense quality at Internet speed."

I thank Dave Thomas, Andy Hunt, Steve Peter, Kim Wimpsett, and the rest of the Pragmatic team who worked behind the scenes to get this book published. The Pragmatic Bookshelf's writing process is agile, and I can't imagine writing a book any other way without the simple yet effective tools, facilities, and practices they've created.

I had the privilege of a number of Groovy and Grails committers reviewing this book. I thank Alexandru Popescu, Dierk Konig, Graeme Rocher, Guillaume Laforge, Jason Rudolph, Jeff Brown, John Wilson, and Russel Winder for their valuable input, corrections, and clarifications. I also thank the other Groovy committers and community for their help through the Groovy users mailing list—for answering my questions, explaining things I didn't understand, and quickly fixing the bugs I found.

I thank Brian Sletten, David Geary, Joe McTee, Nathaniel Schutta, Scott Davis, Scott Leberknight, and Stuart Halloway for taking time away from their extremely busy schedules to review this book and offer their valuable input.

I also thank the developers who purchased this book in the beta form. You started giving feedback within 24 hours of the release of the beta book! Thank you Adam Rinehart, Alan Thompson, Frederic Jean, John Loizeaux, Kevin Hutchinson, Richard Boreiko, Tim Hennekey, and Todd W. Crone for your feedback, suggestions, and corrections.

I thank those wonderful developers who have endured my training, conference presentations, and podcasts. The questions you asked, your genuine interest, and your constructive feedback were very helpful— you gave me confidence and encouraged me to continue writing.

---

10. I was surprised when I checked in a chapter around 6 a.m. on a Sunday and got high-quality feedback from Dan within a couple of hours.

I thank Jay Zimmerman for giving me the opportunity to present a number of these concepts at the No Fluff Just Stuff conferences (http://www.nofluffjuststuff.com) around the world and for creating a community of exceptional speakers and developers.

Special thanks to the NFJS opinionated geeks—excuse me, I mean my friends and fellow speakers—who I meet several weekends each year for their friendship, passion, opinions, and discussions on various topics. Where else do you find guys who argue checked vs. unchecked exceptions for three hours in a London restaurant and then some back at the hotel?

Writing this book would not even have been imaginable without my wife's encouragement, support, and sacrifice. She has been too generous to me over the past several years, especially when I disappeared while writing this book. Thank you, Kavitha, for giving me the wings. My sincere thanks to my sons, Karthik and Krupakar, for being so kind and understanding—you guys are my inspiration.

Part I

Beginning Groovy

Chapter 2

Getting Started

You're probably eager to crank out some Groovy code, right? Well, first you need to get Groovy installed. In this chapter, I'll show you how to quickly install Groovy and make sure everything is working well on your system. Taking care of these basics now will help you move quickly to the fun things ahead.

2.1 Getting Groovy

Getting a stable working copy of Groovy is really simple: just visit the Groovy home page at http://groovy.codehaus.org, and click the Download link. You can download either the binary release or the source release. Download the source release if you want to build Groovy locally on your box or you want to explore the source code. Otherwise, I recommend you download the binary release. (If you're on Windows, you can also get the Windows Installer version, though I find it more fulfilling to get the binary release and set up the necessary path myself.) While you're there, you may also want to grab the documentation for Groovy.

If you're like some of the programmers on the Groovy users mailing list, the previously mentioned releases will not suffice. If you want the latest drop of the evolving language implementation, visit http://build. canoo.com/groovy/. Once there, click the Build Artifacts link and then the Deliverables link. Next, pick the binary or source version as you desire.

You also need—and you most likely already have—the JDK 1.4 or newer (see http://java.sun.com/javase/downloads/index.jsp). I recommend at least JDK 1.5 if you want to enjoy the Java 5 features supported in Groovy.

Finally, make sure to confirm that you have Java installed on your system.

2.2 Installing Groovy

Let's get Groovy installed. In the following sections, I'm assuming you've downloaded the Groovy 1.5.4 binary distribution and have already installed the JDK (Section 2.1, *Getting Groovy*, on the preceding page).

Installing Groovy on Windows

If you have the one-click installer for Windows, run it, and follow the instructions.

If you downloaded the binary distribution package, unzip it. Move the groovy-1.5.4 directory to a desired location.[1] For instance, on my Windows system, I have it in the C:\programs\groovy directory.

The next step is to set the GROOVY_HOME environment variable and the path. Edit your system environment variables (by going into Control Panel and opening the System application). Create an environment variable named GROOVY_HOME, and set it to the location of your Groovy directory (for example, I set it to C:\programs\groovy\groovy-1.5.4). Also, add %GROOVY_HOME%\bin to the path environment variable to set the location of the Groovy bin directory in the path. Remember to separate directories in your path using a semicolon (;).

Next, confirm that the environment variable JAVA_HOME is pointing to the location of your JDK directory (if it's not present, set it).

That's pretty much all you have to do. Remember to close any open command window, because the changes to environment variables don't take effect until you reopen command windows. In a new command window, type groovy -v, and make sure it reports version 1.5.4.

Installing Groovy on Unix-like Systems

Unzip the binary distribution you downloaded.[2] Move the groovy-1.5.4 directory to a desired location. For instance, on my Mac system, I have it in the /opt/groovy directory.

---

1. Since path names with whitespace often cause grief, I recommend a path with no whitespace in its name.
2. Check http://groovy.codehaus.org/Download if there are special distributions and instructions for your flavor of Unix.

The next step is to set the GROOVY_HOME environment variable and the path. Depending on the shell you use, you have to edit different profile files. You probably know where to go—refer to the appropriate documentation if you need help figuring out what to edit. I use bash, so I edited the ~/.bash_profile file. In that file, I added an entry export GROOVY_HOME="/opt/groovy/groovy-1.5.4" to set the environment variable GROOVY_HOME. Also add $GROOVY_HOME/bin to the path environment variable.

Next, confirm that the environment variable JAVA_HOME is pointing to the location of your JDK directory (if it's not present, set it). ls -l `which java` should help you determine the location of your Java installation.

That's pretty much all you have to do. Remember to close any open terminal windows because changes to environment variables don't take effect until you reopen the windows.[3] In a new terminal window, type the command groovy -v, and make sure it reports version 1.5.4. That's all there is to it!

2.3 Test-Drive Using groovysh

OK, you've installed Groovy and checked the version—it's time to take it for a test-drive. The quickest way to play with Groovy is to use the command-line tool groovysh. Open a terminal window, and type groovysh; you'll see a shell as shown in Figure 2.1, on the next page. Go ahead and type some Groovy statements to see how it works.

groovysh is a good tool for interactively trying out small Groovy code examples. It is also useful for experimenting with some code while you're in the middle of coding.[4] The groovysh command compiles and executes completed statements as soon as you hit the Enter/Return key, and it prints the result of that statement execution along with any output from the execution.

If you type Math.sqrt(16), for example, it prints the result 4.0. However, if you type println 'Test drive Groovy', it prints the words in quotes followed by null—indicating that println() returned nothing.

---

3. If you like, you can source your profile file instead, but launching another terminal window is darn cheap, so why bother?
4. Be aware, however, that groovysh has some idiosyncrasies. If you run into problems with it, use the save command to save the code to a file and then try running from the command line using the groovy command to get around any tool-related issues.

```
->groovysh
Groovy Shell (1.5.4, JVM: 1.6.0_01-41-release)
Type 'help' or '\h' for help.
-----------------------------------------------------------------
groovy:000> Math.sqrt(16)
===> 4.0
groovy:000> println 'Test drive Groovy'
Test drive Groovy
===> null
groovy:000> String.metaClass.isPalindrome = {-> ;
groovy:001>    delegate == delegate.reverse()
groovy:002> }
===> groovysh_evaluate$_run_closure1@a08feeb
groovy:000> 'mom'.isPalindrome()
===> true
groovy:000> exit
->
```

Figure 2.1: USING THE GROOVYSH COMMAND-LINE TOOL

You can also type code that spans multiple lines—simply use a semi-colon at the end of the line if it complains, as I've done in the line defining the dynamic method isPalindrome(). When you type a class, a method, or even an if statement, groovysh has to wait until you finish in order to execute that code. You'll see that it tells you how many lines it has accumulated for execution next to the groovy: prompt.

Type help to get a list of supported commands. You can use the up arrow to view commands you have already typed, which is useful for repeating statements or commands. It even remembers commands you typed from previous invocations.

When you're done, type exit to exit from the tool.

2.4 Using groovyConsole

If you're not a command-line person and instead prefer a GUI, Groovy has got you covered—simply double-click groovyConsole.bat in Windows Explorer (you'll find it in the %GROOVY_HOME%\bin directory). Users of Unix-like systems can double-click the groovyConsole executable script using their favorite file/directory-browsing tool. A console GUI will pop up, as shown in Figure 2.2, on the facing page.

Go ahead and type some Groovy code in the top window of the console. When you're ready to execute the code, press Ctrl+R or Ctrl+Enter on your Windows system or Command+R or Command+Enter on your Mac system.

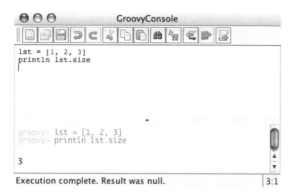

Figure 2.2: USING GROOVYCONSOLE

You can also click the appropriate toolbar button to execute your script. The groovyConsole command has grown fancier over time—you can save your script, open existing scripts, and so on, so take some time to explore the tool.

2.5 Running Groovy on the Command Line

Of course, nothing can give you as much pleasure as getting into the command line and running the program from there, right? You can do that by typing the command groovy followed by the Groovy program filename, as shown in Figure 2.3, on the next page.

If you want to try a couple of statements directly on the command line, you can do that by using the -e option. Type groovy -e "println 'hello'" on the command line, and hit Enter/Return. Groovy will output "hello." You can get a bit fancier and even pass command-line arguments, as shown here:

```
groovy -e 'println "Hello, ${args[0]}. ${args[1]}"' Buddy 'Have a nice day!'
```

Groovy will report the following:

```
Hello, Buddy. Have a nice day!
```

Realistically, though, the groovy command is useful to execute large Groovy scripts and classes. It expects you to either have some executable code outside any class or have a class with a static main(String[] args) method (the traditional Java main() method).

```
~>cat Hello.groovy
println "Hello Groovy!"
~>groovy Hello
Hello Groovy!
~>[]
```

Figure 2.3: RUNNING FROM THE COMMAND LINE

You can also skip the main() method if your class extends GroovyTestCase (see Section 16.2, *Unit Testing Java and Groovy Code*, on page 231 for more information) or if your class implements the Runnable interface.[5]

2.6 Using an IDE

You'll be happy to hear that you'll quickly graduate from the two tools we've talked about so far. Therefore, once you start churning out Groovy code, you'll want to use an IDE. Fortunately, you have several IDEs to choose from for coding Groovy. See http://groovy.codehaus.org/IDE+Supportfor some choices. You can edit your Groovy code, run it from within your IDE, debug your code, and a lot more...depending on which tool you pick.

IntelliJ IDEA and JetGroovy

IntelliJ IDEA offers outstanding support for Groovy through the JetGroovy plug-in (http://www.jetbrains.com/idea). Using it, you can edit Groovy code, take advantage of code completion, get support for Groovy builders, use syntax and error highlighting, use code formatting and inspection, jointly compile Java and Groovy code, refactor and debug both Java and Groovy code, and work with and build Java and Groovy code in the same project. It also supports Grails projects with built-in Grails generators and GSP code completion and assistance.

Eclipse Groovy Plug-In

If you are an Eclipse user, you can use the Groovy Eclipse plug-in (http://groovy.codehaus.org/Eclipse+Plugin). This plug-in allows you to edit Groovy classes and scripts, take advantage of syntax highlighting, and compile and run the code and tests. Using the Eclipse Debugger, you

---

5. If the main() method is present in these cases, it takes precedence.

Figure 2.4: GROOVY CODE EXECUTED WITHIN TEXTMATE

can step into Groovy code or debug unit tests. In addition, you can invoke the Groovy shell or Groovy console from within Eclipse to quickly experiment with Java and Groovy code.

TextMate Groovy Bundle

As a Mac user, I use the Groovy bundle (http://docs.codehaus.org/display/ GROOVY/TextMate) in TextMate (http://macromates.com, [Gra07]) extensively.[6] It provides a number of time-saving snippets that allow code expansion for standard Groovy code such as closures. You can take advantage of syntax highlighting and run Groovy code and tests quickly from within TextMate,[7] as shown in Figure 2.4.

It's nice to have a choice of command-line and IDE tools. However, you need to decide which tool is right for you. Personally, I find it easier to simply run Groovy code directly from within the editor or IDE, letting the groovy tool take care of compiling and executing the code behind the scene. That helps with my "rapid edit, code, and run-my-tests" cycle. At times, I find myself jumping over to groovysh to experiment with code snippets. But you don't have to do what I do. The right tool for you is the one you're most comfortable with. Start with a simple tool and the steps that work for you. Once you get comfortable, you can always scale up to something more sophisticated when you need to do so.

In this chapter, you installed Groovy and took it for a quick test-drive. Along the way you looked at a few command-line tools and IDE support. That means you're all set to explore Groovy in the next chapter.

---

6. Windows users—take a look at E Text Editor at http://www.e-texteditor.com. Also, for editing small code snippets, you can use Notepad2 (see http://tinyurl.com/yqfucf).
7. See my blog entry at http://tinyurl.com/ywotsj for a minor tweak to quickly display results without a pop-up window.

Chapter 3

Groovy for the Java Eyes

I'll help you ease into Groovy in this chapter. Specifically, we'll start on familiar ground and then transition into the Groovy way of writing. Since Groovy preserves Java syntax and semantics, you can mix Java style and Groovy style at will. And, as you get comfortable with Groovy, you can make your code even groovier. So, get ready for a tour of Groovy. We'll wrap this chapter with some "gotchas"—a few things that might catch you off guard if you aren't expecting them.

3.1 From Java to Groovy

Groovy readily accepts your Java code. So, start with the code you're familiar with, but run it through Groovy. As you work, figure out elegant and Groovy ways to write your code. You'll see that your code is doing the same things, but it's a lot smaller. It'll feel like your refactoring is on steroids.

Hello, Groovy

Here a Java sample that's also Groovy code:

```
// Java code
public class Greetings
{
  public static void main(String[] args)
  {
    for(int i = 0; i < 3; i++)
    {
      System.out.print("ho ");
    }

    System.out.println("Merry Groovy!");
  }
}
```

<u>**Default Imports**</u>

You don't have to import some common classes/packages when you write Groovy code. For example, Calendar readily refers to java.util.Calendar. Groovy automatically imports the following Java packages: java.lang, java.util, java.io, and java.net. It also imports the classes java.math.BigDecimal and java.math.BigInteger. In addition, the Groovy packages groovy.lang and groovy.util are imported.

The output from the previous code is as follows:

```
ho ho ho Merry Groovy!
```

That's a lot of code for such a simple task. Still, Groovy will obediently accept and execute it. Simply save that code to a file named Greetings.groovy, and execute it using the command groovy Greetings.

Groovy has a higher signal-to-noise ratio. Hence, less code, more result. In fact, you can get rid of most of the code from the previous program and still have it produce the same result. Start by removing the line-terminating semicolons first. Losing the semicolons not only reduces noise, but it also helps to use Groovy to implement internal DSLs (Chapter 18, *Creating DSLs in Groovy*, on page 273).

Then remove the class and method definition. Groovy is still happy (or is it happier?).

GroovyForJavaEyes/LightGreetings.groovy

```
for(int i = 0; i < 3; i++)
{
  System.out.print("ho ")
}

System.out.println("Merry Groovy!")
```

You can go even further. Groovy understands println() because it has been added on java.lang.Object. It also has a lighter form of the for loop that uses the Range object, and Groovy is lenient with parentheses. So, you can reduce the previous code to the following:

GroovyForJavaEyes/LighterGreetings.groovy

```
for(i in 0..2) { print 'ho ' }

println 'Merry Groovy!'
```

The output from the previous code is the same as the Java code you started with, but the code is a lot lighter. That just goes to show you that simple things are simple to do in Groovy.

Ways to Loop

You're not restricted to the traditional for loop in Groovy. You already used the range 0..2 in the for loop. Wait, there's more.[1]

Groovy has added a convenient upto() instance method to java.lang. Integer, so you can loop using that method, as shown here:

GroovyForJavaEyes/WaysToLoop.groovy
```
0.upto(2) { print "$it "}
```

Here you called upto() on 0, which is an instance of Integer. The output from the previous code is as follows:

```
0 1 2
```

So, what's that it in the code block? In this context, it represents the index value through the loop. The upto() method accepts a closure as a parameter. If the closure expects only one parameter, you can use the default name it for it in Groovy. Keep that in mind, and move on for now; we'll discuss closures in more detail in Chapter 5, *Using Closures*, on page 81. The $ in front of the variable it tells the method println() to print the value of the variable instead of the characters "it"—it allows you to embed expressions within strings, as you'll see in Chapter 6, *Working with Strings*, on page 101.

The upto() method allows you to set both lower and upper limits. If you start at 0, you can also use the times() method, as shown here:

GroovyForJavaEyes/WaysToLoop.groovy
```
3.times { print "$it "}
```

The output from previous code is as follows:

```
0 1 2
```

If you want to skip values while looping, use the step() method:

GroovyForJavaEyes/WaysToLoop.groovy
```
0.step(10, 2) { print "$it "}
```

The output from the previous code is as follows:

```
0 2 4 6 8
```

---

1. http://groovy.codehaus.org/Looping

You've now seen simple looping in action. You can also iterate or traverse a collection of objects using similar methods, as you'll see later in Chapter 7, *Working with Collections*, on page 115.

To go further, you can rewrite the greetings example using the methods you learned earlier. Look at how short the following Groovy code is compared to the Java code you started with:

GroovyForJavaEyes/WaysToLoop.groovy

```groovy
3.times { print 'ho ' }
println 'Merry Groovy!'
```

To confirm, the output from the previous code is as follows:

```
ho ho ho Merry Groovy!
```

A Quick Look at the GDK

Groovy extends the JDK with an extension called the GDK[2] or the Groovy JDK. I'll whet your appetite here with a quick example.

In Java, you can use java.lang.Process to interact with a system-level process. Suppose you want to invoke Subversion's help from within your code; well, here's the Java code for that:

```java
//Java code
import java.io.*;

public class ExecuteProcess
{
  public static void main(String[] args)
  {
    try
    {
      Process proc = Runtime.getRuntime().exec("svn help");
      BufferedReader result = new BufferedReader(
                    new InputStreamReader(proc.getInputStream()));

      String line;
      while((line = result.readLine()) != null)
      {
        System.out.println(line);
      }
    }
    catch(IOException ex)
    {
      ex.printStackTrace();
    }
  }
}
```

---

2. http://groovy.codehaus.org/groovy-jdk.html

java.lang.Process is very helpful, but I had to jump through some hoops to use it in the previous code; in fact, all the exception-handling code and effort to get to the output makes me dizzy. But the GDK, on the other hand, makes this insanely simple:

GroovyForJavaEyes/Execute.groovy

```
println "svn help".execute().text
```

Compare the two pieces of code. They remind me of the sword-fight scene[3] from the movie *Raiders of the Lost Ark*; the Java code is pulling a major stunt like the villain with the sword. Groovy, on the other hand, like Indy, effortlessly gets the job done. Don't get me wrong—I am certainly not calling Java the villain. You're still using Process and the JDK in Groovy code. Your enemy is the unnecessary complexity that makes it harder and time-consuming to utilize the power of the JDK and the Java platform.

Which of the previous two versions would you prefer? The short and sweet one-liner, of course (unless you're a consultant who gets paid by the number of lines of code you write...).

When you called the execute() method on the instance of String, Groovy created an instance that extends java.lang.Process, just like the exec() method of Runtime did in the Java code. You can verify this by using the following code:

GroovyForJavaEyes/Execute.groovy

```
println "svn help".execute().getClass().name
```

The output from the previous code, when run on a Unix-like machine, is as follows:

```
java.lang.UNIXProcess
```

On a Windows machine, you'll get this:

```
java.lang.ProcessImpl
```

When you call text, you're calling the Groovy-added method getText() on the Process to read the process's entire standard output into a String.[4] Go ahead, try the previous code.

---

3. http://www.youtube.com/watch?v=m5TcfywPj0E
4. If you simply want to wait for a process to finish, use either waitFor() or the Groovy-added method waitForOrKill() that takes a timeout in milliseconds.

If you don't use Subversion, substitute svn help with some other program on your system (such as groovy -v), as shown here:

```
GroovyForJavaEyes/Execute.groovy
```

```
println "groovy -v".execute().text
```

The output from the previous code is as follows:

```
GroovyForJavaEyes/Execute.output
```

```
Groovy Version: 1.5.4 JVM: 1.6.0_01-41-release
```

This code sample works on Unix-like systems and on Windows.

Similarly, on a Unix-like system, to get the listing of current directory,
you can call ls:

```
GroovyForJavaEyes/Execute.groovy
```

```
println "ls -l".execute().text
```

If you're on Windows, simply replacing ls with dir will not work. The
reason is that although ls is a program that you're executing on Unix-
like systems, dir is not a program—it's a shell command. So, you have
to do a little more than calling dir. Specifically, you need to invoke cmd
and ask it to execute the dir command, as shown here:

```
GroovyForJavaEyes/Windows/ExecuteDir.groovy
```

```
println "cmd /C dir".execute().text
```

In this section, you've merely scratched the surface of the GDK. You can
find more GDK goodness in Chapter 8, *Exploring the GDK*, on page 133.

Safe Navigation Operator

Groovy has a number of little features that are exciting and help ease
the development effort. You'll find them throughout this book—one
such feature is the safe navigation operator (?.). It eliminates the mundane check for null, as shown in the following code:

```
GroovyForJavaEyes/Ease.groovy
```

```
def foo(str)
{
  //if (str != null) { return str.reverse() }
  str?.reverse()
}

println foo('evil')
println foo(null)
```

The ?. operator in method foo()[5] calls the method or property only if the reference is not null. The output from the previous code is as follows:

```
live
null
```

The call to reverse() on the null reference using ?. resulted in a null instead of a NullPointerException—another way Groovy reduces noise.

Exception Handling

I mentioned that Groovy has less ceremony than Java. One area where that's crystal clear is in exception handling. Java forces you to handle checked exceptions. Consider a simple case: you want to call Thread's sleep() method.[6] Java forces you to catch java.lang.InterruptedException. What does any respectable Java developer do when forced to do things? They find a way around doing it. The result? Lots of empty catch blocks, right? Check this out:

GroovyForJavaEyes/Sleep.java

```
// Java code
try
{
  Thread.sleep(5000);
}
catch(InterruptedException ex)
{
  // eh? I'm losing sleep over what to do here.
}
```

Having an empty catch block is worse than not handling an exception. If you put an empty catch block, you're suppressing the exception. If you don't handle it in the first place, it is propagated to the caller who either can do something about it or can pass it yet again to its caller.

Groovy does not force you to handle exceptions that you don't want to handle or that are inappropriate at your level. Any exception you don't handle is automatically passed on to a higher level. Here's an example of Groovy's answer to exception handling:

GroovyForJavaEyes/ExceptionHandling.groovy

```
def openFile(fileName)
{
  new FileInputStream(fileName)
}
```

---

5. Programming books are required to have at least one method named "foo."
6. Groovy provides an alternate sleep() method; see Section 8.1, *sleep*, on page 136.

The method openFile() does not handle the infamous FileNotFoundException. If the exception occurs, it is not suppressed. Instead, it's passed to the calling code, which can handle it, as shown here:

GroovyForJavaEyes/ExceptionHandling.groovy

```
try
{
  openFile("nonexistentfile")
}
catch(FileNotFoundException ex)
{
  // Do whatever you like about this exception here
  println "Oops: " + ex
}
```

If you are interested in catching all Exceptions that may be thrown, you can write a catch, as shown here:

GroovyForJavaEyes/ExceptionHandling.groovy

```
try
{
  openFile("nonexistentfile")
}
catch(ex)
{
  // Do whatever you like about this exception here
  println "Oops: " + ex
}
```

I used catch(ex) without any type in front of the variable ex so I can catch just about any exception thrown my way. Beware, this doesn't catch Errors or Throwables other than Exceptions. To really catch *all* of them, use catch(Throwable t).

As you can see, Groovy allows you to focus on getting your work done rather than tackling annoying system-level details.

Groovy as Lightweight Java

Groovy has other features that make it lighter and easier to use. Here are some:

- The return statement is almost optional (see Section 3.8, *Gotchas*, on page 55).

- ; is almost optional though can be used to separate statements (see Section 3.8, *The Semicolon (;) Is Almost Optional*, on page 61).

- Methods and classes are public by default.

- The ?. operator dispatches calls only if the object reference is not null.

- You can initialize JavaBeans using named parameters (see Section 3.2, *JavaBeans*).

- You're not forced to catch exceptions that you don't care to handle. They get passed to the caller of your code.

- You can use this within static methods to refer to the Class object. For example, in the following code, the learn() methods return the class so you can chain calls to learn() methods:

```
class Wizard
{
  def static learn(trick, action)
  {
    //...
    this
  }
}

Wizard.learn('alohomora', {/*...*/})
  .learn('expelliarmus', {/*...*/})
  .learn('lumos', {/*...*/})
```

3.2 JavaBeans

The story of JavaBeans is interesting. When the concept was introduced, it was exciting. It was declared that Java objects would be considered JavaBeans if they followed certain conventions and that they would carry *properties*. That raised a lot of excitement and hope. But when it came to accessing these properties, I found that calls to mere getters and setters were required. My excitement came crashing down, and developers moved on to create thousands of silly methods in their applications.[7] If JavaBeans were human, they'd be on Prozac.[8]

Groovy treats JavaBeans with the respect they deserve. In Groovy, a JavaBean truly has properties. Let's start with Java code and reduce it to Groovy so you can see what I mean.

---

7. http://www.javaworld.com/javaworld/jw-09-2003/jw-0905-toolbox.html

8. To be fair, the intent of JavaBean is noble—it made component-based development, application assembling, and integration practical and paved the way for exceptional IDE and plug-in development.

GroovyForJavaEyes/Car.java

```java
//Java code
public class Car
{
  private int miles;
  private int year;

  public Car(int theYear) { year = theYear; }
  public int getMiles() { return miles; }
  public void setMiles(int theMiles) { miles = theMiles; }

  public int getYear() { return year; }

  public static void main(String[] args)
  {
    Car car = new Car(2008);

    System.out.println("Year: " + car.getYear());
    System.out.println("Miles: " + car.getMiles());
    System.out.println("Setting miles");
    car.setMiles(25);
    System.out.println("Miles: " + car.getMiles());
  }
}
```

That's all too familiar Java code, isn't it? The output from the previous code is as follows:

```
Year: 2008
Miles: 0
Setting miles
Miles: 25
```

Let's rewrite the code in Groovy:

GroovyForJavaEyes/GroovyCar.groovy

```groovy
class Car
{
  def miles = 0
  final year

  Car(theYear)
  {
    year = theYear
  }
}

Car car = new Car(2008)
```

```
println "Year: $car.year"
println "Miles: $car.miles"
println 'Setting miles'
car.miles = 25
println "Miles: $car.miles"
```

That code does the same thing (see the following output), but it has less clutter and ceremony.

```
Year: 2008
Miles: 0
Setting miles
Miles: 25
```

def declared a *property* in this context.[9] Groovy quietly created a getter and setter method for you behind the scenes (just like how a constructor is created in Java if you don't write any). When you call miles in your code, you're not referencing a field; instead, you're calling the getter method for the miles property. If you want a property to be read-only, then declare it final. This is not defining a final field but a read-only property—you can change the property from within instance methods of the defining class, but not from outside. Groovy provides a getter in this case and no setter. You can verify these concepts with the following code:

GroovyForJavaEyes/GroovyCar2.groovy

```
class Car
{
  final miles = 0

  def getMiles()
  {
    println "getMiles called"
    miles
  }

  def drive(dist) { if (dist > 0) miles += dist }
}
```

You declared miles as final; however, you can change it from within the drive() instance method. Let's use this class now.

---

9. You can declare properties by either using def as in the example or giving the type (and optional value) as in int miles or int miles = 0.

GroovyForJavaEyes/GroovyCar2.groovy

```
def car = new Car()

println "Miles: $car.miles"
println  'Driving'
car.drive(10)
println "Miles: $car.miles"

try
{
  print 'Can I set the miles? '
  car.miles = 12
}
catch(groovy.lang.ReadOnlyPropertyException ex)
{
  println ex.message
}
```

The output from the previous code is as follows:

```
getMiles called
Miles: 0
Driving
getMiles called
Miles: 10
Can I set the miles? Cannot set readonly property: miles for class: Car
```

If you want to access properties, you don't need to use getters or setters anymore in your call. You can see the elegance of this in the following code:

GroovyForJavaEyes/UsingProperties.groovy

```
Calendar.instance
// instead of Calendar.getInstance()

str = 'hello'

str.class.name
// instead of str.getClass().getName()
// Caution: Won't work for Maps, Builders,...
// use str.getClass().name to be safe
```

Use caution with the class property, however—some classes like Map and builders give special treatment to this property (see Section 7.5, *Using Map*, on page 124, for example). As a result, I recommend you use getClass() instead of class to avoid any surprises.

Groovy gives you the flexibility to initialize a JavaBean class. When constructing an object, simply give values for properties as comma-separated name-value pairs. This is a postconstruction operation if your class has a no-argument constructor. You can also design your methods so they can take named parameters. To take advantage of this feature, define the first parameter as a Map. Let's see these in action:

```
class Robot
{
  def type, height, width

  def access(location, weight, fragile)
  {
    println "Received fragile? $fragile, weight: $weight, loc: $location"
  }
}

robot = new Robot(type: 'arm', width: 10, height: 40)

println "$robot.type, $robot.height, $robot.width"

robot.access(50, x: 30, y: 20, z: 10, true)
```

The output from the previous code is shown next. The instance of Robot took type, height, and width parameters as name-value pairs. In the call to the access() method, you set the first parameter, weight, to a single value, which is an Integer. You set the last parameter, fragile, to a single value as well. The rest of the parameters in the middle are name-value pairs for location. The example did not quite follow the same ordering as in the method definition (though I recommend you do); instead, you took advantage of some Groovy magic.

If the number of parameters you send is more than the number of arguments the method expects and if the excess parameters are name-value pairs, then Groovy assumes the first argument of the method is a Map and groups all the name-value pairs together as values for the first parameter. It then takes the rest of the parameters, in the presented order, as values for the remaining parameters, as shown in the following output:

```
arm, 40, 10
Received fragile? true, weight: 50, loc: ["x":30, "y":20, "z":10]
```

Although the previous Groovy magic is quite powerful, it leads to a problems, such as when you pass three integer arguments. In this case, the arguments will be passed in order, no map is created from the arguments, and the result is not what you desire.

You can avoid confusion like this by explicitly naming the first parameter as a Map, as shown here:

GroovyForJavaEyes/NamedParameters.groovy

```
def access(Map location, weight, fragile)
{
  print "Received fragile? $fragile, weight: $weight, loc: $location"
}
```

Now, if your arguments do not contain two objects plus arbitrary name-value pairs, you will get an error.

As you can see, thanks to the makeover Groovy gave JavaBeans, they're quite vibrant in Groovy.

3.3 Optional Parameters

In Groovy you can make method and constructor parameters optional. In fact, make as many parameters optional as you like, but they have to be trailing. To define an optional parameter, you simply give it a value in the parameter list. Here's an example of a log() function that allows you to optionally give the base (if you don't set that argument, it assumes base 10):

GroovyForJavaEyes/OptionalParameters.groovy

```
def log(x, base=10)
{
  Math.log(x) / Math.log(base)
}

println log(1024)
println log(1024, 10)
println log(1024, 2)
```

The output from the previous code is as follows:

```
3.0102999566398116
3.0102999566398116
10.0
```

Groovy also treats the trailing array parameter as optional. So, in the following example, you can send zero or more values for the last parameter:

GroovyForJavaEyes/OptionalParameters.groovy

```
def task(name, String[] details)
{
  println "$name - $details"
}
```

```
task 'Call', '123-456-7890'
task 'Call', '123-456-7890', '231-546-0987'
task 'Check Mail'
```

The output from the previous code is as follows:

```
Call - {"123-456-7890"}
Call - {"123-456-7890", "231-546-0987"}
Check Mail - {}
```

Providing mundane arguments to methods can get tiring. Optional parameters reduce noise and allow for sensible defaults.

3.4 Implementing Interfaces

In Groovy you can morph a map or a block of code into implementing interfaces. This allows you to implement interfaces with multiple methods quickly. In this section, I'll show a Java way of implementing interfaces, and then you'll learn how to take advantage of Groovy's facilities.

Here's the all-too-familiar Java code to register an event handler to a Swing JButton. The call to addActionListener() expects an instance that implements the ActionListener interface. So, you create an anonymous inner class that implements ActionListener, and you provide the required actionPerformed() method. This method insists on taking ActionEvent as an argument even though you have no use for it in this example.

```
// Java code
button.addActionListener(new ActionListener()
{
  public void actionPerformed(ActionEvent ae)
  {
    JOptionPane.showMessageDialog(frame, "You clicked!");
  }
});
```

Groovy brings a charming idiomatic difference here—no need for that actionPerformed() method declaration or that explicit new anonymous inner class instance!

```
button.addActionListener(
  { JOptionPane.showMessageDialog(frame, "You clicked!") } as ActionListener
)
```

You call the addActionListener method and provide it with a block of code that morphs itself to implement the ActionListener interface because of the as operator.

That's it—Groovy takes care of the rest. Groovy intercepts calls to any method on the interface (actionPerformed(), in this case) and routes it to the block of code you provided.[10]

You don't have to do anything different if you plan to provide one single implementation for all the methods of a multimethod interface.

Suppose you want to update the display of mouse location in a label as the mouse is clicked and moved around in your application. In Java, you have to implement a total of seven methods of the MouseListener and MouseMotionListener interfaces. Since your implementation for all these methods are the same, Groovy makes your life easy.

```
displayMouseLocation = { positionLabel.setText("$it.x, $it.y") }
frame.addMouseListener(displayMouseLocation as MouseListener)
frame.addMouseMotionListener(displayMouseLocation as MouseMotionListener)
```

In this code, you created the variable displayMouseLocation that refers to a block of code. You then morphed it twice using the as operator, once for each of the interfaces, MouseListener and MouseMotionListener. Once again, Groovy takes care of the rest, and you can move on to focus on other things. It took three lines of code instead of...—sorry, I'm still counting—in Java.

In the previous example, you see that variable it again. it represents the method argument. If a method of the interface you're implementing takes multiple arguments, you can define them either as discrete arguments or as a parameter of type array—you'll see how in Chapter 5, *Using Closures*, on page 81.

OK, that was nice, but in most realistic situations, you'd want a different implementation for each method of an interface. No worries, Groovy can handle that. Simply create a map—no, you don't have to endure the map syntax of Java. Simply separate the method names from the code block using a colon (:). Also, you don't have to implement all the methods. You implement only those you really care about. If the methods you don't implement are never called, you didn't waste any effort implementing dummy stubs. Of course, if you fail to provide a method that's called, you'll get a NullPointerException. Let's put these to use in an example.

---

10. If you want to try running this code, you'll need to create the frame and its components; the full listing of the code is shown at the end of this section.

```
handleFocus = [
  focusGained : { msgLabel.setText("Good to see you!") },
  focusLost : { msgLabel.setText("Come back soon!") }
]
button.addFocusListener(handleFocus as FocusListener)
```

Whenever the button in this example gains focus, the first block of code associated with the key focusGained will be called. When the button loses focus, the block of code associated with focusLost is called. The keys in this case correspond to the methods of the FocusListenerInterface.

The as operator is good if you know the name of the interface you're implementing. However, what if your application demands dynamic behavior and you'll know the interface name only at runtime? Well, the asType() method comes to your rescue. You can use this method to morph either a block of code or a map to an interface by sending the Class metaobject of the interface you want to implement as an argument to asType(). Let's look at an example.

Suppose you want to add an event handler for different events: WindowListener, ComponentListener, … the list may be dynamic. Also suppose your handler will perform some common operation such as logging or updating a status bar—some task to help with testing or debugging your application. You can dynamically add handlers for multiple events using a single block of code. Here's how:

```
events = ['WindowListener', 'ComponentListener']
// Above list may be dynamic and may come from some input

handler = { msgLabel.setText("$it") }

for (event in events)
{
  handlerImpl = handler.asType(Class.forName("java.awt.event.${event}"))
  frame."add${event}"(handlerImpl)
}
```

The interfaces you want to implement—that is, the events you want to handle—are in the list events. This list is dynamic; suppose it will be populated with input during code execution. The common handler for the events is in the code block referred to by the variable handler. You loop through the events, and for each event, you're creating a implementation of the interface using the asType() method. This method is called on the block of code and is given the Class metaobject of the interface obtained using the forName() method. Once you have the implementation of the listener interface on hand, you can register it by calling the appropriate add method (like addWindowListener()). The call to the add method itself is dynamic. You'll learn more about such methods later in Section 12.2, *Querying Methods and Properties*, on page 185.

In the previous code, I used the asType() method on the block of code. If you have different implementations for different methods, you'd have a map instead of a single block of code. In that case, you can call the asType() method on the map in a similar way. Finally, as promised, here is the full listing of the Groovy Swing code developed in this section:

GroovyForJavaEyes/Swing.groovy

```groovy
import javax.swing.*
import java.awt.*
import java.awt.event.*

frame = new JFrame(size: [300, 300],
  layout: new FlowLayout(),
  defaultCloseOperation: javax.swing.WindowConstants.EXIT_ON_CLOSE)
button = new JButton("click")
positionLabel = new JLabel("")
msgLabel = new JLabel("")
frame.contentPane.add button
frame.contentPane.add positionLabel
frame.contentPane.add msgLabel

button.addActionListener(
  { JOptionPane.showMessageDialog(frame, "You clicked!") } as ActionListener
)

displayMouseLocation = { positionLabel.setText("$it.x, $it.y") }
frame.addMouseListener(displayMouseLocation as MouseListener)
frame.addMouseMotionListener(displayMouseLocation as MouseMotionListener)

handleFocus = [
  focusGained : { msgLabel.setText("Good to see you!") },
  focusLost : { msgLabel.setText("Come back soon!") }
]
button.addFocusListener(handleFocus as FocusListener)

events = ['WindowListener', 'ComponentListener']
// Above list may be dynamic and may come from some input

handler = { msgLabel.setText("$it") }

for (event in events)
{
  handlerImpl = handler.asType(Class.forName("java.awt.event.${event}"))
  frame."add${event}"(handlerImpl)
}

frame.show()
```

In this section, you saw the Groovy way to implement interfaces. It makes registering for events or passing anonymous implementations of interfaces really simple. You'll find the ability to morph blocks of code and maps into interface implementations a real time-saver.

3.5 Groovy boolean Evaluation

The truth is that boolean evaluation in Groovy is different from evaluation in Java. Depending on the context, Groovy will automatically evaluate expressions as boolean.

Let's see a specific example. The following Java code will not work:

```
//Java code
String obj = "hello";
int val = 4;
if (obj) {} // ERROR
if(val) {} //ERROR
```

Java insists that you provide a boolean expression for the condition part of the if statement. It wants if(obj != null) and if(val > 0) in the previous example, for instance.

Groovy is not that picky. It tries to infer, so you need to know what Groovy is thinking.

If you place an object reference where a boolean expression is expected, Groovy checks whether the reference is null. It considers null as false, and true otherwise, as in the following code:

```
str = 'hello'
if (str) { println 'hello' }
```

The output from the previous code is as follows:

```
hello
```

But, the last part about true that I mentioned earlier is not entirely true. If the object reference is not-null, then the truth depends on the type of the object. For example, if the object is a collection (like java.util.ArrayList), then Groovy checks whether the collection is empty. So, in this case, the expression if (obj) evaluates true only if obj is not null and the collection has at least one element, as shown in the following code example:

```
lst0 = null
println lst0 ? 'lst0 true' : 'lst0 false'
lst1 = [1, 2, 3]
println lst1 ? 'lst1 true' : 'lst1 false'
lst2 = []
println lst2 ? 'lst2 true' : 'lst2 false'
```

Type	Condition for truth
Boolean	true
Collection	not empty
Character	value not 0
CharSequence	length greater than 0
Enumeration	has more elements
Iterator	has text
Number	double value not 0
Map	not empty
Matcher	at least one match
Object[]	length greater than 0
any other type	reference not null

Figure 3.1: TYPES AND THEIR SPECIAL TREATMENT FOR BOOLEAN EVALUATION

You can check your understanding of how Groovy handles boolean for Collections with the following output:

```
1st0 false
1st1 true
1st2 false
```

Collections are not the only things that receive special boolean treatment. For the types with special treatment and how Groovy evaluates their truth, refer to the table in Figure 3.1.

3.6 Operator Overloading

You can use Groovy's support for operator overloading, judiciously, to create DSLs (see Chapter 18, *Creating DSLs in Groovy*, on page 273). When Java has no support for operator overloading, how does Groovy get away with that? It's really simple, actually—each operator has a standard mapping to methods.[11] So, in Java you can use those methods, and on the Groovy side you can use either the operators or their corresponding methods.

---

11. For a list of operators and method mapping, visit http://groovy.codehaus.org/Operator+Overloading.

Here's an example to show operator overloading in action:

GroovyForJavaEyes/OperatorOverloading.groovy
```
for(i = 'a'; i < 'd'; i++)
{
  println i
}
```

You're looping through the characters *a* through *c* using the ++ operator. This operator maps to the next() method on the String class. The output from the previous code is as follows:

```
a
b
c
```

You'll most likely write the previous code as shown next using a lighter form of the loop, but both implementations use the next() method of String:

GroovyForJavaEyes/OperatorOverloading.groovy
```
for (i in 'a'..'c')
{
  println i
}
```

The String class has a number of operators overloaded, as you'll see in Section 6.4, *String Convenience Methods*, on page 110. The collection classes—ArrayList and Map—similarly have operators overloaded for convenience.

If you want to add an element to a collection, you can use the << operator, which translates to the Groovy-added leftShift() method on Collection, as shown here:

GroovyForJavaEyes/OperatorOverloading.groovy
```
lst = ['hello']
lst << 'there'
println lst
```

The output from the previous code is as follows:

```
["hello", "there"]
```

You can provide operators for your own classes by adding the mapping methods, like plus() for +, for example.

Here's an example showing how to add an operator overloaded method to a class:

```
GroovyForJavaEyes/OperatorOverloading.groovy
class ComplexNumber
{
  def real, imaginary

  def plus(other)
  {
    new ComplexNumber(real: real + other.real,
          imaginary: imaginary + other.imaginary)
  }

  String toString() { "$real ${imaginary > 0 ? '+' : ''} ${imaginary}i"}
}

c1 = new ComplexNumber(real: 1, imaginary: 2)
c2 = new ComplexNumber(real: 4, imaginary: 1)

println c1 + c2
```

Because you added the plus() method on the ComplexNumber[12] class, Groovy allows you to use + to add two complex numbers to get a resulting (more?) complex number. The output from the previous code is as follows:

```
5 + 3i
```

Operator overloading can make code expressive when used within a context. However, I'm not a big fan of operator overloading in general because it is hard to get it right—use it at your discretion. Overload only those operators that will make things very obvious. For example, if someone who understands the context or domain asks you what's the purpose of an operator you've provided, then that overloading might not be a good choice there. When overloading, preserve the expected semantics. For instance, + must not change any of the operands in the operation. If an operation must be commutative, symmetric, or transitive, make sure your operator adheres to that.

---

12. In case you skipped school when they taught complex numbers, they're useful for computing complex equations that involve the square root of negative numbers—they have real and imaginary parts, like your actual income and what you report on your tax return.

3.7 Support of Java 5 Language Features

If you use enums, annotations, or some of the other Java 5 language features in your applications, you'll be pleased to find that they work in Groovy also. This means you can mix Java and Groovy quite fluently. To refresh your memory, the Java 5 language features are as follows:

- Autoboxing[13]
- for-each
- enum
- Varargs
- Annotation
- Static import
- Generics

Some of these features (such as autoboxing and varargs) work in Groovy even with Java 1.4; however, to use most of these Java 5 language features in Groovy, you'll need Java 5. In the following sections, I'll discuss the extent of the Groovy support for these features.

Autoboxing

Groovy, because of its dynamic typing, supports autoboxing from the get-go. In fact, Groovy automatically treats all primitives as objects. For instance, execute the following code:

GroovyForJavaEyes/NotInt.groovy

```
int val = 5
println val.getClass().name
```

The previous code reports the type, as shown here:

```
java.lang.Integer
```

In this code, you created an instance of java.lang.Integer and not a primitive int, even though you specified int. How Groovy handles autoboxing is a notch better than Java. In Java, autoboxing and unboxing involve constant casting. Groovy, on the other hand, simply treats them as objects[14]—so there's no repeated casting involved.

---

13. Autoboxing is not new in Groovy 1.5; it's a feature supported from the beginning in Groovy.

14. Don't let that worry you if you're calling a Java method that takes a primitive, because Groovy automatically figures the conversions in.

for-each

Groovy's support for looping is different from and superior than the forms available in Java (see Section 3.1, *Ways to Loop*, on page 27). However, if you want to use the traditional for loop (that is, for(int i = 0; i < 10; i++) {...}), you can use that in Groovy. Or, if you like the simpler form supported in Java 5, you can do that as well. In Java 5, objects that implement the Iterable interface can be used in a for-each loop, as shown here:

GroovyForJavaEyes/ForEach.java

```java
// Java code
String[] greetings = {"Hello", "Hi", "Howdy"};

for(String greet : greetings)
{
  System.out.println(greet);
}
```

The previous code written in Groovy looks like this:

GroovyForJavaEyes/ForEach.groovy

```groovy
String[] greetings = ["Hello", "Hi", "Howdy"]

for(String greet : greetings)
{
  println greet
}
```

Groovy insists that you specify the type (String in the previous example) in the Java style for-each. If you don't want to specify the type, use the in keyword instead of a colon (:), as shown here:

GroovyForJavaEyes/ForEach.groovy

```groovy
for(greet in greetings)
{
  println greet
}
```

enum

Groovy provides support for enum, which is the Java 5 feature that solves problems with enumerations. It's type safe (you can distinguish between shirt sizes and days of the week, for example), printable, serializable, and so on.

Here's an example that defines different sizes of coffee you can order:

`GroovyForJavaEyes/UsingCoffeeSize.groovy`

```groovy
enum CoffeeSize { SHORT, SMALL, MEDIUM, LARGE, MUG }

def orderCoffee(size)
{
  print "Coffee order received for size $size: "

  switch(size)
  {
    case [CoffeeSize.SHORT, CoffeeSize.SMALL]:
      println "you're health conscious"
      break
    case CoffeeSize.MEDIUM..CoffeeSize.LARGE:
      println "you gotta be a programmer"
      break
    case CoffeeSize.MUG:
      println "you should try Caffeine IV"
      break
  }
}

orderCoffee(CoffeeSize.SMALL);
orderCoffee(CoffeeSize.LARGE);
orderCoffee(CoffeeSize.MUG);

print 'Available sizes are: '
for(size in CoffeeSize.values())
{
    print "$size "
}
```

The output from the previous code is as follows:

```
Coffee order received for size SMALL: you're health conscious
Coffee order received for size LARGE: you gotta be a programmer
Coffee order received for size MUG: you should try Caffeine IV
Available sizes are: SHORT SMALL MEDIUM LARGE MUG
```

You can use enum values in case statements. Specifically, you can use a single value, a list of values, or even a range of values.[15] You can find examples of all these flavors in the previous code.

---

15. Support for range of enum values in case statements was introduced after the release of Groovy 1.5.4.

Java 5's enum allows you to define constructors and methods, and Groovy supports that too, as shown here:

```
GroovyForJavaEyes/AgileMethodologies.groovy
enum Methodologies
{
    Evo(5),
    XP(21),
    Scrum(30);

    final int daysInIteration
    Methodologies(days) { daysInIteration = days }

    def iterationDetails()
    {
        println "${this} recommends $daysInIteration days for iteration"
    }
}

for(methodology in Methodologies.values())
{
    methodology.iterationDetails()
}
```

The output from the previous code is as follows:

```
Evo recommends 5 days for iteration
XP recommends 21 days for iteration
Scrum recommends 30 days for iteration
```

There is a limitation in Groovy, however. Java allows you to refine or override a method for specific values of an enum. Groovy does not support that. The following code will result in a compilation error:

```
GroovyForJavaEyes/Activity.groovy
enum WeekendActivity
{
  SATURDAY {
    String activity() { 'Play' } // ERROR, does not work
  },
  SUNDAY;

  String activity() { 'Relax' }
}

for(day in WeekendActivity.values())
{
  println "$day - ${day.activity()}"
}
```

You can expect this feature in Groovy when it supports inner classes. If you need to override methods for specific enum values right now, you can use a workaround. Inject the method into the instance you desire using ExpandoMetaClass,[16] as shown here:

GroovyForJavaEyes/ActivityWorkaround.groovy

```
enum WeekendActivity
{
  SATURDAY, SUNDAY;

  String activity() { 'Relax' }
}

def emc = new ExpandoMetaClass(WeekendActivity)
emc.activity = {-> 'Play'}
emc.initialize()
WeekendActivity.SATURDAY.metaClass = emc

for(day in WeekendActivity.values())
{
  println "$day - ${day.activity()}"
}
```

The output from the previous code is as follows:

```
SATURDAY - Play
SUNDAY - Relax
```

varargs

Remember, Java 5 varargs allows you to pass a variable number of arguments to methods, such as the printf() method. To use this feature in Java, you mark the trailing parameter type of a method with an ellipsis, as in public static Object max(Object... args). This is syntactic sugar—Java rolls all the arguments into an array at the time of call.

Groovy supports Java 5 varargs in two different ways. Groovy's support for varargs is even available with Java 1.4. In addition to supporting parameters marked with ..., you can pass variable arguments to methods that accept an array as a trailing parameter.

---

16. You'll learn about method injection and ExpandoMetaClass later in Chapter 14, *MOP Method Injection and Synthesis*, on page 197.

Let's look at a Groovy example for these two ways:

GroovyForJavaEyes/VarArgs.groovy

```groovy
def foo1(int a, int... b)
{
  println "You passed $a and $b"
}

def foo2(int a, int[] b)
{
  println "You passed $a and $b"
}

foo1(1, 2, 3, 4, 5)
foo2(1, 2, 3, 4, 5)
```

The output from the previous code is as follows:

```
You passed 1 and [2, 3, 4, 5]
You passed 1 and [2, 3, 4, 5]
```

You can send either an array or discrete values to methods that accept varargs or an array as trailing parameters, and Groovy figures out what to do.

Annotations

Annotations in Java allows you to express metadata, and Java 5 ships with a few predefined annotations such as @Override, @Deprecated, and @SuppressWarnings. You can use annotations in Groovy, but you can't define new annotations. However, this is not a huge drawback because application programmers use annotations more often than defining new ones. You can define annotations using Java until Groovy allows you to define them.

You use annotations typically for a framework or a tool to use; for example, JUnit 4.0 makes use of the @Test annotation. So, if you're using frameworks like Hibernate, JPA, Seam, Spring, and so on, you'll find Groovy's current level of support for annotations quite adequate and helpful.

The Groovy compiler does not, however, use the Java annotations like @Deprecated and @Override. If you declare a method with @Deprecated in Groovy, groovyc will compile the code but does not retain the deprecation meta information in the bytecode. Similarly, groovyc ignores @Override.

Static Import

Static import in Java allows you to import static methods of a class into your namespace so you can refer to them without specifying the class name. For instance, if you place the following:

```
import static Math.random;
```

in your Java code, then instead of Math.random(), you can call it like this:

```
double val = random();
```

Static import in Java improves job security. If you define several static imports or use * to import all static methods of a class, you're sure to confuse the heck out of programmers trying to figure out where these methods come from.

Groovy extends that luxury to you in two forms. First, it implements static import. You can use it just like in Java. Feel free to lose the semicolon because that's optional in Groovy. Second, you can define aliases in Groovy—for both static methods and class names. To define an alias, use the as operator in the import statement, as shown here:

```
import static Math.random as rand
import groovy.lang.ExpandoMetaClass as EMC

double value = rand()
def metaClass = new EMC(Integer)
assert metaClass.getClass().name == 'groovy.lang.ExpandoMetaClass'
```

In the previous code, you created rand() as an alias for the Math.random() method. You also created an alias EMC for the ExpandoMetaClass. Now, you can use rand() and EMC instead of Math.random() and ExpandoMeta-Class, respectively.

Generics

Groovy is a dynamic language; however, it is optionally typed and supports Generics. The Groovy compiler does not perform type checks like the Java compiler does (see Section 3.8, *No Compile-Time Type Checking*, on page 58). So, code with type violations that'll be rejected by the Java compiler are quietly accepted by the Groovy compiler. However, Groovy's dynamic typing will interplay here to get your code running, if possible. Let's look at an example in which you'll add a couple of Integers and a String to an ArrayList of Integer. As you iterate over the elements of the ArrayList and do some operations on the elements, notice the effect of Groovy dynamic typing.

Let's first start with Java code:

```
Line 1   // Java code
   -     import java.util.ArrayList;

   -     public class Generics
   5     {
   -       public static void main(String[] args)
   -       {
   -         ArrayList<Integer> lst = new ArrayList<Integer>();
   -         lst.add(1);
  10         lst.add(2);
   -         lst.add("hello");
   -         lst.add(4);
   -         lst.add(5);

  15         int total = 0;
   -         for(Integer i : lst)
   -         {
   -           System.out.println(i);
   -           total += i;
  20         }

   -         System.out.println("Total is " + total);

   -         try
  25         {
   -           for(Integer i : lst)
   -           {
   -             System.out.println(i.intValue());
   -           }
  30         }
   -         catch(Exception ex)
   -         {
   -           System.out.println(ex);
   -         }
  35       }
   -     }
```

When you compile the previous Java code using the Java compiler, you'll get a compilation error:

```
Generics.java:10: cannot find symbol
symbol  : method add(java.lang.String)
location: class java.util.ArrayList<java.lang.Integer>
    lst.add("hello");
        ^
1 error
```

The Java compiler was not happy with you sending a String to the add()
method since it accepts only Integers (or int, which will be autoboxed to
Integer).

So, copy the previous code to a file named Generics.groovy, and then run
groovy Generics.[17] You'll get the following output:

```
1
2
hello
4
5
Total is 3hello45
1
2
groovy.lang.MissingMethodException:
  No signature of method: java.lang.String.intValue()
  is applicable for argument types: () values: {}
```

How's that? The iterator (for loop) treated the elements as objects, so
there was no error on line number 16—Groovy took the type information more as a suggestion. On line number 19, you ended up appending
"hello" to 3, thanks to Groovy/Java's treatment of + as a concatenate
operation when an operand is String. The variable total started out being
defined an int, but Groovy decided to ignore the type definition and treat
it as an Object reference. On line number 28, however, when you tried
to invoke the method intValue() on the elements, you got an exception
since String does not have that method. This call would have worked had
you added that method dynamically to String. Groovy supports Generics
and at the same time favors dynamic behavior. It's quite an interesting
interplay of the two concepts.

3.8 Gotchas

You'll see a number of nice capabilities of Groovy throughout this book.
Groovy, for its share, also has some "gotchas"—ranging from minor
annoyances to surprises if you're not expecting them. In the following
sections, I'll show you a few of them.[18]

---

17. Groovy code is always compiled. When you run groovy, it compiles your code in memory and executes it. To explicitly compile your code, use groovyc (Section 11.2, *Running
Groovy*, on page 166).
18. Visit http://groovy.codehaus.org/Differences+from+Java for a nice list of Groovy-Java
differences.

return Is Not Always Optional

The return statement at the end of a method is optional in Groovy, as shown in the following code:

GroovyForJavaEyes/ReturnGotchas.groovy

```groovy
def isPalindrome(str) { str == str.reverse() }
println "mom is palindrome? ${isPalindrome('mom')}"
```

The output from the previous code is as follows:

```
mom is palindrome? true
```

That charm runs out if the last statement is a conditional statement:

GroovyForJavaEyes/ReturnGotchas.groovy

```groovy
def isPalindrome2(str)
{
  if (str)
  {
    str == str.reverse()
  }
  else
  {
    false
  }
}
println "mom is palindrome? ${isPalindrome2('mom')}"
```

The output from the previous code is as follows:

```
mom is palindrome? null
```

In Groovy, if is not an expression; it is a statement, and it evaluates to null. The problem I just showed you is not confined to if statements—you'll run into this for any statement in Groovy. For example, if you have a try-catch block in your code, examine it to see whether you need to add a return. The fix for the previous code is as follows:

GroovyForJavaEyes/ReturnGotchas.groovy

```groovy
def isPalindromeOK(str)
{
  if (str)
  {
    return str == str.reverse()
  }
  else
  {
    return false
  }
}
println "mom is palindrome? ${isPalindromeOK('mom')}"
```

The output is as follows:

```
mom is palindrome? true
```

You'll catch on to return being optional very quickly, but soon after that you'll trip over cases where it's not optional. It has caught me by surprise a number of times. There has been discussions in the Groovy community to change this behavior, and I hope it happens soon. In the meantime, though, thoroughly review and test your code (which are good practices in general, of course).

Groovy's == Is Equal to Java's equals

== and equals() were already a source of confusion in Java, and Groovy adds to the confusion. Groovy maps the == operator to the equals() method in Java. What if you want to actually perform the reference equals (the original ==, that is)? You have to use is() in Groovy for that. I'll illustrate this difference with the following example:

GroovyForJavaEyes/Equals.groovy

```groovy
str1 = 'hello'
str2 = str1
str3 = new String('hello')
str4 = 'Hello'

println "str1 == str2: ${str1 == str2}"
println "str1 == str3: ${str1 == str3}"
println "str1 == str4: ${str1 == str4}"

println "str1.is(str2): ${str1.is(str2)}"
println "str1.is(str3): ${str1.is(str3)}"
println "str1.is(str4): ${str1.is(str4)}"
```

This is the output from the previous code:

```
str1 == str2: true
str1 == str3: true
str1 == str4: false
str1.is(str2): true
str1.is(str3): false
str1.is(str4): false
```

The observation that Groovy == maps to equals() is only partially true—that mapping happens only if your class does not implement the Comparable interface. If it does, then it maps to the compareTo() method of your class.

Here is an example that shows this behavior:

GroovyForJavaEyes/WhatsEquals.groovy

```groovy
class A
{
  boolean equals(other)
  {
    println "equals called"
    false
  }
}

class B implements Comparable
{
  boolean equals(other)
  {
    println "equals called"
  }

  int compareTo(other)
  {
    println "compareTo called"
    0
  }
}

new A() == new A()
new B() == new B()
```

The output from the previous code shows that the operator picks the compareTo() method over the equals() method for classes that implement the Comparable interface. Here's the output:

```
equals called
compareTo called
```

Use caution when comparing objects—first ask yourself whether you're comparing references or values, and then ask yourself whether you're using the correct operator.

No Compile-Time Type Checking

Groovy is optionally typed; however, the Groovy compiler, groovc, does not perform full type checking. Instead, it performs casting when it encounters type definitions. It also checks for imports to ensure the classes you use exist. Consider the following code:

GroovyForJavaEyes/NoTypeCheck.groovy

```groovy
Integer val = 4
val = 'hello'
```

The code will compile with no errors. When you try to run the Java bytecode created, you will receive a GroovyCastException exception. The output from the previous code is shown here:

```
org.codehaus.groovy.runtime.typehandling.GroovyCastException:
Cannot cast object 'hello' with class 'java.lang.String'
to class 'java.lang.Integer'
```

The Groovy compiler, instead of verifying the type, simply cast it and left it to the runtime to deal with. You can verify this by digging into the bytecode generated (you can use the javap -c ClassFileName command to peek at the human-readable form of the bytecode):

```
...
  58:  ldc       #71; //String hello
  60:  getstatic       #74; //Field class$java$lang$Integer:Ljava/lang/Class;
  63:  ifnonnull        78
  66:  ldc       #76; //String java.lang.Integer
  68:  invokestatic    #21; //Method class$:(Ljava/lang/String;)L...
  71:  dup
  72:  putstatic       #74; //Field class$java$lang$Integer:Ljava/lang/Class;
  75:  goto    81
  78:  getstatic       #74; //Field class$java$lang$Integer:Ljava/lang/Class;
  81:  invokestatic    #80; //Method org/codehaus/groovy/runtime/Scri...
  84:  checkcast       #65; //class java/lang/Integer
  87:  dup
  88:  astore_3
  89:  aload_3
  90:  areturn
...
```

So, in Groovy, x = y is semantically equivalent to x = (ClassOfX)(y).[19]

Similarly, if you call a method that does not exist (such as the method call to the nonexistent method blah in the following example), you will not get any compilation error:

GroovyForJavaEyes/NoTypeCheck.groovy

```
Integer val = 4
val.blah()
```

You will get a MissingMethodException at runtime, as shown next. This is actually an advantage, as you'll see in Chapter 14, *MOP Method Injection and Synthesis*, on page 197. Between the time the code is compiled and before it is executed, you have the ability to inject missing methods dynamically.

---

19. Defining an int in Groovy, for example, actually creates an instance of Integer—see Section 4.6, *Types in Groovy*, on page 74.

```
groovy.lang.MissingMethodException:
No signature of method: java.lang.Integer.blah() is applicable
for argument types: () values: {}
```

The Groovy compiler may appear weak;[20] however, this is necessary for the dynamic and metaprogramming strengths of Groovy.

Be Aware of New Keywords

def and in are examples of new keywords in Groovy. def is used to define methods, properties, and local variables. in is used in for loops to specify the range for looping as in for(i in 1..10).

If you use these keywords as variable names or method names, it may lead to problems. This may especially be critical when taking some existing Java code and using it as Groovy code.

It is also not a smart idea to define a variable named it. Although Groovy will not complain, if you have a field with that name and you use it within a closure, the name refers to the closure parameter and not a field in your class—hiding variables is not going to help you pay your technical debt.[21]

No Inner Classes

Groovy does not support inner classes. This is only a minor annoyance if you take existing Java code and try to run it as a Groovy script. If you are writing fresh Groovy code, you can take advantage of closures in Groovy. For more information, see Chapter 5, *Using Closures*, on page 81.

No Code Block

The following code is valid Java code:

GroovyForJavaEyes/Block.java

```java
// Java code
public void method()
{
  System.out.println("in method1");

  {
    System.out.println("in block");
  }
}
```

---

20. http://groovy.codehaus.org/Runtime+vs+Compile+time,+Static+vs+Dynamic
21. http://martinfowler.com/bliki/TechnicalDebt.html

Code blocks in Java define a new scope. Groovy gets confused at this code, however. It thinks you're defining a closure and complains. You can't have arbitrary code blocks like this within methods in Groovy.

The Semicolon (;) Is Almost Optional

Programmers of C-derived languages who have subjected their pinky fingers to years of abuse will find relief in Groovy. You don't have to place a semicolon (;) at the end of statements. If you want to place multiple statements on the same line, then place a semicolon to separate the statements. Losing semicolons is actually good—it will help you when creating DSLs. However, there's at least one place where the semicolon is not optional. Take a look at the following code:

GroovyForJavaEyes/SemiColon.groovy

```
class Semi
{
  def val = 3

  {
    println "Instance Initializer called..."
  }
}

println new Semi()
```

You intend the code block to be an instance initializer for your class. However, Groovy gets confused, treats the instance initializer as a closure, and gives the following error:

```
Caught: groovy.lang.MissingMethodException:
No signature of method: java.lang.Integer.call()
is applicable for argument types: (Semi$_closure1)
values: {Semi$_closure1@be513c}
  at Semi.<init>(SemiColon.groovy:3)
  at SemiColon.run(SemiColon.groovy:10)
  at SemiColon.main(SemiColon.groovy)
```

Replace def val = 3 with def val = 3;, and the code will run fine. Now Groovy recognizes the block of code as instance initializer, not attached to the property definition.

If you have a static initializer instead of instance initializer, you won't have this problem, however. So if you have a reason to use both static and instance initializers, you can avoid the semicolon if you place the static initializer before the instance initializer.

Different Syntax for Creating Primitive Arrays

In Groovy, if you want to create a primitive array, you can't use the notation you're used to using in Java.

Suppose you want to create an array of integer in Java. You would write the following:

GroovyForJavaEyes/ArrayInJava.java

```
int[] arr = new int[] {1, 2, 3, 4, 5};
```

In Groovy, that will not work. In fact, you will get a compilation error. The Groovy way to define a primitive array of int is as follows:

GroovyForJavaEyes/ArrayInGroovy.groovy

```
int[] arr = [1, 2, 3, 4, 5]

println arr
println "class is " + arr.getClass().name
```

The output from the previous code is shown next. The type of the instance created is [I, which is the JVM representation for int[].

```
[1, 2, 3, 4, 5]
class is [I
```

You've come a long way in this chapter. You know how to write classes in Groovy, you've picked up some Groovy idioms, and you know some Groovy ways to writing code. You also know that you can fall back on Java syntax if necessary. You don't have to wait to finish the rest of this book to start experimenting and playing with Groovy. However, there is a lot in store for you ahead. I mentioned dynamic typing and optional typing a few times, so in the next chapter I will discuss those topics and show how you can take advantage of them in Groovy.

Chapter 4

Dynamic Typing

As a Java programmer, you're used to static typing. Your Java compiler acts as a first level of defense—it checks to see whether the types you're using are the ones expected. And that's not your only defense; your second level of defense is the Java runtime. Dynamic typing allows you to skip that first part. It does not make your code unsafe. You're forgoing static type checking in return for a greater benefit. It's like you were offered a tax deduction—no thanks, you're going for a tax credit. In this chapter, I will walk you through the benefits of Groovy's dynamic typing. Your fingers will thank you because dynamic typing allows you to type less. And you'll also notice that it takes less time and effort to create extensible code. You'll find that relying on dynamic typing takes more discipline, but it's a small pain for a greater gain.

4.1 Typing in Java

As Java programmers we've all come to rely on the "safety" of compile-time type checking.

Several years ago, when I was young and stupid, I wrote my first C program that looked something like this:

```
#include<stdio.h>
    int main(int argc, char* argv)
    {
            int value;
            scanf("%d", value);
            /*...*/
    }
```

It compiled with no errors. When I ran it, after accepting an integer input, it crashed with a segmentation fault.

As a novice C programmer, I was crestfallen.[1] That early experience showed me that just because the compiler produced a binary (or byte-code in Java), it does not mean that the code is correct or will even run. As I came to realize, and as I'm sure you have too, you need to take the time to test the code to make sure it actually meets your expectations.

The safety offered by the Java compiler is not far from my previous experience. I am not discounting the usefulness of the compiler; I am simply arguing that depending heavily on the type checking it offers is rather naive. Java's support for typing at compile time goes only so far—for example, it does not fully help you when working with collections. Consider the following pre-Java 5 code:

TypesAndTyping/UsingList.java

```
Line 1  ArrayList lst1 = new ArrayList();

        lst1.add("hello");

     5  int size = ((String)(lst1.get(0))).length();
```

That casting around the call to the get() method on line number 5 is overwhelming. I am sure you've asked several times why it can't be as simple as lst1.get(0).length(). Generics, in Java 5, makes that possible:

TypesAndTyping/UsingList.java

```
ArrayList<String> lst2 = new ArrayList<String>();

lst2.add("better?");

int size = lst2.get(0).length();
```

The Generics concept is interesting—I've appreciated, for example, the templates in C++ and the implementation of Generics in .NET. Unfortunately, because of the desire to keep backward compatibility, Java had to use so-called type erasure. As a result, Generics in Java do not offer real type safety,[2] as you'll see in the following example:

TypesAndTyping/UsingList.java

```
Line 1  ArrayList<String> lst3 = new ArrayList<String>();

        //lst3.add(1); // Will result in a compilation error if uncommented

     5  ArrayList lst = lst3; // May happen during passing parameters in method calls
        lst.add(1);
        int size = lst3.get(0).length();
```

---

1. I had forgotten a silly & in front of the variable value in the call to scanf().
2. Refer to the article "Good, bad, and ugly of Java Generics" in Appendix A, on page 287.

The previous code—depending on the version of compiler you're using—at best will give you a warning. If you run the generated bytecode, you'll get a ClassCastException because you're trying to treat an Integer as a String. Furthermore, using Generics did not eliminate casting. For example, the statement on line number 7 in the previous code shifted the type casting from the source code to the bytecode. If you examine the generated bytecode using javap, you'll see a call to checkcast. For the amount of complexity involved and the steep learning curve it has, you'd probably expect Generics to offer more than mere type inference and shifting of the cast to bytecode.

Let's look at typing from a different angle. Suppose you have a class Car with a year and an Engine, and you want to implement the ability to clone objects of this class.[3] To do that, you implement the Cloneable interface and provide a public clone() method. Object's clone() can make a shallow copy of the object. However, you want different instances of the Car to have different Engines. So, you clone the Car using the base method but tweak it a little to have its own Engine. The Java code for this is as follows:

```
TypesAndTyping/Car.java
//Java code
public Object clone()
{
  try
  {
    Car cloned = (Car) super.clone();
    cloned.engine = (Engine) engine.clone();
    return cloned;
  }
  catch(CloneNotSupportedException ex)
  {
    return null; // Will not happen, but we need to please the compiler
  }
```

That code is noisy—first, the compiler insists that you must handle CloneNotSupportedException, right in the very method that's implementing the clone. Second, when you're calling super.clone() within your Car class's instance method, you know you're asking for another Car. Yet, your compiler is adamant that you must cast the result of that call. It's the same with the next statement where you're cloning the Engine. Furthermore, when you're ready to actually call the clone() method on an instance of Car, you need to cast again to receive the result of that call

---

3. We'll ignore deeper issues with cloning in Java—see my article "Why Copying an Object Is a Terrible Thing to Do" in Appendix A, on page 287.

into a Car reference. These are examples where the static type checking amounts to mere annoyance and lowers your productivity. Good static type checking should work like a good government—do the essential things, and stay out of your way. However, the Java compiler is in your face most of the time.

Compile-time type checking has its values. However, today's IDEs have made developing code and running the tests so much easier that I often write code and run my tests, leaving it to the IDE to save the relevant files that have been edited and to compile the code as necessary. When my attempt to run the tests fails, I address those issues. Thus, while repeating my fast edit-run-test cycles, I tend not to care so much to distinguish between compilation errors, runtime errors, and failures of the tests. The focus is on getting the code working and having all the tests pass at all time.

4.2 Dynamic Typing

Dynamic typing relaxes the typing requirements. Basically, you let the language figure out the type based on the context. A number of dynamic languages are dynamically typed, but some respectable dynamic languages do provide static typing.

What is the advantage of dynamic typing? Is it worth forgoing the benefit of type verification or confirmation at compile-time or code-editing time? Dynamic typing provides two main advantages, and I contend that the benefits outweigh the cost.

You can write calls to methods on objects without nailing down the details at that moment. During runtime, objects dynamically respond to methods or messages. You can certainly achieve this to a certain extent using polymorphism in statically typed languages. However, most statically typed languages tie inheritance with polymorphism. They force you to conform to a structure rather than to true behavior. True polymorphism does not care about types—send a message to an object, and at runtime it figures out the appropriate implementation to use. So, dynamic typing can help you achieve a greater degree of polymorphism than traditional static languages allow.

The second advantage is you're not fighting the compiler doing trivial casting, like the examples you saw in Section 4.1, *Typing in Java*, on page 63.

You feel like you are working with a language that is intelligent and follows along with you. You're more productive partly because of less ceremony.

Working with static typing feels like having a nagging in-law standing next to you as you work—your every move being scrutinized. It does not give you the full flexibility to defer some implementation to a later time, before the code is actually executed. Working with dynamic typing feels like having an all-too-kind grandfather standing next to you as you work—letting you experiment, figure things out, and be creative but still there to help you when you really need it.

The first advantage—true realization of polymorphism—significantly alters the way you design your application for the better, as you'll see in Section 4.4, *Design by Capability*, on the next page.

4.3 Dynamic Typing != Weak Typing

In a statically-typed language, you specify the types of variables, references, and so on, at compile time—and the compiler insists that you do. Take C/C++, for example. You have to specify the variable type as a primitive type like int, double, ..., or a specific class type. However, what if you cast the variable to a wrong type? Will the compiler stop you? No. What's the fate of the program when you run? It depends. If you are lucky, the program will crash. If not, it may wait until that important demo to crash or misbehave. Depending on how the memory is laid out, whether your call is polymorphic, and how the v-table[4] is organized, things may behave in quite unpredictable ways. If you turn the dial up, you may hear the compiler laugh for relying on the type-safety it pretends to provide. This is an example of static typing with weak typing at runtime.

In Figure 4.1, on the following page, I classify some common languages based on static vs. dynamic typing and strong vs. weak typing.

Java is also a statically typed language, but it's strongly typed. The compiler checks for the types, but if you're coercing to a wrong type, the runtime is there to catch you.

---

4. Some languages like C++ maintain a method dispatch table with addresses of polymorphic methods ([ES90]).

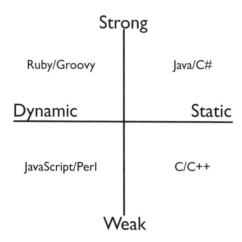

Figure 4.1: CLASSIFICATION OF SELECT LANGUAGES: STATIC VS. DYNAMIC AND STRONG VS. WEAK TYPING

Dynamically typed languages such as Groovy don't perform type checking at code-editing time or compile time. However, if you mistreat an object as a wrong type, you'll hear about it in no uncertain terms at runtime. You postpone the actual verification until runtime; this allows you to modify the structure of your program between the time you write/compile the code and the time it actually executes. These languages show us that dynamic typing does not mean weak typing.

4.4 Design by Capability

As Java programmers we rely heavily on *interfaces*. We value "design by contract," [Mey97] where interfaces define contracts for communication and classes implement and abide by these contracts.

In business, contracts are good. They allow us to agree upon a certain expectations to be fulfilled. At the same time, you don't want the contract to be too restrictive, strict, and controlling. You want the flexibility to meet and exceed the expectations in acceptable ways.

Software contracts must be similar. Interface-based programming, although very powerful, tends to be restrictive beyond a certain point. Let's consider an example that highlights the differences between using static typing and dynamic typing.

Using Static Typing

Say I need to move some heavy stuff. So, I ask a willing and able man to help me out. In Java, this would look like the following code:

TypesAndTyping/TakeHelp.java

```
public void takeHelp(Man man)
{
  //...
  man.helpMoveThings();
  //...
}
```

Because of strong typing, I ignored help from a willing and able woman nearby. Let me extend this so I can seek the help of either a man or a woman. I'll do that by creating a Human abstract class with the help-MoveThings() method. Man and Woman will provide their own implementations for this method:

TypesAndTyping/Human.java

```
// Java code
public abstract class Human
{
  public abstract void helpMoveThings();

  //...
}
```

Here's code that takes the help of a Human:

TypesAndTyping/TakeHelp.java

```
public void takeHelp(Human human)
{
  //...
  human.helpMoveThings();
  //...
}
```

OK, now any human can help me move things. However, if I'm a forest officer in the Serengeti, I failed to take advantage of that nice elephant next to me. I depend on Human, and an elephant does not (want to) conform to that contract. It's time to extend again, this time with an interface Helper with the method helpMoveThings():

TypesAndTyping/Helper.java

```
// Java code
public interface Helper
{
    public void helpMoveThings();
}
```

Then Human, Elephant, and any other helpers implement Helper. I now depend on Helper and can accept help from those implementing that interface:

TypesAndTyping/TakeHelp.java

```
public void takeHelp(Helper helper)
{
  //...
  helper.helpMoveThings();
  //...
}
```

Extending took some effort so far. Using a wide variety of objects meant creating interfaces and modifying the code to depend on it.

Using Dynamic Typing

Let's revisit the "take help" example using the dynamic typing capabilities of Groovy:

TypesAndTyping/TakeHelp.groovy

```
def takeHelp(helper)
{
  //...
  helper.helpMoveThings()
  //...
}
```

The takeHelp() method accepts a helper but does not specify its type—it defaults to an Object. I call, among other things, the helpMoveThings() method on it. This is "design by capability." Instead of asking the helper to conform to some explicit interface, I am making use of the object's capability—relying upon an implicit interface. This is called *duck typing*,[5] which is based on the sentiment that "if it walks like a duck and quacks like a duck, it must be a duck."

Classes that care to have that capability simply implement the method; there's no need to extend or implement anything. The result is low ceremony and high productivity. Now, if a machine has that capability, I can use it without any change to my code. Let's look at a few classes with the capability I want.

---

5.   http://c2.com/cgi/wiki?DuckTyping

```groovy
class Man
{
  void helpMoveThings()
  {
    //...
    println "Man's helping"
  }
  //...
}

class Woman
{
  void helpMoveThings()
  {
    //...
    println "Woman's helping"
  }
  //...
}

class Elephant
{
  void helpMoveThings()
  {
    //...
    println "Elephant's helping"
  }

  void eatSugarcane()
  {
    //...
    println "I love sugarcanes..."
  }
  //...
}
```

Here is an example of calling the takeHelp() method:

```groovy
takeHelp(new Man())
takeHelp(new Woman())
takeHelp(new Elephant())
```

The output from the previous code is as follows:

```
Man's helping
Woman's helping
Elephant's helping
```

Dynamic Typing Needs Discipline

See how simple, elegant, and flexible your code is when you take advantage of dynamic typing? But, is this risky business?

- You might mistype the method name when creating one of the helpers.
- Without the type information, how do you know what to send to your method?
- What if you send a nonhelper (an object that's not capable of moving stuff) to the method?

These are good concerns, but don't let those turn into fear. Instead, take steps to address these effectively. In this section, I highlight some ways to address each of these concerns.

If you're like me, you will make several mistakes typing. Also, our mind constantly fools us; we tend to see what we want to see instead of what's really there. So, ensure that the method names have proper case and take proper parameters. The compiler in a static language does this for you. In a dynamically typed language, either you don't have the compiler or the compiler does not check for these. You'll need to rely on unit testing (see Section 16.2, *Unit Testing Java and Groovy Code*, on page 231) to ensure that you have things right. If you write unit tests only for this purpose, then, yes, I agree that it is an overhead—a rather outlandish ceremony. However, just because a compiler produces byte-code does not mean the code is right either. You still need to verify that it meets your expectations—not just doing what you typed, but doing what you really meant. So, unit testing is a practice that I've come to rely upon quite extensively when I program with static languages. The lack of compiler support (or the lack of compiler) to verify these doesn't bother me so much. Unit testing is a good practice, and dynamic typing requires you to follow that with greater discipline. Programming with dynamic typing without having the discipline of unit testing is playing with wildfire.

To a certain extent, typing helps you figure out what objects or values you need to send to a method. But that is only half the story. Knowing that you must send a double value to a method is hardly enough in practice.[6] Again, two things that can help you a great deal here are disciplined unit testing and following good naming conventions.

---

6. Unless you want to end up on the news for crashing orbiters; see http://www.cnn.com/TECH/space/9909/30/mars.metric.02/.

If a method takes distance as a parameter, rather than naming the variable d, dist, or even distance, you can name them to be very expressive like distanceInMiles. Sure, you can create a type DistanceInMiles, but you don't need that much ceremony if you follow good conventions and testing practices.

Lastly, what about conformance—what if someone sends you an object that does not support the method you're expecting? There are two ways to look at it. You can assume that the callers take the responsibility to make sure they send you only what's valid. If they send you an invalid object, your code will fail, and an exception is thrown their way. Even in compiled code you have to deal with violation of preconditions, so this is along the same lines but broader. Alternately, in special cases, where you want to deal with some alternative or optional behavior, you may ask the object whether it's capable of doing what you're expecting. Groovy's respondsTo() method can help here (see Section 12.2, *Querying Methods and Properties*, on page 185). Assume I own a sugarcane farm and want to share some with my helper, but not all helpers may eat raw sugarcanes. I can ask whether my helper likes sugarcanes, as shown in the following example:

TypesAndTyping/TakeHelp.groovy

```groovy
def takeHelpAndReward(helper)
{
  //...
  helper.helpMoveThings()

  if (helper.metaClass.respondsTo(helper, 'eatSugarcane'))
  {
    helper.eatSugarcane()
  }
  //...
}

takeHelpAndReward(new Man())
takeHelpAndReward(new Woman())
takeHelpAndReward(new Elephant())
```

I'm checking with the helper whether sugarcanes are OK, and if so, I share some. The output from the previous code is as follows:

```
Man's helping
Woman's helping
Elephant's helping
I love sugarcanes...
```

Design by capability with a proper mix of discipline provides you with the flexibility for extensibility and makes you more productive.

4.5 Optional Typing

Groovy is dynamically typed but is also optionally typed; you can adjust the dial of typing all the way to the left where you do not specify any type and let Groovy figure things out, or you can move the dial all the way to the right where you will precisely specify the type of variables or references you use.

Remember that Groovy is a language that runs on top of the JVM. Optional typing helps integrate your Groovy code with Java libraries, frameworks, and tools. Sometimes you will find that Groovy's dynamic mapping of type does not match what these libraries or tools expect. Such a situation is not a showstopper in Groovy—you can switch readily and specify the type information to get moving. Optional typing is also useful in other situations like needing type information to generate database schema or to create validators in GORM/Grails.

As an example, consider writing a JUnit test using Groovy (see Section 16.2, *Unit Testing Java and Groovy Code*, on page 231). In Groovy, you may define methods using the def keyword. This, however, defines a method that returns Object. JUnit, on the other hand, expects test methods to be void. You will get an error if you try to run a test defined using def. Instead, you will have to define the method as a void method to satisfy JUnit. The optional typing of Groovy comes in handy here.

Looking at Figure 4.1, on page 68, you may ask, if Groovy is optionally typed, why didn't I place Groovy in the middle between static and dynamic typing? That's because the Groovy compiler—groovyc—does not really do full type checking (see Section 3.8, *No Compile-Time Type Checking*, on page 58 for details). If you write X obj = 2, where X is a class, it simply places a cast like X obj = (X) 2 and lets the runtime dynamically determine whether that is valid. So, even though Groovy allows typing, it's still dynamically typed.

4.6 Types in Groovy

Since Groovy supports optional typing, you can write code quite flexibly, as shown here:

TypesAndTyping/GroovyTypes.groovy

```
def x = 1
println x

int y = 1
println y
```

Declaring the type as int is optional. However, there is a hidden surprise in the previous code. To see it, ask Groovy the type of variable y:

TypesAndTyping/GroovyTypes.groovy

```
println x.getClass().name
println y.getClass().name
println 1.1.getClass().name
```

The output from the previous code is as follows:

```
java.lang.Integer
java.lang.Integer
java.math.BigDecimal
```

Groovy reports that both the variables x and y are referring to objects of type Integer, even after you defined y as int. Much like Smalltalk and Ruby, Groovy has no primitives—only objects. Also, Groovy treated 1.1 as an instance of java.math.BigDecimal—Groovy computations have higher precision by default, and Groovy readily supports the java.math classes so you don't have to do special things to get more accurate results.[7]

The fact that everything is an object allows you to call methods easily on just about anything. So, as a trivial example, you can do the following:

TypesAndTyping/GroovyTypes.groovy

```
println 1.byteValue()
```

You may wonder why in the world anyone would want to call that method on a number. Instead, understand that you can call methods on numbers as shown. This paves the way to easily create DSLs in Groovy and write code like this:

```
5.days.ago.at 4:30
25.dollars.and.15.cents
```

You'll learn how to write code like this in Section 18.9, *Categories and DSLs*, on page 282.

4.7 Multimethods

Dynamic typing and dynamic languages change the behavior and hence your understanding of how objects respond to method calls.

---

7. http://groovy.codehaus.org/Groovy+Math

Take the following Java example:

TypesAndTyping/Employee.java

```java
// Java code
public class Employee
{
  public void raise(Number amount)
  {
    System.out.println("Employee got raise");
  }
}
```

The Employee class's raise() method takes a Number and simply reports that it was called. Now look at the Executive class:

TypesAndTyping/Executive.java

```java
// Java code
public class Executive extends Employee
{
  public void raise(Number amount)
  {
    System.out.println("Executive got raise");
  }

  public void raise(java.math.BigDecimal amount)
  {
    System.out.println("Executive got outlandish raise");
  }
}
```

The executive has overloaded raise() methods—what else do you expect? The version that takes Number reports its call; the version that takes BigNumber announces the outlandish raise.

Finally, here's Java code that puts these to use:

TypesAndTyping/GiveRaiseJava.java

```java
// Java code
import java.math.BigDecimal;
public class GiveRaiseJava
{
  public static void giveRaise(Employee employee)
  {
    employee.raise(new BigDecimal(10000.00));
  }

  public static void main(String[] args)
  {
    giveRaise(new Employee());
    giveRaise(new Executive());
  }
}
```

You create an Employee and an Executive and send them to the same giveRaise() method, which then calls the raise() method on these objects. The output from the previous code, shown next, is quite expected in Java:

```
Employee got raise
Executive got raise
```

The raise() method in Employee is polymorphic, meaning at runtime the actual method invoked depends not on the type of the target reference but on the type of the object to which it refers. There's one restriction, however. The method called at runtime has to take Number as a parameter because that's what Employee—the base—has defined. So, the compiler treats the instance of BigNumber as Number.

That's a standard, everyday operation in Java. Not a big deal, right? All that changes when it comes to the dynamic nature of Groovy. Groovy knows that "premature optimization is the root of all evil."

So, when you call the raise() method in Groovy, it does not go through the previous sequence as in Java. Instead, it walks up to the object and asks—figuratively speaking, that is—"Hey, do you have a raise() method that takes a java.math.BigDecimal()?"[8] An Employee would say, "No, but you can give it to me as a Number." On the other hand, an Executive does have a raise() that takes a BigDecimal and so the call is routed to that implementation. Here's the code that illustrates this behavior— you're still using Java classes for Employee and Executive from earlier, so there's no change to those:

TypesAndTyping/GiveRaise.groovy

```
void giveRaise(Employee employee)
{
  employee.raise(new BigDecimal(10000.00))
  // same as
  //employee.raise(10000.00)
}

giveRaise new Employee()
giveRaise new Executive()
```

The output from the previous code is as follows:

```
Employee got raise
Executive got outlandish raise
```

---

8. Remember, Groovy treats primitives as objects. I could've sent it a double, and Groovy would've treated it as BigDecimal.

You see how dynamic Groovy is? If you have overloaded methods in your class, Groovy smartly picks the correct implementation not only based on the target object—the object on which the method is invoked—but also based on the parameter(s) you send to the call. Since the method dispatching is based on multiple objects—the target plus the parameters—this is called *multiple dispatch* or *multimethods*.

Multimethods fix a problem in Java.[9] Take a look at the following Java code that uses Generics. lst refers to an instance of ArrayList<String>, and col, which is of type Collection<String>, is referring to the same instance. You added three elements to lst and removed one. The remove got rid of the first element in the list. Now, you intend the call col.remove(0) to remove another element. However, the remove() method in the Collection interface expects an Object, so Java boxes the 0 into an Integer. And since an instance of Integer is not part of the list, it did not remove anything.

```
TypesAndTyping/UsingCollection.java
//Java code
import java.util.*;
public class UsingCollection
{
  public static void main(String[] args)
  {
    ArrayList<String> lst = new ArrayList<String>();
    Collection<String> col = lst;
    lst.add("one");
    lst.add("two");
    lst.add("three");
    lst.remove(0);
    col.remove(0);
    System.out.println("Added three items, remove two, so 1 item to remain.");
    System.out.println("Number of elements is: " + lst.size());
    System.out.println("Number of elements is: " + col.size());
  }
}
```

The output from the previous code is as follows:

```
Added three items, remove two, so 1 item to remain.
Number of elements is: 2
Number of elements is: 2
```

Now, don't make any change to the previous code. Simply copy and paste it as is into a file named UsingCollection.groovy, and run groovy

---

9. Thanks to Neal Ford for this Java example.

UsingCollection. The output from the Groovy execution of the previous code is as follows:

```
Added three items, remove two, so 1 item to remain.
Number of elements is: 1
Number of elements is: 1
```

Groovy's dynamic and multimethod capability nicely handles this case. At runtime it figures you meant to remove the first element and did not go into the unnecessary trouble of boxing that would lead to incorrect behavior here.

4.8 Dynamic: To Be or Not to Be?

Since Groovy is a dynamic language that supports optional typing, a good question to ask is, should you specify the type or rely on dynamic typing?

There are no real rules in this area, but you can certainly develop some preferences.

When programming in Groovy, I generally lean toward leaving out the type and instead making the parameter/variable names very expressive. Not specifying the type has the added advantages of benefiting from duck typing (Section 4.4, *Design by Capability*, on page 68) and from the ease of applying mocks for testing (Section 16.2, *Unit Testing Java and Groovy Code*, on page 231).

I opt to specify the type if I am forced to (such as when JUnit requires test methods to be void) or if that provides a significant benefit (such as when mapping types to databases in GORM).

If you're developing an API that's intended for use by someone using a static language, then I suggest you specify the parameter types for methods in the statically typed client-facing API.

In this chapter, you journeyed through the typing-related issues, benefits, and features of Groovy. You saw how the dynamic typing of Groovy allows you to make typing implicit when you don't care to specify. At the same time, you saw how easily the optional typing allows you to reach for the type declaration where you need it. You learned that method dispatching is quite different and powerful in Groovy, how to enjoy true polymorphism, and also how take advantage of the design by capability. In the next chapter, I'll take you into one of the most interesting features in Groovy—closures.

Chapter 5

Using Closures

Closures[1] are one of the Groovy features you'll use the most. You can pass closures to methods and invoke them. In fact, one of the biggest contributions of the GDK is extending the JDK with methods that take closures. Closures provide you with the power of function pointers, but with the elegance of objects and the ease of duck typing. Once you get the hang of using closures, you'll be eager to put them to good use in your own projects. So, in this chapter, we'll start with what closures are, why you should care, and how to use them. Along the way, you'll learn some inner mechanics of closures in Groovy and quickly pick up some advanced uses of closures.

5.1 Closures

Suppose you have a function that traverses a collection of values or objects. You may want to perform different operations on the selected values. You can fetch the selected values as an array and then operate on them. Alternately, you can work on them as they're selected—closures help you do that.

The Traditional Way

Let's consider a simple example—assume you want to find the sum of even values from 1 to a certain number n.

---

1. You may view Groovy closures more as lambda expressions, but Groovy uses a relaxed definition of the term *closures*. See http://groovy.codehaus.org/Closures+-+Formal+Definition for more information.

Here is the traditional approach:

UsingClosures/UsingEvenNumbers.groovy

```
def sum(n)
{
  total = 0
  for(int i = 2; i <= n; i += 2)
  {
    total += i
  }

  total
}
```

```
println "Sum of even numbers from 1 to 10 is ${sum(10)}"
```

In the method sum(), you're running a for loop that iterates over even numbers and sums them. Now, suppose instead that you want to find the product of even numbers from 1 to n.

UsingClosures/UsingEvenNumbers.groovy

```
def product(n)
{
  prod = 1
  for(int i = 2; i <= n; i += 2)
  {
    prod *= i
  }

  prod
}
```

```
println "Product of even numbers from 1 to 10 is ${product(10)}"
```

You again iterate over even numbers, this time computing their product. Now, what if you want to get a collection of squares of these values? The code that returns an array of squared values might look like the following:

UsingClosures/UsingEvenNumbers.groovy

```
def sqr(n)
{
  squared = []
  for(int i = 2; i <= n; i += 2)
  {
    squared << i ** 2
  }

  squared
}
```

```
println "Squares of even numbers from 1 to 10 is ${sqr(10)}"
```

The code that does the looping is the same (and duplicated) in each of the previous code examples. What's different is the part dealing with the sum, product, or squares. If you want to perform some other operation over the even numbers, you'd be duplicating the code that traverses the numbers. Let's find ways to remove that duplication.

The Groovy Way

Let's start with a function that allows you to simply pick even numbers. Once the function picks a number, it immediately sends it to a code block for processing. Let the code block simply print that number for now:

UsingClosures/PickEven.groovy
```
def pickEven(n, block)
{
  for(int i = 2; i <= n; i += 2)
  {
    block(i)
  }
}

pickEven(10, { println it } )
```

The pickEven()[2] method is iterating over values (like before), but this time, it yields or sends the value over to a block of code—or closure. The variable block holds a reference to a closure. Much like the way you can pass objects around, you can pass closures around. The variable name does not have to be named block; it can be any legal variable name. When calling the method pickEven(), you can now send a code block as shown in the earlier code. The block of code (the code within {}) is passed for the parameter block, like the value 10 for the variable n. In Groovy, you can pass as many closures as you want. So, the first, third, and last arguments for a method call, for example, may be closures. If a closure is the last argument, however, there is an elegant syntax, as shown here:

UsingClosures/PickEven.groovy
```
pickEven(10) { println it }
```

---

2. pickEven() is a *higher-order function*—a function that takes functions as arguments or returns a function as a result (http://c2.com/cgi/wiki?HigherOrderFunction).

If the closure is the last argument to a method call, you can attach the closure to the method call as shown earlier. The code block, in this case, appears like a parasite to the method call. Unlike Java code blocks, Groovy closures can't stand alone; they're either attached to a method or assigned to a variable.

What's that it in the block? If you are passing only one parameter to the code block, then you can refer to it with a special variable name it. You can give an alternate name for that variable if you like, as shown here:

UsingClosures/PickEven.groovy

```
pickEven(10) { evenNumber -> println evenNumber }
```

The variable evenNumber now refers to the argument that is passed to this closure from within the pickEven() method.

Now, let's revisit the computations on even numbers. You can use pick-Even() to compute the sum, as shown here:

UsingClosures/PickEven.groovy

```
total = 0
pickEven(10) { total += it }
println "Sum of even numbers from 1 to 10 is ${total}"
```

Similarly, you can compute the product, as shown here:

UsingClosures/PickEven.groovy

```
product = 1
pickEven(10) { product *= it }
println "Product of even numbers from 1 to 10 is ${product}"
```

The block of code in the previous example does something more than the block of code you saw earlier. It stretches its hands and reaches out to the variable product in the scope of the caller of pickEven(). This is an interesting characteristic of closures. A closure is a function with variables bound to a context or environment in which it executes.

Closures are derived from the lambda expressions from functional programming: "A lambda expression specifies the parameter and the mapping of a function." ([Seb04]) Closures are one of the most powerful features in Groovy, yet they are syntactically elegant.[3]

---

3. "A little bit of syntax sugar helps you to swallow the λ calculus." —Peter J. Landin

5.2 Use of Closures

What makes closures interesting? Other than the syntactic elegance, closures provide a simple and easy way for a function to delegate part of its implementation logic.

In C you can delegate using function pointers. They're very powerful, but they're bound to hurt your head. Java uses anonymous inner classes, but they tie you to an interface. Closures do the same thing but are lighter and more flexible. In the following example, totalSelectValues() accepts a closure to help decide the set of values used in computation:

UsingClosures/Strategy.groovy

```
def totalSelectValues(n, closure)
{
  total = 0
  for(i in 1..n)
  {
    if (closure(i)) { total += i }
  }

  total
}

print "Total of even numbers from 1 to 10 is "
println totalSelectValues(10) { it % 2 == 0 }

print "Total of odd numbers from 1 to 10 is "
println totalSelectValues(10) { it % 2 != 0}
```

The method totalSelectValues() iterates from 1 to n. For each value it calls the closure[4] to determine whether the value must be used in the computation, and it delegates the selection process to the closure.

The closure attached to the first call to totalSelectValues() selects only even numbers; the closure in the second call, on the other hand, selects only odd numbers. If you're a fan of design patterns [GHJV95], celebrate that you just implemented, effortlessly, the Strategy pattern.

Let's look at another example. Assume you're creating a simulator that allows you to plug in different calculations for equipment. You want to perform some computation but want to use the appropriate calculator.

---

4. return is optional even in closures; the value of the last expression (possibly null) is automatically returned to the caller if you don't have an explicit return (see Section 3.8, *return Is Not Always Optional*, on page 56).

The following code shows an example of how to do that:

UsingClosures/Simulate.groovy

```groovy
class Equipment
{
  def calculator

  Equipment(calc) { calculator = calc }

  def simulate()
  {
    println "Running simulation"
    calculator() // You may send parameters as well
  }
}

eq1 = new Equipment() { println "Calculator 1" }

aCalculator = { println "Calculator 2" }

eq2 = new Equipment(aCalculator)
eq3 = new Equipment(aCalculator)

eq1.simulate()
eq2.simulate()
eq3.simulate()
```

Equipment's constructor takes a closure as a parameter and stores that in a property named calculator. In the simulate() method, you call the closure to perform the calculations. When an instance eq1 of Equipment is created, a calculator is attached to it as a closure. What if you need to reuse that code block? You can save the closure into a variable—like the aCalculator in the previous code. You've used this in the creation of two other instances of Equipment, namely, eq2 and eq3. The output from the previous code is as follows:

```
Running simulation
Calculator 1
Running simulation
Calculator 2
Running simulation
Calculator 2
```

A great place to look for examples of closures is in the Collections classes, which make extensive use of closures. Refer to Section 7.2, *Iterating Over an ArrayList*, on page 117 for details.

5.3 Working with Closures

In the previous sections, you saw how to define and use closures. In this section, you'll learn how to send multiple parameters to closures.

it is the default name for a single parameter passed to a closure. You can use it as long as you know that only one parameter is passed in. If you have more than one parameter passed, you need to list those by name, as in this example:

UsingClosures/ClosureWithTwoParameters.groovy

```
def tellFortune(closure)
{
  closure new Date("11/15/2007"), "Your day is filled with ceremony"
}

tellFortune() { date, fortune ->
  println "Fortune for ${date} is '${fortune}'"
}
```

The method tellFortune() calls its closure with two parameters, namely an instance of Date and a fortune message String. The closure refers to these two with the names date and fortune. The symbol -> separates the parameter declarations in the closure from its body. The output from the previous code is as follows:

```
Fortune for Thu Nov 15 00:00:00 MST 2007 is 'Your day is filled with ceremony'
```

Since Groovy supports optional typing, you can define the types of parameters in the closure, if you like, as shown here:

UsingClosures/ClosureWithTwoParameters.groovy

```
tellFortune() { Date date, fortune ->
  println "Fortune for ${date} is '${fortune}'"
}
```

5.4 Closure and Resource Cleanup

Java's automatic garbage collection is a mixed blessing. You don't have to worry about resource deallocation, provided you release references. But, there's no guarantee when the resource may actually be cleaned up, because it's up to the discretion of the garbage collector. In certain situations, you might want the cleanup to happen straightaway. This is the reason you see methods such as close() and destroy() on resource-intensive classes.

Execute Around Method

If you have a pair of actions that have to be performed together—such as open and close—you can use the Execute Around Method pattern, a Smalltalk pattern (Bec96). You write a method—the "execute around" method—that takes a block as a parameter. In the method, you sandwich the call to the block in between calls to the pair of methods; that is, call the first method, then invoke the block, and finally call the second method. Users of your method don't have to worry about the pair of action; they're called automatically. Make sure you take care of exceptions within the "execute around" method.

One problem, though, is the users of your class may forget to call these methods. Closures can help ensure that these get called. I will show you how.

The following code creates a FileWriter, writes some data, but forgets to call close() on it. If you run this code, the file output.txt will not have the data/character you wrote.

UsingClosures/FileClose.groovy

```groovy
writer = new FileWriter('output.txt')
writer.write('!')
// forgot to call writer.close()
```

Let's rewrite this code using the Groovy-added withWriter() method. with-Writer() flushes and closes the stream automatically when you return from the closure.

UsingClosures/FileClose.groovy

```groovy
new FileWriter('output.txt').withWriter { writer ->
  writer.write('a')
} // no need to close()
```

Now you don't have to worry about closing the stream; you can focus on getting your work done. You can implement such convenience methods for your own classes also, making the users of your class happy and productive. For example, suppose you expect users of your class Resource to call open() before calling any other instance methods and then call close() when done.

Here is an example of the Resource class:

UsingClosures/ResourceCleanup.groovy

```groovy
class Resource
{
  def open() { print "opened..." }
  def close() { print "closed" }
  def read() { print "read..." }
  def write() { print "write..." }
  //...
```

Here is a usage of this class:

UsingClosures/ResourceCleanup.groovy

```groovy
def resource = new Resource()
resource.open()
resource.read()
resource.write()
```

Sadly, the user of your class failed to close(), and the resource was not closed, as you can see in the following output:

```
opened...read...write...
```

Closures can help here—you can use the Execute Around Method pattern (see the sidebar on the preceding page) to tackle this problem. Create a static method named use(), in this example, as shown here:

UsingClosures/ResourceCleanup.groovy

```groovy
def static use(closure)
{
  def r = new Resource()
  try
  {
    r.open()
    closure(r)
  }
  finally
  {
   r.close()
  }
}
```

In the previous static method, you create an instance of Resource, call open() on it, invoke the closure, and finally call close(). You guard the call with a try-finally, so you'll close() even if the closure call throws an exception.

Now, the users of your class can use it, as shown here:

UsingClosures/ResourceCleanup.groovy

```groovy
Resource.use { res ->
  res.read()
  res.write()
}
```

The output from the previous code is as follows:

```
opened...read...write...closed
```

Thanks to the closure, now the call to close() is automatic, deterministic, and right on time. You can focus on the application domain and its inherent complexities and let the libraries handle system-level tasks such as guaranteed cleanup in file I/O, and so on.

5.5 Closures and Coroutines

Calling a function or method creates a new scope in the execution sequence of a program. You enter the function at one entry point (top). Once you complete the method, you return to the caller's scope.

Coroutines,[5] on the other hand, allow a function to have multiple entry points, each following the place of the last suspended call. You can enter a function, execute part of it, suspend, and go back to execute some code in the context or scope of the caller. You can then resume execution of the function from where you suspended. Coroutines are handy to implement some special logic or algorithms, such as in a producer-consumer problem. A producer receives some input, does initial processing on it, and notifies a consumer to take that processed value for further computation and output or storage. The consumer does its part and, when done, notifies the producer to get more input.

In Java, wait() and notify() help you implement coroutines when combined with multithreading. Closures give the impression (or illusion) of coroutines in a single thread.

---

5. "In contrast to the unsymmetric relationship between a main routine and a subroutine, there is complete symmetry between coroutines, which call on each other." —Donald E. Knuth in [Knu97]

For example, take a look at this:

`UsingClosures/Coroutine.groovy`

```groovy
def iterate(n, closure)
{
  1.upto(n) {
    println "In iterate with value ${it}"
    closure(it)
  }
}

println "Calling iterate"
total = 0
iterate(4) {
  total += it
  println "In closure total so far is ${total}"
  }
println "Done"
```

In this code, the control transfers back and forth between the iterate() method and the closure. The output from the previous code is as follows:

```
Calling iterate
In iterate with value 1
In closure total so far is 1
In iterate with value 2
In closure total so far is 3
In iterate with value 3
In closure total so far is 6
In iterate with value 4
In closure total so far is 10
Done
```

In each call to the closure, you're resuming with the value of total from the previous call. It feels like the execution sequence is like the one shown in Figure 5.1, on the following page—you're switching between the context of two functions back and forth.

5.6 Curried Closure

There's a feature that adds spice to Groovy—it's called *curried closures*.[6] When you curry() a closure, you're asking the parameters to be pre-bound, as illustrated in Figure 5.2, on page 93. This can help remove redundancy or duplication in your code.

---

6. It has really nothing to do with my favorite Indian dish.

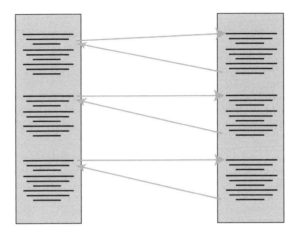

Figure 5.1: EXECUTION SEQUENCE OF A COROUTINE

Here's an example:

UsingClosures/Currying.groovy

```
def tellFortunes(closure)
{
  Date date = new Date("11/15/2007")

  //closure date, "Your day is filled with ceremony"
  //closure date, "They're features, not bugs"
  // You can curry to avoid sending date repeatedly

  postFortune = closure.curry(date)

  postFortune "Your day is filled with ceremony"
  postFortune "They're features, not bugs"
}

tellFortunes() { date, fortune ->
  println "Fortune for ${date} is '${fortune}'"
}
```

The tellFortunes() method calls a closure multiple times. The closure takes two parameters. So, tellFortunes() would have to send the first parameter date in each call. Alternately, you can curry that parameter. Call curry() with date as an argument. postFortune holds a reference to the curried closure. The curried object prebinds the value of date.

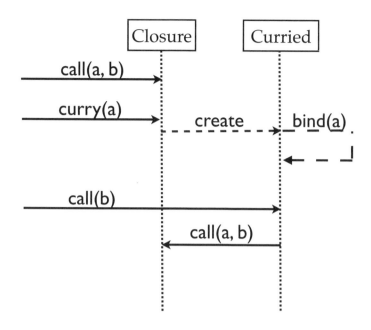

Figure 5.2: CURRYING A CLOSURE

You can now call the curried closure and pass only the second parameter (fortune) that is intended for the original closure. The curried closure takes care of sending the fortune along with the prebound parameter date to the original closure. The output of the code is as follows:

```
Fortune for Thu Nov 15 00:00:00 MST 2007 is 'Your day is filled with ceremony'
Fortune for Thu Nov 15 00:00:00 MST 2007 is 'They're features, not bugs'
```

You can curry any number of parameters, but you can curry only leading parameters. So if you have n parameters, you can curry any of the first k parameters, where 0 <= k <= n.

Currying is to express a function that takes multiple parameters using functions that take fewer (typically one) parameter. The name *Curry* was coined after Haskell B. Curry by Christopher Strachey. Moses Schönfinkel and Friedrich Ludwig Gottlob Frege invented the concept. The curry function on the function f(X,Y) -> Z is defined as curry(f): X -> (Y -> Z). Currying helps reduce and simplify methods for mathematical proofs. For our purpose, in Groovy, currying can reduce the noise in code.

5.7 Dynamic Closures

You can determine whether a closure has been provided to you. Otherwise, you may decide to use a default implementation for, say, an algorithm in place of a specialized implementation the caller failed to provide. Here's an example to figure out whether a closure is present:

UsingClosures/MissingClosure.groovy

```groovy
def doSomeThing(closure)
{
  if (closure) { return closure() }

  println "Using default implementation"
}

doSomeThing() { println "Use specialized implementation" }

doSomeThing()
```

The output from the previous code is as follows:

```
Use specialized implementation
Using default implementation
```

You can also dynamically determine the number of parameters to a closure and the types of those parameters, which gives you a greater flexibility. Assume you use a closure to compute the tax for a sale. The tax amount depends on the sale amount and the tax rate. Also assume that the closure may or may not need you to provide the tax rate. Here's an example to examine the number of parameters:

UsingClosures/QueryingClosures.groovy

```groovy
def completeOrder(amount, taxComputer)
{
  tax = 0
  if (taxComputer.maximumNumberOfParameters == 2)
  {// expects tax rate
    tax = taxComputer(amount, 6.05)
  }
  else
  {// uses a default rate
    tax = taxComputer(amount)
  }

  println "Sales tax is ${tax}"
}

completeOrder(100) { it * 0.0825 }

completeOrder(100) { amount, rate -> amount * (rate/100) }
```

The maximumNumberOfParameters property (or getMaximumNumberOfParameters() method) tells you the number of parameters the given closure accepts. You can determine the types of these parameters using the parameterTypes property (or getParameterTypes() method). The output from the previous code is as follows:

```
Sales tax is 8.2500
Sales tax is 6.0500
```

Here is an example examining the parameters of the closures provided:

UsingClosures/ClosuresParameterTypes.groovy

```groovy
def examine(closure)
{
  println "$closure.maximumNumberOfParameters parameter(s) given:"
  for(aParameter in closure.parameterTypes) { println aParameter.name }

  println "--"
}

examine() { }
examine() { it }
examine() {-> }
examine() { val1 -> }
examine() {Date val1 -> }
examine() {Date val1, val2 -> }
examine() {Date val1, String val2 -> }
```

The output from the previous code is as follows:

```
1 parameter(s) given:
java.lang.Object
--
1 parameter(s) given:
java.lang.Object
--
0 parameter(s) given:
--
1 parameter(s) given:
java.lang.Object
--
1 parameter(s) given:
java.util.Date
--
2 parameter(s) given:
java.util.Date
java.lang.Object
--
2 parameter(s) given:
java.util.Date
java.lang.String
--
```

Even when a closure is not using any parameters as in {} or { it }, it takes one parameter (whose name defaults to it). If the caller does not pass any values to the closure, then the first parameter (it) refers to null. If you want your closure to absolutely take no parameter, then you have to use the syntax {-> }—the lack of parameter before -> indicates that your closure takes 0 parameters.

Using the maximumNumberOfParameters and parameterTypes properties, you can examine the given closures dynamically and implement logic with greater flexibility.

Talking about examining objects, what does this mean within a closure? We will take a look at this next.

5.8 Closure Delegation

Three properties of a closure determine which object handles a method call from within a closure. These are this, owner, and delegate. Generally, the delegate is set to owner, but changing it allows you to exploit Groovy for some really good metaprogramming capabilities. In this section, we'll examine these properties for closures:

```
UsingClosures/ThisOwnerDelegate.groovy
def examiningClosure(closure)
{
  closure()
}

examiningClosure() {
  println "In First Closure:"
  println "class is " + getClass().name
  println "this is " + this + ", super:" + this.getClass().superclass.name
  println "owner is " + owner + ", super:" + owner.getClass().superclass.name
  println "delegate is " + delegate +
              ", super:" + delegate.getClass().superclass.name

  examiningClosure() {
    println "In Closure within the First Closure:"
    println "class is " + getClass().name
    println "this is " + this + ", super:" + this.getClass().superclass.name
    println "owner is " + owner + ", super:" + owner.getClass().superclass.name
    println "delegate is " + delegate +
                ", super:" + delegate.getClass().superclass.name
  }
}
```

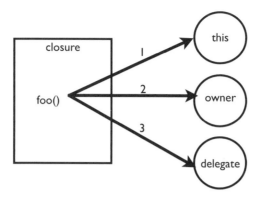

Figure 5.3: ORDER OF METHOD RESOLUTION ON METHOD CALLS FROM CLOSURES

Within the first closure, you fetch the details about the closure, finding out what this, owner, and delegate refer to. Then within the first closure, you call a method and send it another closure defined within the first closure, making the first closure the owner of the second closure. Within this second closure, you print those details again. The output from the previous code is as follows:

```
In First Closure:
class is ThisOwnerDelegate$_run_closure1
this is ThisOwnerDelegate@55e6cb2a, super:groovy.lang.Script
owner is ThisOwnerDelegate@55e6cb2a, super:groovy.lang.Script
delegate is ThisOwnerDelegate@55e6cb2a, super:groovy.lang.Script
In Closure within the First Closure:
class is ThisOwnerDelegate$_run_closure1_closure2
this is ThisOwnerDelegate@55e6cb2a, super:groovy.lang.Script
owner is ThisOwnerDelegate$_run_closure1@15c330aa, super:groovy.lang.Closure
delegate is ThisOwnerDelegate$_run_closure1@15c330aa, super:groovy.lang.Closure
```

The previous code example and the corresponding output show that closures are created as inner classes. It also shows that the delegate is set to owner. Certain Groovy functions—such as identity()—modify delegate to perform dynamic routing. this within a closure refers to the object to which the closure is bound (the executing context). Variables and methods referred to within the closure are bound to this—it has dibs on handling any methods calls or access to any properties or variables. The owner stands in next and then the delegate. This sequence is illustrated in Figure 5.3.

Here's an example of method resolution:

UsingClosures/MethodRouting.groovy

```
class Handler
{
  def f1() { println "f1 of Handler called ..."}
  def f2() { println "f2 of Handler called ..."}
}

class Example
{
  def f1() { println "f1 of Example called ..."}
  def f2() { println "f2 of Example called ..."}

  def foo(closure)
  {
    closure.delegate = new Handler()
    closure()
  }
}

def f1() { println "f1 of Script called..." }

new Example().foo {
  f1()
  f2()
}
```

In this code, calls to methods within the closure are first routed to the context object—this—for the closure. If they're not found, they're routed to the delegate:

```
f1 of Script called...
f2 of Handler called ...
```

If you set the delegate property of a closure, ask whether it will have side effects, especially if the closure can be used in other functions or in other threads. If you're absolutely sure that the closure is not used elsewhere, you can set the delegate. If it is used elsewhere, avoid the side effect—clone the closure, set the delegate on the clone, and use the clone.

Refer to Section 18.6, *Closures and DSLs*, on page 278 to see how the concepts you learned in this section are used to build DSLs. Also refer to Section 8.1, *Object Extensions*, on page 133 and Section 14.2, *Injecting Methods Using ExpandoMetaClass*, on page 203. ExpandoMetaClass uses delegate to proxy methods of your class.

5.9 Using Closures

You saw the power and elegance of closures in this chapter, but let's now discuss how to approach them in your projects. You need to decide whether you want to implement a certain functionality or task as a regular function/method or whether you should use a closure.

I view closures as pieces of code that augment, refine, or enhance another piece of code. For example, a closure may be useful to express a predicate or condition that will refine the selection of objects. Use closures where you want to take advantage of coroutines such as control flow (like in iterators).

Closures are very helpful in two specific areas. They can help manage resource cleanup (see Section 5.4, *Closure and Resource Cleanup*, on page 87). They also help create internal DSLs (see Chapter 18, *Creating DSLs in Groovy*, on page 273).

If I want to implement a certain well-identified task, I prefer a regular function instead of a closure. A good time to introduce closures is during refactoring. Why not get the code working first? Then revisit it to see whether you can make it better and more elegant. Let a closure emerge from this effort rather than forcing the use of a closure.

Keep your closures small and cohesive. These are intended to be small chunks of code (a few lines) that are attached to method calls. When writing a method that uses a closure, don't overuse dynamic properties of closures. It must be very simple and obvious to implement a closure to call your method.

In this chapter, you became familiar with one of the most important concepts in Groovy—one that you'll use repeatedly. You now know how to work with closures in a dynamic context. You also understand how closures dispatch method calls. As you read the following chapters, you'll see several examples where closures stand out, so you'll have plenty of opportunity to appreciate their charm.

orking with Strings

...t with strings in Java. As fundamental
...you would think it would be easier. But
...ring manipulation, to evaluate multiple
...string representation, and even to do
...string that spans multiple lines. Groovy
...ray the pain of dealing with strings on
...ttern matching of strings with regular
...roviding special operators. You'll learn
...his chapter.

...erals using single quotes—like 'hello'—
...creating strings with single quotes in
...ile "a" is a String. Groovy makes no such
...stances of String in Groovy. However, if
...instance of Character—remember, there
...you can't use char—simply type 'a' as
...nplicitly create Character objects if any

...at you can put into a literal. For exam-
...double quotes in your string if you want.

WorkingWithStrings/Literals.groovy

```
println 'He said, "That is Groovy"'
```

---

1. Just as int is treated as Integer, char is treated as Character. Groovy is an equal opportunity language.

The output from the previous code is as follows:

```
He said, "That is Groovy"
```

Let's examine the type of the object that was created using the single quotes:

WorkingWithStrings/Literals.groovy
```
str = 'A string'
println str.getClass().name
```

The following output shows that the object is the popular String:

```
java.lang.String
```

Groovy treats a String created using single quotes as a pure literal. So, if you put any expressions in it, Groovy won't expand them; instead, it will use them literally as you provided them. You'll have to use double quotes for that, as you'll see soon:

WorkingWithStrings/Literals.groovy
```
value = 25
println 'The value is ${value}'
```

The output from the previous code is as follows:

```
The value is ${value}
```

Java Strings are immutable, and Groovy honors that immutability.[2] Once you create an instance of String, you can't modify its content by calling setters, and so on. You can read a character using [] operator; however, you can't modify it, as you can see from the following code:

WorkingWithStrings/Literals.groovy
```
str = 'hello'
println str[2]

try
{
  str[2] = '!'
}
catch(Exception ex)
{
  println ex
}
```

---

2. Both in Java and Groovy you can find ways to get around encapsulation and break immutability. In Groovy that's a bit easier than in Java. But, you're a good citizen interested in the good practices, so we'll ignore those how-to-break-stuff approaches in this book.

The previous code produces the following output:

```
1
groovy.lang.MissingMethodException: No signature of method:
  java.lang.String.putAt() is applicable for argument types:
  (java.lang.Integer, java.lang.String) values: {2, "!"}
```

To create an expression, use either double quotes ("") or slashes (//). You can use either one; however, double quotes are often used to define string expressions, and forward slashes are used for regular expressions. Here's an example for creating an expression:

WorkingWithStrings/Expressions.groovy

```
value = 12

println "He paid \$${value} for that."
```

The output from the previous code is as follows:

```
He paid $12 for that.
```

The variable value was expanded within the string. I had to use the escape character (\) to print the $ symbol since Groovy uses that symbol for embedding expressions. You don't have to escape the $ if you use slashes to define the string instead of double quotes. The {} around expressions are optional if the expression is a simple variable name like value or access to a property. So, you could write the statement println "He paid \$${value} for that." as println "He paid \$$value for that." or println (/He paid $$value for that/). Try leaving out the {} in expressions and see whether Groovy complains. You can always add it if needed.

You can store an expression in a string and print it later—Groovy uses lazy evaluation. Let's look at an example:

WorkingWithStrings/Expressions.groovy

```
what = new StringBuffer('fence')
text = "The cow jumped over the $what"
println text

what.replace(0, 5, "moon")
println text
```

The output from the previous code is as follows:

```
The cow jumped over the fence
The cow jumped over the moon
```

When you print the string expression in text, the current value in the object referred to by what is used. So, the first time you printed text, you got "The cow jumped over the fence." Then, after changing the value in the StringBuffer when you reprinted the string expression—you did not modify the content of text—you got a different output, this time the phrase "The cow jumped over the moon" from the popular rhyme "Hey Diddle Diddle."

From this behavior you see that strings created using single quotes are different from those created using double quotes or slashes. Strings created using single quotes are regular java.lang.Strings. However, those created using double quotes and slashes are special. The authors of Groovy have a weird sense of humor—they called them GStrings, short for *Groovy strings*. Let's look at the type of the objects created using different string syntax:

WorkingWithStrings/Expressions.groovy

```
def printClassInfo(obj)
{
  println "class: ${obj.getClass().name}"
  println "superclass: ${obj.getClass().superclass.name}"
}

val = 125
printClassInfo ("The Stock closed at ${val}")
printClassInfo (/The Stock closed at ${val}/)
printClassInfo ("This is a simple String")
```

From the output for the previous code, shown next, you can see the actual types of the objects created:

```
class: org.codehaus.groovy.runtime.GStringImpl
superclass: groovy.lang.GString
class: org.codehaus.groovy.runtime.GStringImpl
superclass: groovy.lang.GString
class: java.lang.String
superclass: java.lang.Object
```

Groovy does not readily create an instance of GString simply because you use double quotes or slashes. It intelligently analyzes the string to determine whether it can get away with a simple regular String. You can see that in the example, the argument to the last call of printClassInfo() is an instance of String even though you used double quotes to create it.

6.2 GString Lazy Evaluation Problem

When I first encountered GString lazy evaluation, I tripped over this really badly, and some bright people pulled me up and helped me grasp this concept. So, I think it deserves some discussion.

Here's the example that worked well in the previous section:

`WorkingWithStrings/LazyEval.groovy`

```
what = new StringBuffer('fence')
text = "The cow jumped over the $what"
println text

what.replace(0, 5, "moon")
println text
```

The output from the previous code is as follows:

```
The cow jumped over the fence
The cow jumped over the moon
```

The GString (text) contains the variable what. The expression is evaluated just in time each time you print it—when the toString() method is called on it. If you changed the value in the StringBuffer object referred by what, the expression reflects it when printed. That seems reasonable, right?

Unfortunately, this is not the behavior you'll see if you modify the reference what instead of changing the referenced object's properties—that's what you'd naturally do if the object were immutable. Here's an example that shows the problem:

`WorkingWithStrings/LazyEval.groovy`

```
price = 568.23
company = 'Google'
quote = "Today $company stock closed at $price"
println quote

stocks = [Apple : 130.01, Microsoft : 35.95]

stocks.each { key, value ->
  company = key
  price = value
  println quote
}
```

This code stores an expression in quote that has the variables company and price. When you print it the first time, it correctly prints Google and the its stock price. You have the stocks of a few other companies, and you want to use the expression you created before to print the quote for these companies as well. So, you iterate over the stocks map—within the closure you have the company as the key and the price as the value. However, when you print the quote, the result (shown next) is not what you expected. You have to fix this problem before your colleagues start another "Google has taken over the world" debate.

```
Today Google stock closed at 568.23
Today Google stock closed at 568.23
Today Google stock closed at 568.23
```

First, let's figure out why it did not work as expected, and then we can figure out a solution. When you defined the GString—quote—you bound the variables company and price to a String holding the value Google and an Integer holding that obscene stock price, respectively. You can change the company and price references all you want (both of these are referring to immutable objects) to refer to other objects, but you're not changing what the GString instance has been bound to.

"The cow jumping over..." example worked because you modified the object that the GString was bound to; however, in this example, you don't. You can't because of immutability. The solution? You need to ask the GString to reevaluate the reference.[3]

Closures come to the rescue again. Closures in Groovy are what help you define some code now but execute it later. GString does something special when evaluating expressions—if you have a variable, it prints its value to a writer, typically a StringWriter. However, instead of a variable, if you have a closure, it invokes the closure. If your closure takes a parameter (remember that if you don't specify any parameters, by default it takes one[4]), then GString sends the Writer object to the parameter of your closure. If your closure takes no parameters at all, then it simply calls your closure and prints the result you return to the writer. If your closure takes more than one parameter, then the call fails with an exception. Let's not go there.

So, let's put that wisdom to use. Here's the first attempt:

WorkingWithStrings/LazyEval.groovy

```
companyClosure = { it.write(company) }
priceClosure = { it.write("$price") }
quote = "Today ${companyClosure} stock closed at ${priceClosure}"

stocks.each { key, value ->
  company = key
  price = value
  println quote
}
```

---

3. "Any problem in computer science can be solved with another level of indirection." —David Wheeler
4. See Section 5.7, *Dynamic Closures*, on page 94.

The output from the previous code is as follows:

```
Today Apple stock closed at 130.01
Today Microsoft stock closed at 35.95
```

So, you got the output you desire, but the code does not look that groovy. Even though you don't want to implement your final code this way, I think seeing this example will help you in two ways. First, you can see what's really going on—the GString is calling your closure at the time when the expression needs to be evaluated/printed. Second, if you have a need to do some computations that are more than merely displaying a property's value, you know how to do it.

Let's first get rid of that parameter it. Like I mentioned earlier, if your closure has no parameters, then GString uses what you return. You know how to create a closure with no parameters—define it with the syntax {->. So, let's refactor the previous code:

WorkingWithStrings/LazyEval.groovy

```
companyClosure = {-> company }
priceClosure = {-> price }
quote = "Today ${companyClosure} stock closed at ${priceClosure}"

stocks.each { key, value ->
  company = key
  price = value
  println quote
}
```

The output from this code is as follows:

```
Today Apple stock closed at 130.01
Today Microsoft stock closed at 35.95
```

That's a notch better, but still, you don't want to define the closures separately. Instead, you want your code to be self-contained for simple cases, and you're willing to write a separate closure if you have more code to compute the values. Here's the self-contained code that solves the problem (we'll call it the "Google taking over the world problem"):

WorkingWithStrings/LazyEval.groovy

```
quote = "Today ${-> company } stock closed at ${-> price }"

stocks.each { key, value ->
  company = key
  price = value
  println quote
}
```

The output from the previous code is as follows:

```
Today Apple stock closed at 130.01
Today Microsoft stock closed at 35.95
```

GString's lazy evaluation is a very powerful concept. However, use caution not to trip over that string. If you expect your references used in expressions to change and you want their current value to be used in the lazy evaluation, remember not to place them directly in the expressions. Instead, place them within a no-parameter closure.

6.3 Multiline String

When you want to create a multiline string in Java, you have to use code like str += ..., concatenated multiple lines using the + operator, or multiple calls to the append() method of StringBuffer or StringBuilder.

You'd have to use a lot of escape characters, and writing that usually is followed by a long grimace. You might have complained that "there's gotta be a better way to do that." In Groovy there is. You can define a multiline literal by enclosing the string within three single quotes (''...'')—that's Groovy's support of here documents, or *heredocs*:

WorkingWithStrings/MultilineStrings.groovy

```
memo = '''Several of you raised concerns about long meetings.
To discuss this, we will be holding a 3 hour meeting starting
at 9AM tomorrow. All getting this memo are required to attend.
If you can't make it, please have a meeting with your manager to explain.
'''

println memo
```

The output from the previous code is as follows:

```
Several of you raised concerns about long meetings.
To discuss this, we will be holding a 3 hour meeting starting
at 9AM tomorrow. All getting this memo are required to attend.
If you can't make it, please have a meeting with your manager to explain.
```

What if you want to create a string with embedded values of variables? Just as you can create GStrings that can hold expressions using double-quoted strings, you can create multiline expressions using three double quotes.

WorkingWithStrings/MultilineStrings.groovy

```
price = 251.12

message = """We're very pleased to announce
that our stock price hit a high of \$${price} per share
on December 24th. Great news in time for...
"""
println message
```

The previous code gives the following output:

```
We're very pleased to announce
that our stock price hit a high of $251.12 per share
on December 24th. Great news in time for...
```

I write a monthly newsletter, and a couple of years ago I decided to convert the program I use to send email notifications to Groovy. Groovy's ability to create multiline strings with embedded values came in handy. Groovy even makes it easy to spam! (Hey, I'm just kidding.)

Let's take a look at an example of using the feature you learned just now. Assume you have a map of languages and authors and want to create an XML representation of it. Here is a way to do that:[5]

WorkingWithStrings/CreateXML.groovy

```
langs = ['C++' : 'Stroustrup', 'Java' : 'Gosling', 'Lisp' : 'McCarthy']

content = ''
langs.each {language, author ->
fragment = """
  <language name="${language}">
    <author>${author}</author>
  </language>
"""

content += fragment
}

xml = "<languages>${content}</languages>"

println xml
```

---

5. If you are impressed with this, wait until you see the XML builders (Section 17.1, *Building XML*, on page 255).

The output from the previous code is as follows:

```
<languages>
  <language name="C++">
    <author>Stroustrup</author>
  </language>

  <language name="Java">
    <author>Gosling</author>
  </language>

  <language name="Lisp">
    <author>McCarthy</author>
  </language>
</languages>
```

You're using the multiline string with embedded expressions to create the desired content. The content is generated by iterating over the map that contains the data.

6.4 String Convenience Methods

You already heard me praise the execute method of String. In fact, it helped you create a Process object so you can execute system-level processes with only a couple of lines of code.[6]

You can get fancier with String using other methods. For example, take a look at the following code that uses an overloaded operator of String:

WorkingWithStrings/StringConvenience.groovy

```
str = "It's a rainy day in Seattle"

println str

str -= "rainy "

println str
```

The output from the previous code is as follows:

```
It's a rainy day in Seattle
It's a day in Seattle
```

The -= operator is useful to manipulate a string, because it removes part of the string that matches the string on the right side. This is made possible by the Groovy-added minus() method on the String class (see

---

6. See Section 3.1, *A Quick Look at the GDK*, on page 28.

Section 3.6, *Operator Overloading*, on page 44). Groovy adds other convenience methods[7] to String: plus() [+], multiply() [*], next() [++], replaceAll(), and tokenize(), to mention a few.

You can iterate over a range of Strings as well, as shown here:

```
WorkingWithStrings/StringRange.groovy
for(str in 'held'..'helm')
{
  print "${str} "
}
println ""
```

The output from the previous code is as follows:

```
held hele helf helg helh heli helj helk hell helm
```

Here you are still using the same java.lang.String; however, all these added facilities will help you get your work done quickly.

6.5 Regular Expressions

The JDK package java.util.regex contains the API for pattern matching with regular expressions[8] (RegEx). String's replaceFirst() and replaceAll() methods, among other methods, make good use of RegEx pattern matching. Groovy adds operators and symbols to make it easier to program with RegEx.

Groovy provides the operator ~ to easily create a RegEx pattern. This operator maps to String's negate() method:

```
WorkingWithStrings/RegEx.groovy
obj = ~"hello"

println obj.getClass().name
```

The output from the previous code is as follows:

```
java.util.regex.Pattern
```

The previous example shows that ~ applied to String creates an instance of Pattern. You can use either (single or double) quotes or slashes to create a RegEx. The slashes have an added advantage that you don't have to escape backslashes. So, /\d*\w*/ is an equivalent and elegant cousin of "\\d*\\w*".

---

7. Refer to http://groovy.codehaus.org/groovy-jdk/java/lang/String.html for more details.
8. For a detailed discussion of RegEx, refer to [Fri97].

Groovy provides a couple of operators to facilitate matching regular expressions: =~ and ==~. Let me explain the capabilities of and differences between these operators:

WorkingWithStrings/RegEx.groovy

```
pattern = ~"(G|g)roovy"
text = 'Groovy is Hip'
if (text =~ pattern)
  println "match"
else
  println "no match"

if (text ==~ pattern)
  println "match"
else
  println "no match"
```

The previous code gives you the following output:

```
match
no match
```

The =~ performs a RegEx partial match, while the ==~ performs a RegEx exact match. So, in the previous code example, the first pattern match reports a "match," while the second one reports a "no match."

The =~ operator returns a matcher object,[9] which is an instance of java.util.regex.Matcher. If the match results in multiple matches, then the matcher contains an array of the matches. This helps quickly get access to different parts of the text that match the given RegEx.

WorkingWithStrings/RegEx.groovy

```
matcher = 'Groovy is groovy' =~ /(G|g)roovy/
print "Size of matcher is ${matcher.size()} "
println "with elements ${matcher[0]} and ${matcher[1]}."
```

The previous code reports the details of the Matcher, as follows:

```
Size of matcher is 2 with elements ["Groovy", "G"] and ["groovy", "g"].
```

You can replace matching contents of text easily using the replaceFirst() method (for replacing only the first match as the name indicates) or the replaceAll() method (for replacing all matches).

---

9. Groovy handles boolean evaluation of Matcher differently; it returns true if there's at least one match. See Section 3.5, *Groovy boolean Evaluation*, on page 43.

`WorkingWithStrings/RegEx.groovy`

```
str = 'Groovy is groovy, really groovy'
println str
result = (str =~ /groovy/).replaceAll('hip')
println result
```

The original text and the replaced text is as follows:

```
Groovy is groovy, really groovy
Groovy is hip, really hip
```

To summarize, here are the Groovy operators related to RegEx:

- To create a pattern from a string, use the ~ operator.

- To define a RegEx, use forward slashes as in /[G|g]roovy/.

- To determine whether there's a match, use =~.

- For an exact match, use ==~.

In this chapter, you saw how Groovy makes creating and using string so much easier than in Java. It is a breeze to create multiline strings and strings with expressions. You also saw how Groovy simplifies the effort to work with RegEx. Groovy strings will make you feel turbocharged when you get down to regular string manipulations or working with regular expressions.

Chapter 7

Working with Collections

We constantly work with collections of objects in Java. You collect them, pass them around as lists, look in a dictionary or map for values based on keys, sort them, iterate over them, and so on. I imagine you want such common everyday operations to be easy, flexible, and intuitive. Groovy takes the already powerful Java collections and makes their API simpler and easier. Groovy has added a number of convenience methods, effectively using closures as parameters to several methods. In this chapter, you'll dive into two collections—List and Map—and learn the Groovy way of using them. After this chapter, you'll never want to use collections again the way you did.

7.1 Using List

Creating an instance of java.util.ArrayList is easier in Groovy than in Java. You don't have to use new or specify the class name. Simply list the initial values you want in the List, as shown here:

WorkingWithCollections/CreatingArrayList.groovy

```
lst = [1, 3, 4, 1, 8, 9, 2, 6]
println lst
println lst.getClass().name
```

The output from the previous code is as follows:

```
[1, 3, 4, 1, 8, 9, 2, 6]
java.util.ArrayList
```

When you declared a list in Groovy, the reference lst actually refers to an instance of java.util.ArrayList, as you can see from the previous output.

You can fetch the elements of the List by using the [] operator, as shown in the following example:

```
println lst[0]

println lst[lst.size() - 1]
```

The following output shows the values of the first and last elements in the list:

```
1
6
```

But, you don't have to jump that many hoops to get to the last element of the list—Groovy has a simpler way. You can use negative index values, and Groovy will traverse from right instead of left:

```
println lst[-1]

println lst[-2]
```

The previous code gets you the last two elements of the list, as shown in the following output:

```
6
2
```

You can even get contiguous values from the collection using the Range object, as shown here:

```
println lst[2..5]
```

The previous code returns four contiguous values in the list starting from the element at position 2, as shown here:

```
[4, 1, 8, 9]
```

You can even use negative index in the range as in the following code, which produces the same result as the previous code:

```
println lst[-6..-3]
```

Let's quickly examine what lst[2..5] actually returned:

```
WorkingWithCollections/CreatingArrayList.groovy
subLst = lst[2..5]
println subLst.dump()
subLst[0] = 55
println "After  subLst[0]=55 lst = $lst"
```

The output from the previous code is as follows:

```
<java.util.RandomAccessSubList@fedbf l=[1, 3, 4, 1, 8, 9, 2, 6]
    offset=2 size=4 expectedModCount=1 modCount=0>
After  subLst[0]=55 lst = [1, 3, 55, 1, 8, 9, 2, 6]
```

If you use a range like 2..5 as the index, java.util.ArrayList returns an instance of java.util.RandomAccessSubList, which holds an offset into the original list. So be aware, you did not get a copy—if you change an element using one list, you're affecting the other.

You can see how Groovy has made the API for List much simpler. You are using the same, good old ArrayList, but when seen through your Groovy eyes, it looks a lot prettier and lighter, doesn't it?

7.2 Iterating Over an ArrayList

One of the first things you're likely to want to do on a list is to navigate or iterate. Groovy provides elegant ways to not only iterate but to perform operations on the values as you iterate over your lists.

List's each Method

As you saw in Chapter 5, *Using Closures*, on page 81, Groovy provides convenient ways to iterate collections. This iterator, the method named each(), is also known as an *internal iterator*. For more information, see the sidebar on the following page.

```
WorkingWithCollections/IteratingArrayList.groovy
lst = [1, 3, 4, 1, 8, 9, 2, 6]

lst.each { println it }
```

Internal vs. External Iterators

You're used to external iterators in languages like C++ and Java. These are iterators that allow the user or client of the iterator to control the iteration. You have to check whether you're at the end and explicitly move to the next element.

Internal iterators are popular in languages that support closures—the user or client of the iterator does not control the iteration. Instead, they send a block of code that will be executed for each element in the collection.

Internal iterators are easier to use—you don't have to control the iteration. External iterators are more flexible; you can take control of the iteration sequence, skip elements, terminate, restart iteration, and so on, more easily.

Implementors of internal iteration can take extra effort to give you that flexibility and the convenience at the same time. You'll find not one but different methods on List for this reason.

In this code example, you iterate over the elements of a List using the each() method[1] and print each element, as shown in the following output:

```
1
3
4
1
8
9
2
6
```

You can also do other operations (see Section 5.2, *Use of Closures*, on page 85), such as summing the elements of the collection, as shown here:

WorkingWithCollections/IteratingArrayList.groovy

```
total = 0
lst.each { total += it }
println "Total is $total"
```

The result of executing the previous code is as follows:

```
Total is 34
```

---

1. Use reverseEach() if you want to iterate elements in reverse order. If you need a count or an index during iteration, use eachWithIndex().

Suppose you want to double each element of the collection. Let's take a stab at it using the each() method:

WorkingWithCollections/IteratingArrayList.groovy
```
doubled = []
1st.each { doubled << it * 2 }

println doubled
```

The output from the previous code is as follows:

```
[2, 6, 8, 2, 16, 18, 4, 12]
```

You create an empty ArrayList named doubled to hold the result. While iterating through the collection, you double each element and push the value into the result using the << operator (leftShift()).

If you want to perform some operations on each element in a collection, the each() method is your friend.

List's collect Method

If you want to operate on each element in a collection and return a resulting collection, there is a simpler way in Groovy to do that—the collect() method, as shown here:

WorkingWithCollections/IteratingArrayList.groovy
```
println 1st.collect { it * 2 }
```

The collect() method, like each(), invokes the closure for each element of the collection. However, it *collects* the return value from the closure into a collection and finally returns that resulting collection. The closure, in the previous example, is returning[2] double the value it's given. You get back an ArrayList with the input values doubled, as shown in the following output:

```
[2, 6, 8, 2, 16, 18, 4, 12]
```

If you want to perform operations on each element of a collection, use each(); however, if you want a collection of the result of such a computation, use the collect() method.

---

2. There's an implicit return in the closure. For more information, see Section 3.8, *return Is Not Always Optional*, on page 56.

7.3 Finder Methods

You know how to iterate over a collection and perform operations on each element. However, if you want to search for a particular element, each() or collect() are not convenient. Instead, you should use find(), like so:

WorkingWithCollections/Find.groovy

```
lst = [4, 3, 1, 2, 4, 1, 8, 9, 2, 6]

println lst.find { it == 2 }
```

The output from the previous code is as follows:

```
2
```

In this code, you're looking for an object that matches value 2 in the collection. find() gets you the first occurrence of the matching object. In this case, it returns the object at position 3. Just like the each() method, the find() method iterates over the collection, but only until the closure returns a true. On receiving a true, find() breaks from the iteration and returns the current element. If it never receives a true, then find() returns a null.

Specify any condition you want in the closure you attach to find(). Here's how you'd look for the first element greater than 4:

WorkingWithCollections/Find.groovy

```
println lst.find { it > 4 }
```

The output from the previous code is as follows:

```
8
```

You can also find all occurrences of 2. Just as the find() method behaves like each(), the findAll() method behaves like collect():

WorkingWithCollections/Find.groovy

```
println lst.findAll { it == 2 }
```

The previous code returns all the 2s it can find, as shown in the following output:

```
[2, 2]
```

You looked for 2s, and it's returning the objects and not the positions.[3]

---

3. If you want to find the position of the first matching object, use the findIndexOf() method.

In the simplest case, this does not sound very useful. However, in general, if you're looking for objects that match some criteria, you will get those objects. For example, if you look for all cities over a certain population, the result will be a list of the appropriate cities. Returning to the previous example, if you want all numbers that are greater than 4, here's how to get them:

```
WorkingWithCollections/Find.groovy
println lst.findAll { it > 4 }
```

The result of the previous code is as follows:

```
[8, 9, 6]
```

In general, if you have a collection of arbitrary objects, find() and findAll() will help you filter out those objects that meet a certain criteria.

7.4 Collections' Convenience Methods

There are a number of convenience methods that Groovy adds to Collections.[4] Let's take an example and implement it first using the method you're already familiar with—the each() method. Then we'll refactor that example using methods that will make your code self-contained and expressive. Along the way, you'll see how Groovy treats code blocks as first-class citizens, like functional programming languages do.

Suppose you have a collection of strings and want to count the total number of characters. Here's a way to do that using the each() method:

```
WorkingWithCollections/CollectionsConvenienceMethods.groovy
lst = ['Programming', 'In', 'Groovy']

count = 0
lst.each { count += it.size() }

println count
```

The output from the previous code is as follows:

```
19
```

Groovy gives you more than one way to do stuff.

---

4. For a list of methods added to Collections, refer to http://groovy.codehaus.org/groovy-jdk/java/util/Collection.html.

Here's another way using collect() and sum() (both are Groovy-added methods on Collections):

```
println lst.collect { it.size() }.sum()
```

I am calling the sum() method on the Collection returned by the collect() method. The output from the previous code is as follows:

```
19
```

The previous code is a bit terse but is self-contained: each() is useful to work on each individual element of a collection and get a cumulative result. However, collect() is useful if you want to apply some computation on each element of a collection but still retain the result as a collection. You can take advantage of this to apply other operations (such as the sum() method) that can cascade down on the collection.

You can also do the same using the inject() method:

```
println lst.inject(0) { carryOver, element ->  carryOver + element.size() }
```

The output from the previous code is as follows:

```
19
```

inject() calls the closure for each element of the collection. The element is represented, in this example, by the element parameter. inject() takes as a parameter an initial value that it will inject, through the carryOver parameter, into the first call to the closure. It then injects the result from the closure into the subsequent call to the closure. You'll prefer the inject() method over the collect() method if you want a cumulative result of applying a computation on each element of a collection.

Suppose you want to concatenate the elements of the collection into a sentence. You can do that easily with join():

```
println lst.join(' ')
```

The output from the previous code is as follows:

```
Programming In Groovy
```

join() iterates over each element, concatenating each of them with the character given as the input parameter. In this example, the parameter given is a whitespace, so join() returns the string "Programming In Groovy." The join() method comes in handy when you want to take a collection of paths and concatenate them—for instance, using a colon (:) to form a classpath—all using one simple call.

You can replace an element of a List by assigning to an index. In the following code, you're setting ['Be', 'Productive'] to element 0:

```
lst[0] = ['Be', 'Productive']
println lst
```

This results in a List within the collection, as shown here:

```
[["Be", "Productive"], "In", "Groovy"]
```

If that's not what you want, flatten the List with flatten():

```
lst = lst.flatten()
println lst
```

This results in a flattened single List of objects, as shown here:

```
["Be", "Productive", "In", "Groovy"]
```

You can also use the - operator (minus() method) on List, as shown here:

```
println lst - ['Productive', 'In']
```

The elements in the right operand are removed from the collection on the left. If you provide a nonexistent element, no worries—it's simply ignored. The - operator is flexible, so you can provide either a list or a single value for the right operand. The output from the previous code is as follows:

```
["Be", "Groovy"]
```

Use the reverse() method if you want to get a copy of the list with the elements in reverse order.

Here's another convenience in Groovy: you can easily perform an operation on each element without actually using an iterator:

```
println lst.size()
println lst*.size()
```

The output from the previous code is as follows:

```
4
[2, 10, 2, 6]
```

The first call to size() is on the list, so it returns 4, the current number of elements in the list. The second call (because of the influence of *) is on each element (String in this example) of the list, so it returns a List with each element holding the size of corresponding elements in the original collection. The effect of lst*.size() is the same as lst.collect { it.size() }.

Finally, I'll show how you can use an ArrayList in method calls. If a method takes a number of parameters, instead of sending individual arguments, you can explode an ArrayList as arguments, that is, split the collection into individual objects using the * operator (the *spread* operator), as shown next. For this to work correctly, the size of the ArrayList must be the same as the number of parameters the method expects.

WorkingWithCollections/CollectionsConvenienceMethods.groovy

```
def words(a, b, c, d)
{
  println "$a $b $c $d"
}

words(*lst)
```

The output from the previous code is as follows:

```
Be Productive In Groovy
```

7.5 Using Map

Java's java.util.Map is useful when you want to work with an associative set of key and value pairs. Again, Groovy makes working with Maps simpler and elegant with the use of closures. Creating an instance of Map is also simple, because you don't need to use new or specify any class names. Simply create pairs of values, as shown here:

WorkingWithCollections/UsingMap.groovy

```
langs = ['C++' : 'Stroustrup', 'Java' : 'Gosling', 'Lisp' : 'McCarthy']

println langs.getClass().name
```

The output from the code is as follows:

```
java.util.LinkedHashMap
```

This example creates a hash map of some languages as keys and their authors as values. The keys are separated from their values using the colon (:), and the entire map is placed in a []. This simple Groovy syntax created an instance of java.util.LinkedHashMap. You can see that by calling getClass() and getting the name property of it.[5]

You can access the value for a key using the [] operator, as in the following code:

```
println langs['Java']
println langs['C++']
```

The output from the previous code is as follows:

```
Gosling
Stroustrup
```

I'm sure you're expecting something fancier here, and Groovy is sure not going to let you down. You can access the values by using the key as if it were a property of the Map:

```
println langs.Java
```

The output from the previous code is as follows:

```
Gosling
```

That is neat—it's convenient to send a key as if it were a property of the object, and the Map smartly returns the value. Of course, an experienced programmer immediately asks "What's the catch?" You already saw a catch or gotcha. You're not able to call the class property on the Map since it assumes that to be a key, it returns a null value, and the call to the name property on null fails obviously.[6] So, you had to call the getClass() method. But what about the key C++? Let's try that:

```
println langs.C++ // Invalid code
```

The output from the previous code is as follows:

```
java.lang.NullPointerException: Cannot invoke method next() on null object
```

What the...? You may discard this example code by saying C++ is always a problem, no matter where you go.

---

5. As an astute reader, you may have observed the call to the getClass() method instead of access to the class property. Read further to see the reason for that little gotcha.
6. Instances of Map and a few other classes don't return the Class metaobject when you call the class property. To avoid surprises, always use the getClass() method instead of the class property on instances.

But, this problem is actually because of another feature of Groovy inter-fering here—operator overloading (see Section 3.6, *Operator Overloading*, on page 44). Groovy took the previous request as a get with key "C," which doesn't exist. So, it returned a null and then tried to call the next() method (the operator ++ maps to it). Luckily, there is a workaround for special cases like this. Simply present the key with offending characters as a String, as shown here:

WorkingWithCollections/UsingMap.groovy
```
println langs.'C++'
```

Now you can be happy to get the following output:

```
Stroustrup
```

When defining a Map in Groovy, you can skip the quotes around well-behaved key names. For instance, you can write the map of languages and their authors, as shown here:

WorkingWithCollections/UsingMap.groovy
```
langs = ['C++' : 'Stroustrup', Java : 'Gosling', Lisp : 'McCarthy']
```

7.6 Iterating Over Map

You can iterate over a Map,[7] just like how you iterated over an ArrayList (see Section 7.2, *Iterating Over an ArrayList*, on page 117).

Map has a flavor of the each() and collect() methods.

Map's each Method

Let's look at an example of using the each() method:

WorkingWithCollections/NavigatingMap.groovy
```
langs = ['C++' : 'Stroustrup', 'Java' : 'Gosling', 'Lisp' : 'McCarthy']

langs.each { entry ->
  println "Language $entry.key was authored by $entry.value"
}
```

The output from the previous code is as follows:

```
Language C++ was authored by Stroustrup
Language Java was authored by Gosling
Language Lisp was authored by McCarthy
```

---

7. For details on methods added to Map, visit http://groovy.codehaus.org/groovy-jdk/java/util/Map.html.

If the closure you attach to each() takes only one parameter, then each() sends an instance of MapEntry[8] for that parameter. If, however, you want to get the key and the value separately, simply provide two parameters in the closure as in the following example:

WorkingWithCollections/NavigatingMap.groovy

```
langs.each { language, author ->
  println "Language $language was authored by $author"
}
```

The output from the previous code is as follows:

```
Language C++ was authored by Stroustrup
Language Java was authored by Gosling
Language Lisp was authored by McCarthy
```

This code example iterates over the langs collection using the each() method. The each() method calls the closure with a key and value. You refer to these two parameters in the closure using the variable names language and author, respectively.

Map's collect Method

Let's next examine the collect() method in Map. First, it's similar to the method in ArrayList in that both methods return a list. However, if you want Map's collect() to send your closure a MapEntry, define one parameter; otherwise, define two parameters for the key and value, as shown here:

WorkingWithCollections/NavigatingMap.groovy

```
println langs.collect { language, author ->
  language.replaceAll("[+]", "P")
  }
```

The output from the previous code is as follows:

```
["CPP", "Java", "Lisp"]
```

In the previous code, you replace all occurrences of + in the closure with the character P.

You can easily transform the data in a Map into other representations. For example, in Section 17.1, *Building XML*, on page 255, you'll see how easy it is to create an XML representation.

---

8. For other methods like collect(), find(), and so on, use one parameter if you want only the MapEntry and two parameters if you want the key and the value separately.

Map's find and findAll Methods

Groovy also adds the find() and findAll() methods to Map. Let's take a look at an example:

WorkingWithCollections/NavigatingMap.groovy

```
println "Looking for the first language with name greater than 3 characters"
entry = langs.find { language, author ->
  language.size() > 3
  }
println "Found $entry.key written by $entry.value"
```

The output from the previous code is as follows:

```
Looking for the first language with name greater than 3 characters
Found Java written by Gosling
```

The find() method accepts a closure that takes the key and value (again, use a single parameter to receive a MapEntry). Similar to its counterpart in ArrayList, it breaks from the iteration if the closure returns true. In the previous example code, you're finding the first language with more than three characters in its name. The method returns null if the closure never returns a true. Otherwise, it returns an instance of a matching entry in the Map.

You can use the findAll() method to get all elements that match the condition you're looking for, as in the following example:

WorkingWithCollections/NavigatingMap.groovy

```
println "Looking for all languages with name greater than 3 characters"
selected = langs.findAll { language, author ->
  language.size() > 3
  }
selected.each { key, value ->
  println "Found $key written by $value"
}
```

The output from the previous code is as follows:

```
Looking for all languages with name greater than 3 characters
Found Lisp written by McCarthy
Found Java written by Gosling
```

7.7 Map Convenience Methods

We'll wrap up our discussion on collections in this section by looking at a few convenience methods of Map.

You saw how the find() method is useful to fetch an element that satisfied a given condition. However, instead of getting the element, if you're simply interested in determining whether any elements in the collection satisfies some condition, you can use the any() method.

Let's continue with the example of languages and authors from Section 7.6, *Iterating Over Map*, on page 126. You can use the any() method to determine whether any language name has a nonalphabetic character:

WorkingWithCollections/NavigatingMap.groovy

```
print "Does any language name have a nonalphabetic character? "
println langs.any {language, author ->
  language =~ "[^A-Za-z]"
  }
```

With *C++* among the key values, your code reports as shown here:

```
Does any language name have a nonalphabetic character? true
```

any() takes a closure with two parameters, just like the other methods of Map we discussed. The closure in this example uses a regular expression comparison (see Section 6.5, *Regular Expressions*, on page 111) to determine whether the language name has a nonalphabetic character.

While the method any() looks for at least one element of the Map to satisfy the given condition (predicate), the method named every() checks whether *all* elements satisfy the condition:

WorkingWithCollections/NavigatingMap.groovy

```
print "Do all language names have a nonalphabetic character? "
println langs.every {language, author ->
  language =~ "[^A-Za-z]"
  }
```

The output from the previous code is as follows:

```
Do all language names have a nonalphabetic character? false
```

If you want to group the elements of a map based on some criteria, don't bother iterating or looping through the map—groupBy() does that for you. All you have to do is specify your criteria as a closure. Here's an example: friends refers to a map of some of my friends (many of my friends share their first names). If I want to group my friends by their first name, I can do that with just one call to groupBy(), as shown in the following code. In the closure attached to groupBy(), I specify what I like to group—in this example, I strip out the first name from the full name and return it. In general, you can simply return the property you're interested in grouping by. For example, if I store my friend's names in a Person object with the properties firstName and lastName instead of a simple String, I write the closure as { it.firstName }. In the following code, groupByFirstname is a map with the first name as the key and an array of full names as the value. Finally, I iterate over it and print the values.

WorkingWithCollections/NavigatingMap.groovy

```
friends = [ briang = 'Brian Goetz', brians = 'Brian Sletten',
        davidb = 'David Bock', davidg = 'David Geary',
        scottd = 'Scott Davis', scottl = 'Scott Leberknight',
        stuarth = 'Stuart Halloway']

groupByFirstName = friends.groupBy { it.split(' ')[0] }

groupByFirstName.each { firstName, buddies ->
  println "$firstName : ${buddies.join(', ')}"
}
```

The output from the previous code is as follows:

```
David : David Bock, David Geary
Brian : Brian Goetz, Brian Sletten
Stuart : Stuart Halloway
Scott : Scott Davis, Scott Leberknight
```

One final convenience I'd like to mention is that Groovy uses Map for named parameters. We discussed this in Section 3.2, *JavaBeans*, on page 33. Also, you can see how you can use Maps to implement interfaces in Section 3.4, *Implementing Interfaces*, on page 39.

In this chapter, you saw the power of closures mixed into the Java collections API. As you apply these concepts on your projects, you'll find that working with collections is easier and faster, your code is shorter, and it's fun. Yes, the Groovy way of using collection brings excitement into what otherwise is a mundane task of traversing and manipulating collections.

Part II

Using Groovy

Chapter 8

Exploring the GDK

Groovy not only brings the strength of dynamic languages onto the JVM, but it also enhances the good old JDK. So, when programming with Groovy, you're productive because you enjoy a better, lighter, and fancier Java API.

Groovy enhances the JDK with convenience methods, quite a few of which make extensive use of closures. This extension is called the Groovy JDK or the GDK.[1] The relationship between the JDK and the GDK is shown in Figure 8.1, on the following page. The GDK sits on top of the JDK, so when you pass objects between your Java code and Groovy code, you are not dealing with any conversions. It's the same object on both sides of the languages when you're within the same JVM. However, what you see on the Groovy side is an object that looks hip, thanks to the methods added by Groovy to make it convenient to use and make you productive.

You'll find extensions to several classes from the JDK. We discussed a number of these in various chapters in this book. In this chapter, we'll focus on two areas—extensions to the java.lang.Object class and various other extensions to popular classes.

8.1 Object Extensions

In this section, we'll explore some additions to the mother of all classes, the java.lang.Object class. In Chapter 7, *Working with Collections*, on

---

1. You can find details about the GDK enhancements at http://groovy.codehaus.org/groovy-jdk.

Figure 8.1: THE JDK AND THE GDK

page 115, you saw Groovy-added methods on Collections: each(), collect(), find(), findAll(), any(), and every(). These are not only available on Collections, but you can also use them on any object. This gives you a consistent API to work with individual objects and collections alike—one of the benefits elicited in the Composite pattern ([GHJV95]). There are also other noncollections-related convenience methods that Groovy has added to Object. I won't go over all the methods added to Object in this section—my objective is not to write a complete reference to the GDK library. Instead, I'll focus on methods that are likely to pique your interest and those that you'll find useful for your everyday tasks.

The dump and inspect Methods

If you're curious about what makes an instance of your class, you can easily find that at runtime using the dump() method:

ExploringGDK/ObjectExtensions.groovy

```
str = 'hello'

println str
println str.dump()
```

The output from the previous code is as follows:

```
hello
<java.lang.String@5e918d2 value=[h, e, l, l, o] offset=0 count=5 hash=99162322>
```

dump() lets you take a peek into an object. You can use it for debugging, logging, and learning. It tells you about the class of the target instance, its hash code, and its fields.

Groovy also adds another method, inspect(), to Object. This method is intended to tell you what input would be needed to create an object. If unimplemented on a class, it simply returns what toString() returns. If your object takes extensive input, this method will help users of your class figure out at runtime what input they should provide.

identity: The Context Method

There's a nice feature in JavaScript and VBScript called with that allows you to create a *context*. Any method called within the scope of with is directed to the context object. The method identity()[2] of Object in Groovy provides the same capability. It accepts a closure as a parameter. Any method call you make within the closure is automatically resolved to the context object. Let's take a look at an example:

```
ExploringGDK/Identity.groovy
lst = [1, 2]

lst.add(3)
lst.add(4)

println lst.size()
println lst.contains(2)
```

In the previous code you're calling methods on lst, which refers to an instance of ArrayList. There's no implicit context, and you're repeatedly (redundantly) using the object reference lst. In Groovy, you can set a context using the identity() method, so you can change the code to the following:

```
ExploringGDK/Identity.groovy
lst = [1, 2]
lst.identity {
  add(3)
  add(4)

  println size()
  println contains(2)
}
```

The output from the previous code is as follows:

```
4
true
```

---

2. with() was introduced as a synonym to identity() in Groovy 1.5, so you can use them interchangeably.

How does the identity() method *know* to route calls within the closure to the context object? The magic happens because of the delegate property of the closure (for more information, see Section 5.8, *Closure Delegation*, on page 96). Let's examine the delegate property along with the this and owner properties within the closure attached to identity():

ExploringGDK/Identity.groovy

```
lst.identity {
  println "this is ${this},"
  println "owner is ${owner},"
  println "delegate is ${delegate}."
}
```

The output from the previous code is as follows:

```
this is Identity@ce56f8,
owner is Identity@ce56f8,
delegate is [1, 2, 3, 4].
```

When you invoke the identity() method, it sets the delegate property of the closure (actually it is done with the with() method of the Default-GroovyMethods class, which is called by identity()) to the object on which identity() is called. As discussed in Section 5.8, *Closure Delegation*, on page 96, the delegate has dibs on methods that this doesn't pick up.

Use the identity method if you need to call multiple methods on an object. Take advantage of the context and reduce clutter. You'll find this method very useful when building DSLs. You can implement scriptlike calls to be implicitly routed to your instance behind the scenes, as you'll learn in Chapter 18, *Creating DSLs in Groovy*, on page 273.

sleep

The sleep() method added to Object should be called *soundSleep*. It ignores interrupts while sleeping for the given number of milliseconds (approximately).

Let's take a look at an example of the sleep() method:[3]

ExploringGDK/Sleep.groovy

```
thread = Thread.start {
  println "Thread started"
  startTime = System.nanoTime()
  new Object().sleep(2000)
  endTime = System.nanoTime()
  println "Thread done in ${(endTime - startTime)/10**9} seconds"
}
```

---

3. I'm using the Groovy-added Thread.start() method here. It's a convenient way to execute a piece of code in a different thread.

```
new Object().sleep(100)
println "Let's interrupt that thread"
thread.interrupt()
thread.join()
```

The output is as follows:

```
Thread started
Let's interrupt that thread
Thread done in 2.000272 seconds
```

The difference between calling sleep() on Object and using the Java-provided Thread.sleep() is that the former suppresses the Interrupted-Exception. If you do care to be interrupted, you don't have to endure try-catch. Instead, in Groovy, you can use a variation of the previous sleep() method that accepts a closure to handle the interruption:

ExploringGDK/Sleep.groovy

```
def playWithSleep(flag)
{
  thread = Thread.start {
    println "Thread started"
    startTime = System.nanoTime()
    new Object().sleep(2000) {
      println "Interrupted... " + it
      flag
    }
    endTime = System.nanoTime()
    println "Thread done in ${(endTime - startTime)/10**9} seconds"
  }

  thread.interrupt()
  thread.join()
}

playWithSleep(true)
playWithSleep(false)
```

The output from the previous code is as follows:

```
Thread started
Interrupted... java.lang.InterruptedException: sleep interrupted
Thread done in 0.00437 seconds
Thread started
Interrupted... java.lang.InterruptedException: sleep interrupted
Thread done in 1.999077 seconds
```

Within the interrupt handler, you can take any appropriate actions. If you need to access the InterruptedException, it is available as a parameter to your closure. If you return a false from within the closure, sleep() will continue as if uninterrupted, as you can see in the second call to playWithSleep() in the previous example.

Indirect Property Access

You know that Groovy already makes it easy to access properties. For example, to get property miles of an instance car of a class Car, you can simply call car.miles. However, this syntax is not helpful if you don't know the property name at coding time, such as if the property name depends on user input and you don't want to hard-code a branch for all possible input. You can use the [] operator—the Groovy-added getAt() method maps to this operator—to access properties dynamically. If you use this operator on the left side of an assignment, then it maps to the putAt() method. Let's take a look at an example:

ExploringGDK/IndirectProperty.groovy

```
class Car
{
  int miles, fuelLevel
}

car = new Car(fuelLevel: 80, miles: 25)

properties = ['miles', 'fuelLevel']
// the above list may be populated from some input or
// may come from a dynamic form in a web app

properties.each { name ->
  println "$name = ${car[name]}"
}

car[properties[1]] = 100

println "fuelLevel now is ${car.fuelLevel}"
```

The output from the code previous is as follows:

```
miles = 25
fuelLevel = 80
fuelLevel now is 100
```

Here you're accessing the miles and fuelLevel properties using the [] operator. You can use this approach if the names of properties are given to you as input; you can dynamically create and populate web forms, for example. You can easily write a higher-level function that takes a list of property names[4] and an instance and outputs the names and values in XML, HTML, or any other format you desire.

---

4. To get a list of all the properties of an object, use its properties property, namely, the getProperties() method.

Indirect Method Invoke

If the method name is given to you as a String and you want to call
that method, you know how to use reflection to do that—you have to
first fetch the Class metaobject from the instance, call getMethod() to get
the Method instance, and finally call the invoke() method on it. And, oh
yeah, don't forget those exceptions you'll be forced to handle.

No, you don't have to do all that in Groovy. In Groovy, you need only
one line of code—just call the invokeMethod(). All objects support this
method in Groovy. Here's an example:

ExploringGDK/IndirectMethod.groovy

```
class Person
{
  def walk() { println "Walking..." }
  def walk(int miles) { println "Walking $miles miles..." }
  def walk(int miles, String where) { println "Walking $miles miles $where..." }
}

peter = new Person()

peter.invokeMethod("walk", null)
peter.invokeMethod("walk", 10)
peter.invokeMethod("walk", [2, 'uphill'] as Object[])
```

The output from the previous code is as follows:

```
Walking...
Walking 10 miles...
Walking 2 miles uphill...
```

So if you don't know the method names at coding time but receive
the names at runtime, you can turn that into a dynamic call on your
instance with a single line of code, as shown in the previous example.

Groovy also provides getMetaClass() to get the metaclass object, which
is a key object that allows you to take advantage of dynamic capabilities
in Groovy, as you'll see in later chapters.

8.2 Other Extensions

The GDK extensions go beyond the Object class. Several other JDK
classes and interfaces have been enhanced in the GDK. Again, the list
is vast, and my objective is not to create a comprehensive reference. So,
I will introduce only a small subset of extensions in this section. These
are the extensions that I think you're likely to put to regular use.

Array Extensions

You can use the Range object as an index on all the array types[5] like int[], double[], and char[]. Here's how you can access contiguous values in an int array using the range of index:

```
int[] arr = [1, 2, 3, 4, 5, 6]

println arr[2..4]
```

The output from the previous code is as follows:

```
[3, 4, 5]
```

You're already familiar with a number of convenience methods that the GDK added to Lists, Collections, and Maps. Refer to Chapter 7, *Working with Collections*, on page 115 if you want to review them.

java.lang Extensions

One of the noticeable additions to the primitive type wrappers like Character, Integer, and so on, is the overloaded operator mapping methods. These are the methods such as plus() for operator +, next() for operator ++, and so on. You'll find these methods, *operators* I should say, useful when creating DSLs.

Number (which Integer and Double extend) has picked up the iterator methods upto() and downto(). It also has the step() method (see Section 3.1, *Ways to Loop*, on page 27). These allow you to iterate over a range of values easily.

You looked at a few examples to interact with system-level processes in Section 3.1, *A Quick Look at the GDK*, on page 28. The Process class has convenience methods to access the stdin, stdout, and stderr commands—the out, in, and err properties, respectively. It also has the text property that can give you the entire standard output or response from the process. If you want to read the entire standard error in one shot, use err.text on the process instance. You can use the << operator to pipe into a process.[6] Here's an example to illustrate communicating with a

---

5. For the syntax for creating arrays, see Section 3.8, *Different Syntax for Creating Primitive Arrays*, on page 62.
6. A pipe (|) on Unix-like systems allows you to chain the output from one process into the input of another process.

process—the wc program, which is a popular utility on Unix-like systems that prints to the standard output the number of words, lines, and characters it finds in its standard input:

ExploringGDK/UsingProcess.groovy

```
process = "wc".execute()

process.out.withWriter {
  // Send input to process
  it << "Let the World know...\n"
  it << "Groovy Rocks!\n"
}

// Read output from process
println process.in.text
// or
//println process.text
```

The output from the previous code is the result returned by wc—two lines, six words, and thirty-six characters:

```
2      6      36
```

In this code, first you obtain an instance of the process by calling String's execute() method. You want to write to wc's standard input, so you need an OutputStream from our program. You can obtain that from the process by calling the out property.

To write content, you can use the << operator. However, once you write to the stream, you want to flush and close it. You can handle both with one method: withWriter(). This method attaches an OutputStreamWriter to the OutputStream and hands it to the closure. When you return from the closure, it flushes and closes the stream automatically.[7] Try implementing the previous code using Java, and you'll truly appreciate not only the time savings but also the elegance Groovy provides.

If you want to send command-line parameters to the process, you have two options. You can format it as one string or create a String array of parameters. String[] supports the execute() method as well; the first element is treated as the command to execute, and the remaining elements are considered as command-line arguments to that command. Instead, you can also use the execute() method of List.

---

7. See Section 5.4, *Closure and Resource Cleanup*, on page 87.

Here's an example of passing command-line parameters to the groovy command:

ExploringGDK/ProcessParameters.groovy

```
String[] command = ['groovy', '-e', 'print "Groovy!"']
println  "Calling ${command.join(' ')}"
println command.execute().text
```

The output from the previous code is as follows:

```
Calling groovy -e print "Groovy!"
Groovy!
```

You can start a process, send parameters, and interact with the process fairly easily in Groovy. It takes only a couple of lines of code.

If you have to create threads and assign tasks to execute in those separate threads, Groovy will save you quite a bit of typing. You can start a Thread and provide it a closure that will be run in a separate thread using the start() method. If you want that thread to be daemon thread,[8] use the startDaemon() method instead. Let's take a look at an example that shows these two methods in action:

ExploringGDK/ThreadStart.groovy

```
def printThreadInfo(msg)
{
  def currentThread = Thread.currentThread()
  println "$msg Thread is ${currentThread}. Daemon? ${currentThread.isDaemon()}"
}

printThreadInfo 'Main'

Thread.start {
  printThreadInfo "Started"
  sleep(3000) { println "Interrupted" }
  println "Finished Started"
}

sleep(1000)

Thread.startDaemon {
  printThreadInfo "Started Daemon"
  sleep(5000) { println "Interrupted" }
  println "Finished Started Daemon" // Will not get here
}
```

---

8. A daemon thread quits if there are no active nondaemon threads currently running—kind of like employees who work only when the boss is around.

The output from the previous code is as follows:

```
Main Thread is Thread[main,5,main]. Daemon? false
Started Thread is Thread[Thread-1,5,main]. Daemon? false
Started Daemon Thread is Thread[Thread-2,5,main]. Daemon? true
Finished Started
```

The daemon thread in the previous example was aborted as soon as the main thread and the nondaemon thread you created quit. You can see that to create threads in Groovy, you don't need to work with instances of Thread or Runnable. It's very simple and easy to get going with thread creation.

java.io Extensions

A lot of methods have been added to the File class in the java.io package. It has methods such as eachFile() and eachDir() (and variations of these) that accept closures and provide easy navigation or iteration through directories and files.

Suppose you want to read the contents of a file. Here's the Java code for that:

```
// Java code
import java.io.*;
public class ReadFile
{
  public static void main(String[] args)
  {
    try
    {
      BufferedReader reader = new BufferedReader(
                  new FileReader("thoreau.txt"));

      String line = null;
      while((line = reader.readLine()) != null)
      {
        System.out.println(line);
      }
    }
    catch(FileNotFoundException ex)
    {
      ex.printStackTrace();
    }
    catch(IOException ex)
    {
      ex.printStackTrace();
    }
  }
}
```

That's quite an effort to read a file. Groovy makes this much simpler. Groovy has added a text property to BufferedReader, InputStream, and File, so you can read the entire content of the reader into a String. This is useful if you want to take the entire output for processing or printing. Here's the previous code rewritten in Groovy:

ExploringGDK/ReadFile.groovy

```
println new File('thoreau.txt').text
```

The output from the previous code—the content of my file thoreau.txt—is as follows:

```
"I went to the woods because I wished to live deliberately,
to front only the essential facts of life, and see if I could
not learn what it had to teach, and not, when I came to die,
to discover that I had not lived..."
- Henry David Thoreau
```

Instead of reading the entire file in one shot, if you want to read and process one line at a time, use the eachLine() method, which calls a closure for each line of text read:

ExploringGDK/ReadFile.groovy

```
new File('thoreau.txt').eachLine { line ->
  println line // or do whatever you like with that line here
}
```

If you want to fetch only those lines of text that meet a certain condition, you can use filterLine(), as shown here:

ExploringGDK/ReadFile.groovy

```
println new File('thoreau.txt').filterLine { it =~ /life/ }
```

The output from the previous code is as follows:

```
to front only the essential facts of life, and see if I could
```

You filtered only the line(s) in the input file that contained the word "life."

If you want to automatically flush and close an input stream when you're done, you can use the withStream() method. This method calls the closure it accepts as a parameter and sends the instance of Input-Stream as a parameter. It then flushes and closes the stream as soon as you return from the closure. The Writer has a similar method named withWriter(); you saw an example of this earlier.

The withReader() method of InputStream creates a BufferedReader that's attached to the input stream and sends it to the closure that it accepts as a parameter. You can also obtain a new instance of BufferedReader by calling the newReader() method.

You can iterate over the stream of input in InputStream and DataInputStream using an Iterator you obtain by calling the iterator() method. Talking about iterating, you can conveniently iterate over objects in an ObjectInputStream as well.

If you want to use a Reader instead, the convenience methods added to InputStream are still available on it.

You can easily write contents to a file or stream in Groovy. The OutputStream, ObjectOutputStream, and Writer classes have received a face-lift via the leftShift() method (the << operator). The following code example uses that operator to write to a file:

ExploringGDK/ShiftOperator.groovy

```
new File("output.txt").withWriter{ file ->
 file << "some data..."
}
```

There are several other extensions to classes in the java.io package to make your life easier and coding time shorter.

java.util Extensions

We discussed Groovy extensions to the collection classes in Chapter 7, *Working with Collections*, on page 115. In this section, we'll check out a few other extensions to classes in the java.util package.

List, Set, SortedMap, and SortedSet have gained the method asImmutable() to obtain an immutable instance of their respective instances. They also have a method asSynchronized() to create an instance that is thread-safe.

The Iterator supports the inject() method we discussed in Section 7.4, *Collections' Convenience Methods*, on page 121.

A runAfter() method has been added to the java.util.Timer class. The syntax is easier to use because this method accepts a closure that will run after a given delay in milliseconds.

As you learned in this chapter, Groovy adds a number of methods at the java.lang.Object level. There are methods that allow you to peek into an object for debugging, logging, or informational purposes. You can also use methods that allow you to treat a single object and a collection of objects using a consistent interface, such as using the Composite pattern.

Object also supports methods for metaprogramming—to dynamically access properties and invoke methods. The higher level of abstraction that these methods have collectively built reduces your application code size and the time you need for routine tasks.

And then there are specialized methods that you can use on different classes—Groovy enhances the API for several classes and interfaces—Matcher, Writer, Reader, List, Map, Socket...the list goes on. In Groovy 1.5 the GDK has extensions for more than fifty-eight JDK classes and interfaces. The GDK is far too large for us to cover entirely in this book. Visit http://groovy.codehaus.org/groovy-jdkfor a comprehensive and updated list of the GDK API.

When you're programming in Groovy, you need to refer to both the JDK and the GDK. If you don't find what you're looking for in the JDK, remember to check the GDK to see whether it supports the feature.

Chapter 9

Working with XML

Working with XML can be so tedious, can't it? Working with traditional Java APIs and libraries to create and parse XML documents tends to lower my spirits. And navigating the document hierarchy using the DOM API is one sure way to drive me insane.

Groovy brings relief to both parsing and creating XML documents. You already saw a few ways to create XML documents. We'll revisit that topic in this chapter and look at Groovy facilities for parsing XML documents.

9.1 Parsing XML

You can use the Java-based parsing approaches and tools you are already familiar with in Groovy. Use them if you have some special need or reasons to depend on the older APIs or have legacy code that already uses them. If you have working Java code to parse your XML documents, reuse those readily in Groovy. Groovy does not force you to duplicate your efforts.

However, if you're creating new code to parse XML, you can benefit from the Groovy facilities.

In this section, we'll focus on Groovy's support for parsing XML. Groovy parsers are fairly powerful, convenient to use, and support namespaces as well.

For the examples in the rest of this chapter, you'll work with an XML document (shown next) with a list of languages and authors:

```
WorkingWithXML/languages.xml
```

```xml
<languages>
  <language name="C++">
    <author>Stroustrup</author>
  </language>
  <language name="Java">
    <author>Gosling</author>
  </language>
  <language name="Lisp">
    <author>McCarthy</author>
  </language>
  <language name="Modula-2">
    <author>Wirth</author>
  </language>
  <language name="Oberon-2">
    <author>Wirth</author>
  </language>
  <language name="Pascal">
    <author>Wirth</author>
  </language>
</languages>
```

Using DOMCategory

Groovy categories allow you to define dynamic methods on classes. I'll discuss categories in detail in Section 14.1, *Injecting Methods Using Categories*, on page 198. Groovy provides a category for working with the DOM—DOMCategory. Groovy simplifies the DOM API by adding convenience methods.

DOMCategory allows you to navigate the DOM structure using GPath-like notation.

You can access all child elements simply using the child name. For example, instead of calling getElementsByTagName('name'), use the property name to get it, as in rootElement.language. That is, given the root element, languages, you can obtain all the language elements by simply calling rootElement.language. The rootElement can be obtained using a DOM parser; in the following example, you'll use the DOMBuilder's parse() method to get it.

You can obtain the value for an attribute by placing an @ before the attribute name, as in language.@name.

> ### What's GPath?
>
> Much like how XPath allows you to navigate the hierarchy of an XML document, GPath allows you to navigate the hierarchy of objects (POJOs and POGOs) and XML—you can traverse the hierarchy using the . (dot) notation. In the case of objects, for example, car.engine.power accesses the engine property of Car using getEngine() and then accesses its power property using the getPower() method. In the case of an XML document, you obtained the child element power of the element engine, which in turn is a child element of an element car. To access the year attribute of a car, use car.'@year' (or car.@year). The @ symbol allows you to traverse to an attribute instead of a child element.

In the following code, you use DOMCategory to fetch language names and authors from the document:

`WorkingWithXML/UsingDOMCategory.groovy`

```groovy
document = groovy.xml.DOMBuilder.parse(new FileReader('languages.xml'))

rootElement = document.documentElement

use(groovy.xml.dom.DOMCategory)
{
  println "Languages and authors"
  languages = rootElement.language

  languages.each { language ->
    println "${language.'@name'} authored by ${language.author[0].text()}"
  }

  def languagesByAuthor = { authorName ->
      languages.findAll { it.author[0].text() == authorName }.collect {
                                              it.'@name' }.join(', ')
    }

  println "Languages by Wirth:" + languagesByAuthor('Wirth')
}
```

The output from the previous code is as follows:

```
Languages and authors
C++ authored by Stroustrup
Java authored by Gosling
Lisp authored by McCarthy
Modula-2 authored by Wirth
```

```
Oberon-2 authored by Wirth
Pascal authored by Wirth
Languages by Wirth:Modula-2, Oberon-2, Pascal
```

DOMCategory is useful for parsing an XML document using the DOM API with the convenience of GPath queries and Groovy's dynamic elegance mixed in.

To use the DOMCategory, you must place the code within the use() block. The other two approaches you'll see in this chapter don't have that restriction. In the previous example, you extracted the desired details from the document using the GPath syntax. You also wrote a custom method or filter to get only those languages written by Wirth.

Using XMLParser

The class groovy.util.XMLParser exploits the dynamic tying and metaprogramming capabilities of Groovy. You can access the members of your document directly by name. For example, you can access an author's name using it.author[0].

Let's use the XMLParser to fetch the desired data from the language's XML document:

> WorkingWithXML/UsingXMLParser.groovy

```groovy
languages = new XmlParser().parse('languages.xml')

println "Languages and authors"

languages.each {
  println "${it.@name} authored by ${it.author[0].text()}"
}

def languagesByAuthor = { authorName ->
    languages.findAll { it.author[0].text() == authorName }.collect {
                                          it.@name }.join(', ')
  }


println "Languages by Wirth:" + languagesByAuthor('Wirth')
```

The code is much like the example you saw in Section 9.1, *Using DOMCategory*, on page 148. The main difference is the absence of the use() block. XMLParser has added the convenience of iterators to the elements, so you can navigate easily using methods such as each(), collect(), find(), and so on.

There are a few downsides to using XMLParser, which may be a concern to you depending on your needs. It does not preserve the XML InfoSet. It ignores the XML comments and processing instructions in your document. The convenience it provides makes it a great tool for most common processing needs. If you have other specific needs, you have to explore more traditional parsers.

Using XMLSlurper

For large document sizes, the memory usage of XMLParser might become prohibitive. The class XMLSlurper comes to rescue in these cases. It is similar to XMLParser in usage. The following code is almost the same as the code in Section 9.1, *Using XMLParser*, on the facing page:

WorkingWithXML/UsingXMLSlurper.groovy

```groovy
languages = new XmlSlurper().parse('languages.xml')

println "Languages and authors"

languages.language.each {
  println "${it.@name} authored by ${it.author[0].text()}"
}

def languagesByAuthor = { authorName ->
    languages.language.findAll { it.author[0].text() == authorName }.collect {
                                          it.@name }.join(', ')
  }

println "Languages by Wirth:" + languagesByAuthor('Wirth')
```

You can parse XML documents with namespaces in it as well. Namespaces remind me of an incident. I got a call from a company in Malaysia interested in training that involved extensive coding to emphasize test-driven development. So, I asked, in the middle of the conversation, what language would I be using? After a pause, the gentleman said reluctantly, "English, of course. Everyone on my team speaks English well." What I had actually meant was "What computer language would I be using?" This is an example of contexts and confusion in daily conversations. XML documents have the same issue, and namespaces can help you deal with name collisions.

Remember that namespaces are not URLs, but they are required to be unique. Also, the prefixes you use for namespaces in your XML document are not unique. You can make them up as you please with some naming restrictions. So, to refer to a namespace in your query, you need to associate prefix to namespaces. You can do that using the declareNamespaces() method, which takes a map of prefixes as keys and namespaces as values. Once you define the prefixes, your GPath queries can contain prefixes for names as well. element.name will return all child elements with name, independent of the namespace; however, element.'ns:name' will return only elements with the namespace that ns is associated with. Let's look at an example. Suppose you have an XML document with names of computer and natural languages, as shown here:

```
<languages xmlns:computer="Computer" xmlns:natural="Natural">
  <computer:language name="Java"/>
  <computer:language name="Groovy"/>
  <computer:language name="Erlang"/>
  <natural:language name="English"/>
  <natural:language name="German"/>
  <natural:language name="French"/>
</languages>
```

The element name language falls into either a "Computer" namespace or a "Natural" namespace. The following code shows how to fetch all language names and also only languages that are "Natural":

> WorkingWithXML/UsingXMLSlurperWithNS.groovy

```
languages = new XmlSlurper().parse(
  'computerAndNaturalLanguages.xml').declareNamespace(human: 'Natural')

print "Languages: "
println languages.language.collect { it.@name }.join(', ')

print "Natural languages: "
println languages.'human:language'.collect { it.@name }.join(', ')
```

The output from this code is as follows:

> WorkingWithXML/UsingXMLSlurperWithNS.output

```
Languages: Java, Groovy, Erlang, English, German, French
Natural languages: English, German, French
```

For large XML documents, you'd want to use the XMLSlurper. It performs a lazy evaluation, so it's kind on memory usage and has low overhead.

9.2 Creating XML

In this section, I'll summarize different ways to create XML documents. We discuss these topics in depth in different chapters in this book where you'll see more detailed code examples.

You can use the full power of Java APIs to generate XML. If you have a particular favorite Java-based XML processor such as Xerces (http://xerces.apache.org/xerces-j), for example, you can use it with Groovy as well. This might be a good approach if you already have working code in Java to create XML documents in a specific format and want to use it in your Groovy projects.

If you want to create an XML document using a pure-Groovy approach, you can use GString's ability to embed expressions into a string along with Groovy's facility for creating multiline strings. I find this facility useful for creating small XML fragments that I might need in code and tests. Here's a quick example (you can refer to Section 6.3, *Multiline String*, on page 108 for more details):

WorkingWithStrings/CreateXML.groovy

```
langs = ['C++' : 'Stroustrup', 'Java' : 'Gosling', 'Lisp' : 'McCarthy']

content = ''
langs.each {language, author ->
fragment = """
  <language name="${language}">
    <author>${author}</author>
  </language>
"""

content += fragment
}

xml = "<languages>${content}</languages>"

println xml
```

Here's the output:

```
<languages>
  <language name="C++">
    <author>Stroustrup</author>
  </language>

  <language name="Java">
    <author>Gosling</author>
  </language>

  <language name="Lisp">
    <author>McCarthy</author>
  </language>
</languages>
```

Alternately, you can use the MarkupBuilder or StreamingMarkupBuilder to create XML-formatted output of data from an arbitrary source. This would be the desired approach in Groovy applications, because the convenience provided by the builders make it easy to create XML documents. You don't have to mess with complex APIs or string manipulation; it's all plain simple Groovy. Again, here's a quick example (refer to the discussion in Section 17.1, *Building XML*, on page 255 for details on using both the MarkupBuilder and StreamingMarkupBuilder):

UsingBuilders/BuildUsingStreamingBuilder.groovy

```
langs = ['C++' : 'Stroustrup', 'Java' : 'Gosling', 'Lisp' : 'McCarthy']

xmlDocument = new groovy.xml.StreamingMarkupBuilder().bind {
  mkp.xmlDeclaration()
  mkp.declareNamespace(computer: "Computer")
  languages {
    comment << "Created using StreamingMarkupBuilder"
    langs.each { key, value ->
      computer.language(name: key) {
        author (value)
      }
    }
  }
}

println xmlDocument
```

The output from the previous code is as follows:

```
<?xml version="1.0"?>
<languages xmlns:computer='Computer'>
  <!--Created using StreamingMarkupBuilder-->
    <computer:language name='C++'>
      <author>Stroustrup</author>
    </computer:language>
    <computer:language name='Java'>
      <author>Gosling</author>
    </computer:language>
    <computer:language name='Lisp'>
      <author>McCarthy</author>
    </computer:language>
</languages>
```

If your data resides in a database or a Microsoft Excel file, you can mix that with the techniques you'll look at in Chapter 10, *Working with Databases*, on page 157. Once you fetch the data from the database, insert it into the document using any of the approaches we have discussed.

In this chapter, you saw how Groovy helps you parse XML documents. Groovy can make working with XML bearable. If your users don't like maintaining XML configuration files (who does?), they can create and maintain Groovy-based DSLs that you can transform to the XML formats your underlying frameworks or libraries expect. If you are on the receiving end of the XML documents, you can rely on Groovy to give you an object representation of the XML data. Using regular Groovy syntax, you make parsing XML easy and less painful.

Chapter 10

Working with Databases

I have a remote database (located in some exotic place far away) that I update a few times each week. I used to connect to the database using the browser, but navigating the database that way was slow. I considered creating a Java client program to let me update the database quickly and easily.

But I never got around to creating it because such a program would not easily support ad hoc queries, it would take time to develop, and the task was not exciting—not much really new to learn in that exercise. Then I came across Groovy SQL (GSQL). I found it very simple yet very flexible to create queries and updates. One thing that excited me the most was that I had more data than code in my script—that is a great signal-to-noise ratio. Updating my database has since been a breeze, and GSQL has given me a great amount of agility.[1]

GSQL is a wrapper around JDBC that provides a number of convenience methods to access data. You can easily create SQL queries and then use built-in iterators to traverse the results. The examples in this chapter use MySQL; however, you can use any database that you can access using JDBC. You'll want to create one table named weather to follow along with the examples in this chapter. The table contains the names of some cities and temperature values.

---

1. See my blog entry related to this at http://tinyurl.com/327dmm.

Here is the script to create the database:

```
create database if not exists weatherinfo;
use weatherinfo;

drop table if exists weather;
create table weather (
        city varchar(100) not null,
        temperature integer not null
        );

insert into weather (city, temperature) values ('Austin', 48);
insert into weather (city, temperature) values ('Baton Rouge', 57);
insert into weather (city, temperature) values ('Jackson', 50);
insert into weather (city, temperature) values ('Montgomery', 53);
insert into weather (city, temperature) values ('Phoenix', 67);
insert into weather (city, temperature) values ('Sacramento', 66);
insert into weather (city, temperature) values ('Santa Fe', 27);
insert into weather (city, temperature) values ('Tallahassee', 59);
```

I will walk you through various examples to access this database.

10.1 Connecting to a Database

To connect to a database, simply create an instance of groovy.sql.Sql by calling the static method newInstance(). One version of this method accepts the database URL, user ID, password, and database driver name as parameters. If you already have a java.sql.Connection instance or a java.sql.DataSource, then you can use one of the constructors for Sql that accepts those instead of using newInstance().

You can obtain the information about the connection by calling the getConnection() method (the connection property) of the Sql instance. When you're done, you can close the connection by calling the close() method. Here is an example of connecting to the database I created for this chapter:

WorkingWithDatabases/Weather.groovy

```
def sql = groovy.sql.Sql.newInstance('jdbc:mysql://localhost:3306/weatherinfo',
            userid, password, 'com.mysql.jdbc.Driver')

println sql.connection.catalog
```

The previous code reports the name of the database, as shown here:

```
weatherinfo
```

10.2 Database Select

You can use the Sql object to conveniently iterate through data in a table. Simply call the eachRow() method, provide it with a SQL query to execute, and give it a closure to process each row of data, thusly:

WorkingWithDatabases/Weather.groovy

```
println "City                    Temperature"
sql.eachRow('SELECT * from weather') {
  printf "%-20s%s\n", it.city, it[1]
}
```

The previous code produces the following output:

```
City                 Temperature
Austin               48
Baton Rouge          57
Jackson              50
Montgomery           53
Phoenix              67
Sacramento           66
Santa Fe             27
Tallahassee          59
```

You asked eachRow() to execute the SQL query on the weather table to process all its rows. You then iterate (as the name each indicates) over each row. There's more grooviness here—the GroovyResultSet object that eachRow() provides allows you to access the columns in the table either directly by name (as in it.city) or using the index (as in it[1]).

In the previous example, you hard-coded the header for the output. It would be nice to get this from the database instead. Another over-loaded version of eachRow() will do that. It accepts two closures—one for metadata and the other for data. The closure for metadata is called only once after the execution of the SQL statement with an instance of ResultSetMetaData, and the other closure is called once for each row in the result. Let's give that a try in the following code:

WorkingWithDatabases/Weather.groovy

```
processMeta = { metaData ->
  metaData.columnCount.times { i ->
    printf "%-21s", metaData.getColumnLabel(i+1)
  }

  println ""
}

sql.eachRow('SELECT * from weather', processMeta) {
  printf "%-20s %s\n", it.city, it[1]
}
```

The output from the previous code is shown here:

```
city            temperature
Austin          48
Baton Rouge     57
Jackson         50
Montgomery      53
Phoenix         67
Sacramento      66
Santa Fe        27
Tallahassee     59
```

If you want to process all the rows but don't want to use an iterator, you can use the rows() method on the Sql instance. It returns an instance of ArrayList of result data, as shown here:

WorkingWithDatabases/Weather.groovy

```
rows = sql.rows('SELECT * from weather')
println "Weather info available for ${rows.size()} cites"
```

The previous code reports this:

```
Weather info available for 8 cites
```

Call the firstRow() method instead if you're interested in getting only the first row of result.

You can perform stored procedure calls using the call() methods of Sql. The withStatement() method allows you to set up a closure that will be called before the execution of queries. This is useful if you want to intercept the SQL queries before execution so you can alter it or set some properties.

10.3 Transforming Data to XML

You can get the data from the database and create different representations using Groovy builders. Here is an example that creates an XML representation (see Section 17.1, *Building XML*, on page 255) of the data in the weather table:

WorkingWithDatabases/Weather.groovy

```
bldr = new groovy.xml.MarkupBuilder()

bldr.weather {
  sql.eachRow('SELECT * from weather') {
    city(name: it.city, temperature: it.temperature)
  }
}
```

The XML output from the previous code is as follows:

```
WorkingWithDatabases/Weather.output
<weather>
  <city name='Austin' temperature='48' />
  <city name='Baton Rouge' temperature='57' />
  <city name='Jackson' temperature='50' />
  <city name='Montgomery' temperature='53' />
  <city name='Phoenix' temperature='67' />
  <city name='Sacramento' temperature='66' />
  <city name='Santa Fe' temperature='27' />
  <city name='Tallahassee' temperature='59' />
</weather>
```

With hardly any effort, Groovy and GSQL help you create an XML representation of data from the database.

10.4 Using DataSet

In Section 10.2, *Database Select*, on page 159, you saw how to process the results set obtained from executing a SELECT query. If you want to receive only a filtered set of rows, such as only cities with temperature values below 33, you can set up the query accordingly. Alternately, you can receive the result as a groovy.sql.DataSet, which allows you to filter data. Let's examine this further.

The dataSet() method of the Sql class takes the name of a table and returns a virtual proxy—it does not fetch the actual rows until you iterate. You can then iterate over the rows using the each() method of the DataSet (like the eachRow() method of Sql). In the following code, however, you'll use the findAll() method to filter the result to obtain only cities with below-freezing temperature. When you invoke findAll(), the DataSet is further refined with a specialized query based on the select predicate you provide. The actual data is still not fetched until you call the each() method on the resulting object. As a result, DataSet is highly efficient, bringing only data that is actually selected.

```
WorkingWithDatabases/Weather.groovy
dataSet = sql.dataSet('weather')
citiesBelowFreezing = dataSet.findAll { it.temperature < 32 }
println "Cities below freezing:"
citiesBelowFreezing.each {
  println it.city
}
```

The output from the code using the previous DataSet is as follows:

```
Cities below freezing:
Santa Fe
```

10.5 Inserting and Updating

You can use the DataSet object to add data in addition to using it to filter data. The add() method accepts a map of data to create a row, as shown in the following code:

WorkingWithDatabases/Weather.groovy

```
println "Number of cities : " + sql.rows('SELECT * from weather').size()
dataSet.add(city: 'Denver', temperature: 19)
println "Number of cities : " + sql.rows('SELECT * from weather').size()
```

The following output shows the effect of executing the previous code:

```
Number of cities : 8
Number of cities : 9
```

More traditionally, however, you can insert data using the Sql class's execute() or executeInsert() methods, as shown here:

WorkingWithDatabases/Weather.groovy

```
temperature = 50
sql.executeInsert("""INSERT INTO weather (city, temperature)
                     VALUES ('Oklahoma City', ${temperature})""")
println sql.firstRow(
  "SELECT temperature from weather WHERE city='Oklahoma City'")
```

The output from the previous code is as follows:

```
["temperature":50]
```

You can perform updates and deletes in a similar way by issuing the appropriate SQL commands.

10.6 Accessing Microsoft Excel

You can use the Sql class to access Microsoft Excel as well.[2] In this section, you'll create a really simple example using things you've seen already, except that you'll be talking to Excel instead of MySQL. Let's first create an Excel file named weather.xlsx.[3]

---

2. If you want to interact with COM or ActiveX, take a look at Groovy's Scriptom API (http://groovy.codehaus.org/COM+Scripting).
3. Or weather.xls if you're using older versions of Excel.

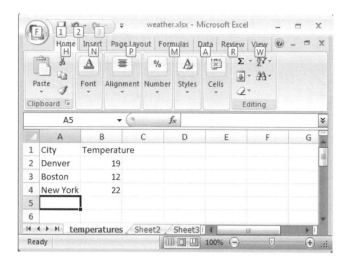

Figure 10.1: An Excel file that you will access using GSQL

Create it in the c:\temp directory. The file will contain a worksheet with the name temperatures (see the bottom of the worksheet) and the content shown in Figure 10.1.

The code to access Excel is as follows:

WorkingWithDatabases/Excel/Windows/AccessExcel.groovy

```groovy
def sql = groovy.sql.Sql.newInstance(
"""jdbc:odbc:Driver=
{Microsoft Excel Driver (*.xls, *.xlsx, *.xlsm, *.xlsb)};
DBQ=C:/temp/weather.xlsx;READONLY=false""", '', '')

println "City\t\tTemperature"
sql.eachRow('SELECT * FROM [temperatures$]') {
 println "${it.city}\t\t${it.temperature}"
}
```

The output from the previous code is as follows:

```
City            Temperature
Denver          19.0
Boston          12.0
New York        22.0
```

In the call to newInstance(), you've specified the driver for Excel and the location of the Excel file. Instead of this, you could set up a DSN to the Excel file and use the good old JDBC-ODBC driver bridge if you want.

If you do that, you won't put the file location in the code. Instead, you'll configure the DSN data source on Windows. The rest of the code to execute the query and process the result is familiar.

In this chapter, you used GSQL to access relational data. You can benefit from the simple yet powerful capability of this API for your data access. It takes only a few lines of code and a few minutes before your application can read and write real data in a relational database.

Chapter 11

Working with Scripts and Classes

In any nontrivial application you'll need to work with multiple classes and scripts. I define a *script* as a file with Groovy code that's not part of a class and that you intend to execute or use without going through an explicit compilation step[1] (a script may also include classes). I define a Groovy *class* as a file in which all code is contained within a class and you can use it with or without an explicit compilation step. I'll use the term *Groovy code* to refer to both.

Groovy is by far the only language that seamlessly allows you to mix and jointly compile both Groovy and Java code. In this chapter, I'll show you how to work with multiple Groovy scripts and both Java and Groovy classes.

11.1   The Melting Pot of Java and Groovy

In your applications, you can implement a certain functionality in a Java class, a Groovy class, or a Groovy script. Then, you can call this functionality from within Java classes, Groovy classes, or Groovy scripts. The various options to mix Java classes, Groovy classes, and Groovy scripts is shown in Figure 11.1, on the next page.

To use Groovy classes from Groovy code, you don't have to do anything. It just works. Simply make sure the classes you depend on are in the classpath either as source or as bytecode. To pull in a Groovy script into your Groovy code, you can use GroovyShell. To use it from within your Java classes, you can use the ScriptEngine API provided by JSR

---

1.   Remember, all Groovy code is compiled in memory when you run the groovy command.

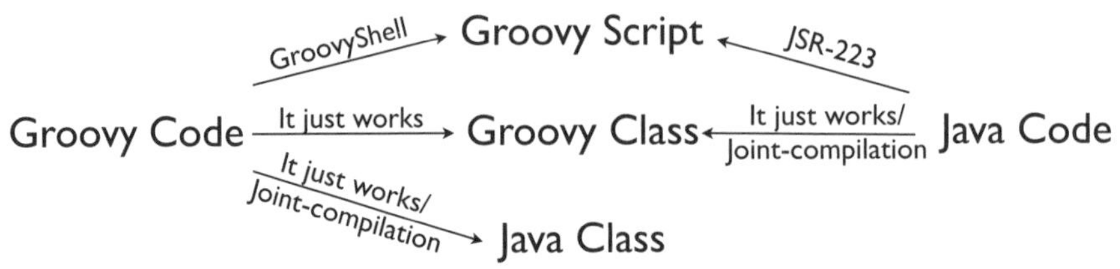

Figure 11.1: Ways to mix Java classes, Groovy classes, and scripts

223. If you want to use a Groovy class from within Java class, or vice versa, you can take advantage of the Groovy joint-compilation facility. All these are really simple, as you'll see in the rest of this chapter.

First I will walk you through options for running Groovy. Then I will discuss how to mix Groovy classes and scripts with both Java and Groovy.

11.2 Running Groovy

There are two options to choose from to run your Groovy code. You can use the groovy command on your source code. Then Groovy automatically compiles your code in memory and executes it. You don't have to take an explicit step to compile it.

If you want to take a more traditional Javalike approach of explicitly compiling code to create bytecode—the .class file—you can do that using the groovyc compiler. To execute the bytecode, you'll use the java command just like you'd execute your compiled Java code. The only difference is you need to have the groovy-all-1.5.4.jar file in the classpath. Remember to add . for the current directory so it can find your classes in the current directory. This JAR is located in the embeddable directory under your GROOVY_HOME. As an example, suppose you have the following Groovy code in a file named Greet.groovy:

ClassesAndScripts/Greet.groovy

```
println (['Groovy', 'Rocks!'].join(' '))
```

If you want to run it, you can simply type groovy Greet. However, if you want to explicitly compile this into Java bytecode, type groovyc Greet.groovy. This will create a file named, as you'd expect, Greet.class.[2] Use the -d option to specify a destination directory other than the current directory. You can run the bytecode by typing this:[3]

```
java –classpath $GROOVY_HOME/embeddable/groovy-all-1.5.4.jar:. Greet
```

Here's the output:

```
Groovy Rocks!
```

These steps show that you can compile and distribute your Groovy code as bytecode much like you would compile and distribute your Java code. You can release it as .class files or JAR it up. java sees no difference. You can use this approach to distribute your Groovy code as bytecode along with rest of your bytecode, if your deployment settings demand it.

11.3 Using Groovy Classes from Groovy

To use a Groovy class from within your Groovy code, you really don't have to do anything other than make sure the Groovy class is in your classpath. You can use the Groovy source code as is, or you can compile it into .class file and use it—it's your choice. When your Groovy code references a Groovy class, Groovy looks for the .groovy file with the name of the class in your classpath; if it does not find it, it looks for a .class file with the same name.

Suppose you have a Groovy source code Car.groovy, shown here, in a directory named src:

`ClassesAndScripts/src/Car.groovy`

```
class Car
{
  int year = 2008
  int miles

  String toString() { "Car: year: $year, miles: $miles" }
}
```

---

2. If your code has a package declaration, then the file will be created in the appropriate directory following the Java package-directory format. Unlike Groovy classes, Groovy scripts usually don't have package declarations.

3. On Windows, use %GROOVY_HOME% instead of $GROOVY_HOME.

Also, suppose you're using this class in a file named useCar.groovy, as shown here:

`ClassesAndScripts/useCar.groovy`

```
println new Car()
```

To use this class, type groovy -classpath src useCar. This will automatically fetch the Car class, create an instance, and produce the following:

```
Car: year: 2008, miles: 0
```

If instead of source code you have bytecode for the Car, the steps are the same—Groovy can readily use classes from .groovy or .class files.

11.4 Using Groovy Classes from Java

If the Groovy classes are precompiled, then you can use the .class files or JARs readily in Java. Java sees no difference between the bytecode from Java and Groovy; you'll have to add the Groovy JAR (discussed earlier) in your classpath much like how you'll have JARs for Spring, Hibernate, or other frameworks/libraries you use.

What if you have a Groovy source code instead of bytecode? Remember, when your Java class depends on other Java classes, javac will compile any Java classes it deems necessary if it does not find their bytecode. However, javac does not extend that kindness to Groovy. Fortunately, groovyc supports *joint compilation* in Groovy 1.5. When you compile Groovy code, it determines whether any Java classes need to be compiled and takes care of compiling them. So, you can freely mix Java source code and Groovy source code in a project. You don't have to go through separate compilation steps; instead, simply call groovyc.

To take advantage of joint compilation, you need to use the -j compilation flag. Use the -J prefix to pass flags to the Java compiler. Here's an example. Suppose you have a Java class in a file named AJavaClass.java:

`ClassesAndScripts/AJavaClass.java`

```
//Java code
public class AJavaClass
{
  {
        System.out.println("Created Java Class");
  }

  public void sayHello() { System.out.println("hello"); }
}
```

You also have a Groovy script in a file UseJavaClass.groovy that uses that Java class:

`ClassesAndScripts/UseJavaClass.groovy`

```
new AJavaClass().sayHello()
```

To compile these two files jointly, issue the command groovyc -j AJava-Class.java UseJavaClass.groovy -Jsource 1.6. The option -Jsource 1.6 sends the optional option source = 1.6 to the Java compiler. Examine the byte-code generated using javap. You'll notice that AJavaClass, as a regular Java class, extends java.lang.Object, while UseJavaClass extends groovy.lang.Script.

Execute the code to confirm all went well. Try the following command:

```
java -classpath $GROOVY_HOME/embeddable/groovy-all-1.5.4.jar:. UseJavaClass
```

You should see the following output:

```
Created Java Class
hello
```

You can intermix Groovy and Java seamlessly in your project, making Groovy a fantastic language for clean Java integration in your enterprise applications. You can focus on leveraging the advantages of each language without having to fight any integration battles.

11.5 Using Java Classes from Groovy

Using Java classes in Groovy is simple and direct. If the Java classes you want to use are part of the JDK, import the classes or their packages in Groovy just like in Java. Groovy imports by default a number of packages and classes (see Section 3.1, *From Java to Groovy*, on page 25), so if the class you want to use is imported already (such as java.util.Date), then just use it—no import is needed.

If you want to use one of your own Java classes, or classes that are not part of the standard JDK, you can import them in Groovy, just like you would in Java. Make sure to import the necessary packages or classes, or refer to the classes by their fully qualified name. When running groovy, specify the path to the .class files or JARs using the -classpath option. If the class files are in same directory where your Groovy code is, there's no need to specify that directory using the classpath option.

Let's look at an example. Say you have a Java class named GreetJava that belongs to package com.agiledeveloper and has a static method called sayHello(), as shown here:

ClassesAndScripts/GreetJava.java

```java
// Java code
package com.agiledeveloper;

public class GreetJava
{
        public static void sayHello()
        {
                System.out.println("Hello Java");
        }
}
```

Now say you want to call this method from a Groovy script. First, compile the Java class GreetJava so the class file GreetJava.class is located in the directory ./com/agiledeveloper, where . is the current directory. Now create a Groovy script in a file UseGreetJava.groovy with the following:

ClassesAndScripts/UseGreetJava.groovy

```
com.agiledeveloper.GreetJava.sayHello()
```

To run this script, simply type groovy UseGreetJava. The script runs with no trouble and uses the sayHello() method in class GreetJava, as shown in the following output:

```
Hello Java
```

If the class file is not under the current directory, you can still use it, but you need to remember to set the classpath option. Assume that the class file GreetJava.class is located under ~/release/com/agiledeveloper, where ~ is your home directory.

To run the previously mentioned Groovy script (UseGreetJava.groovy), use the following command:

```
groovy -classpath ~/release UseGreetJava
```

In this example, you compiled the Java code explicitly and then used the bytecode with your Groovy script. If you intend to explicitly compile your Groovy code, then you don't have to use a separate compilation step for Java and Groovy. Use the joint compilation facility instead.

11.6　Using Groovy Scripts from Groovy

You saw how easy it is to use Groovy classes in Groovy and Java. But, what about Groovy scripts, those Groovy statements not necessarily confined to a particular class in the source code? You can have those scripts executed using GroovyShell class. Let's take a look at an example:

ClassesAndScripts/Script1.groovy

```
println "Hello from Script1"
```

Here you have a file named Script1.groovy, and you want to execute that script as part of executing another Groovy script, Script2.groovy, shown here:

ClassesAndScripts/Script2.groovy

```
println "In Script2"
shell = new GroovyShell()
shell.evaluate(new File('Script1.groovy'))

// or simply
evaluate(new File('Script1.groovy'))
```

The output from the previous code is as follows:

```
In Script2
Hello from Script1
Hello from Script1
```

GroovyShell allows you to execute the evaluate() script in any file (or string). That was easy. But (and there is always a "but"), what if you want to pass some parameters to the scripts?

ClassesAndScripts/Script1a.groovy

```
println "Hello ${name}"
name = "Dan"
```

This script is expecting a variable name. You can use an instance of Binding to bind variables, as shown here:

ClassesAndScripts/Script2a.groovy

```
println "In Script2"

name = "Venkat"

shell = new GroovyShell(binding)
result = shell.evaluate(new File('Script1a.groovy'))

println "Script1a returned : $result"

println "Hello $name"
```

In the calling script, you created a variable name (the same variable name as in the called script). When you create the instance of Groovy-Shell, pass the current Binding object to it (each script execution has one of these). So, the called script can now use (read and set) variables that the calling script knows about. The output of executing the previous code is as follows:

```
In Script2
Hello Venkat
Script1a returned : Dan
Hello Dan
```

If the script returns a value, you can receive that from the evaluate() method as the return value as well, as you saw in the previous example.

In the previous example, you passed the Binding of the calling script to GroovyShell. If you don't want your current binding to be affected and want to keep the called script's binding separate, simply create a new instance of Binding, call setProperty() on it to set variable names and values, and provide it as an argument when creating an instance of GroovyShell, as shown here:

ClassesAndScripts/Script3.groovy

```
println "In Script3"

binding1 = new Binding()
binding1.setProperty('name', 'Venkat')
shell = new GroovyShell(binding1)
shell.evaluate(new File('Script1a.groovy'))

binding2 = new Binding()
binding2.setProperty('name', 'Dan')
shell.binding = binding2
shell.evaluate(new File('Script1a.groovy'))
```

The output from the previous code is as follows:

```
In Script3
Hello Venkat
Hello Dan
```

If you want to pass some command-line arguments to the script, use the run() methods of the GroovyShell class instead of the evaluate() methods.

GroovyShell allows you to easily load arbitrary scripts and execute them as part of your Groovy code. This feature is very useful to not only run routine tasks that may be saved in reusable scripts but also to build and execute DSLs.

11.7 Using Groovy Scripts from Java

You saw so far how to mix Java and Groovy classes and also how to mix Groovy classes and scripts within Groovy. You can compile your Groovy script and use it with Java. However, if you want to use Groovy script as is in Java, you may use JSR 223 for that.

JSR 223 bridges[4] the JVM and scripting languages. It provides a standard way to interact between Java and several languages with implementations of the JSR 223 scripting engine API. You can download and use JSR 223 with Java 5. It is included in Java 6.

JSR 223 currently works only with Groovy 1.0 and not with Groovy 1.5. JSR 223 is an option more suited for other languages on the JVM than for Groovy. Groovy's ability to jointly compile Java and Groovy lessens the need for something like JSR 223.

To call a (not precompiled) script from Java, use the script engine. You can obtain it from ScriptEngineManager by calling the getEngineByName() method. To execute your scripts from within your Java code, call its eval() method. To use Groovy scripts, you need to make sure .../jsr223-engines/groovy/build/groovy-engine.jar is in your classpath.

Let's look at an example to execute a little Groovy script from within Java:[5]

```
MixingJavaAndGroovy/CallingScript.java
```
```java
// Java code
package com.agiledeveloper;

import javax.script.*;

public class CallingScript
{
  public static void main(String[] args)
  {
    ScriptEngineManager manager = new ScriptEngineManager();

    ScriptEngine engine = manager.getEngineByName("groovy");

    System.out.println("Calling script from Java");
```

---

4. See the Java Scripting Programmer's Guide in Appendix A, on page 287.
5. With Java comes the pleasure of handling exceptions I don't care about. In the rest of the examples in this chapter I won't show you exception-handling code, but remember to put it in when you code.

```
    try
    {
      engine.eval("println 'Hello from Groovy'");
    }
    catch(ScriptException ex)
    {
      System.out.println(ex);
    }
  }
}
```

The output from the previous code is as follows:

```
Calling script from Java
Hello from Groovy
```

In this example, your Groovy script is embedded in the string parameter to the eval() method. Unlike this example, in reality, the script may not be hard-coded. It may be in a file, an input stream, a dialog box, and so on. In that case, you'll find other overloaded versions of the eval() method that take a Reader useful.

If the script returns any result to the calling Java program, you can receive it from the Object return value of the eval() method.

Using this approach, you can call any arbitrary Groovy script from within your Java application. If you want to pass some parameters to the script—a Java object, created in Java but accessed in Groovy—you can use Bindings.

Bindings are an implementation of Map<String, Object> that makes objects available through a named value. ScriptContext allows the script engines to connect to the Java objects such as Bindings in the hosting application. You can either explicitly get access to these objects and interact with them[6] or simply use get() and put() on the ScriptEngine instance. Let's look now at an example of passing parameters to Groovy scripts from Java:

MixingJavaAndGroovy/ParameterPassing.java

```
engine.put("name", "Venkat");
engine.eval("println \"Hello ${name} from Groovy\"; name += '!' ");
String name = (String) engine.get("name");
System.out.println("Back in Java:" + name);
```

---

6. If you want to execute the same script but with different set of values for the variables, create different contexts and use them in a call to eval().

The output from the previous code is as follows:

```
Hello Venkat from Groovy
Back in Java:Venkat!
```

You're sending a String object (with value Venkat) to the engine using the put() method. You've given the name name for the variable binding. Within the script, you use that variable (name). You can also set values to it. This value can be obtained on the Java side by calling the get() method on the engine.

JSR 223 provides the capability to call instance methods and also functions not associated with any particular class. You can use the invokeMethod() and invokeFunction() of the Invocable for that. If you plan to use a script repeatedly, use the Compilable interface to avoid repeatedly recompiling the script.

11.8 Ease of Integration

You typically compile your Java code into .class files and JAR them up. To use other Java classes, all you need is the .class files or the JARs that contain those files to be in your classpath. Groovy pretty much expects the same if you call into Java classes from Groovy. Groovy also makes your life easy by providing you with joint compilation. This allows you to not only use both Groovy and Java code side by side, but you can also debug and work seamlessly with the two languages on the same project.

You saw how easily you can mix and work with Groovy scripts as well. You've seen examples of using Java classes from the JDK throughout this book. In this chapter, you figured out how to use your own Java classes and also Groovy classes with your application. There's no impediment to creating enterprise applications mixing Java and Groovy.

Part III

MOPping Groovy

Chapter 12

Exploring
Meta-Object Protocol (MOP)

In Java, you can use reflection at runtime to explore the structure of your program, its classes, their methods, and the parameters they take. However, you're still restricted to the static structure you've created. You can't change the type of an object or let it acquire behavior dynamically at runtime—at least not yet. Imagine if you could add methods and behavior dynamically based on the current state of your application or the inputs it receives. This would make your code flexible, and you could be creative and productive. Well, you don't have to imagine that anymore—metaprogramming provides this functionality. *Metaprogramming* means writing programs that manipulate programs, including itself. Dynamic languages such as Groovy provide this capability through the Meta-Object Protocol (MOP). Creating classes, writing unit tests, and introducing mock objects are all easy with Groovy's MOP.

In Groovy, you can use MOP to invoke methods dynamically and also synthesize classes and methods on the fly. This can give you the feeling that your object favorably changed its class. Grails/GORM uses this facility, for example, to synthesize methods for database queries. With MOP you can create internal DSLs in Groovy.[1] Groovy builders[2] rely on MOP as well. So, MOP is one of the most important concepts you'll want to learn and exploit. There are several concepts in MOP you'll need to investigate, and I'll cover them across the next few chapters.

---

1. See Chapter 18, *Creating DSLs in Groovy*, on page 273.
2. See Chapter 17, *Groovy Builders*, on page 255.

In this chapter, you will explore MOP by looking at what makes a Groovy object and how Groovy resolves method calls for Java objects and Groovy objects. You'll then look at ways to query for methods and properties and finally learn how to access objects dynamically.

Once you absorb the fundamentals in this chapter, you'll be ready to learn how to intercept method calls in Chapter 13, *Intercepting Methods Using MOP*, on page 189. You'll then see how to inject and synthesize methods into classes at runtime in Chapter 14, *MOP Method Injection and Synthesis*, on page 197. Finally, we'll wrap up the discussion on MOP in Chapter 15, *MOPping Up*, on page 219.

12.1 Groovy Object

The flexibility offered by Groovy can be confusing at first. So, if you want to take full advantage of MOP, you need to first understand Groovy objects and Groovy's method handling.

In Section 1.3, *Why Groovy?*, on page 5, I should've said Groovy objects are *at least* Java objects. In fact, Groovy objects have additional capabilities. Groovy objects have more dynamic behavior than compiled Java objects in Groovy. Also, Groovy handles method calls to Java objects differently than to Groovy objects.

In a Groovy application you'll work with three kinds of objects: POJOs, POGOs, and Groovy interceptors. Plain Old Java Objects (POJOs) are regular Java objects—you can create them using Java or other languages on the JVM. Plain Old Groovy Objects (POGOs) are classes written in Groovy. They extend java.lang.Object but implement the groovy.lang.GroovyObject interface. Groovy interceptors are Groovy objects that extend GroovyInterceptable and have a method interception capability, which we'll soon discuss.

Groovy defines the GroovyObject interface as shown here:

```
//This is an excerpt of GroovyObject.java from Groovy source code

package groovy.lang;

public interface GroovyObject {
    Object invokeMethod(String name, Object args);
    Object getProperty(String property);
    void setProperty(String property, Object newValue);
    MetaClass getMetaClass();
    void setMetaClass(MetaClass metaClass);
}
```

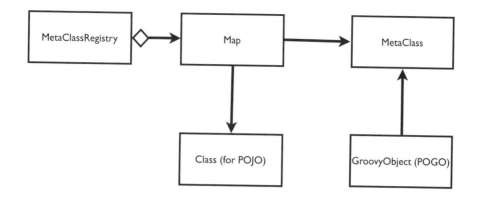

Figure 12.1: POJOs, POGOs, AND THEIR METACLASS

invokeMethod(), getProperty(), and setProperty() make Groovy objects highly dynamic. You can use them to work with methods and properties created on the fly. getMetaClass() and setMetaClass() make it very easy to create proxies to intercept and also inject methods on a POGO. Once a class is loaded into the JVM, you can't change the metaobject Class for it. However, you can change its MetaClass by calling setMetaClass(). This gives you a feeling that the object changed its class at runtime.

The GroovyInterceptable interface is shown next. It's a marker interface that extends GroovyObject, and all method calls—both existing methods and nonexisting methods—on an object that implements this interface are intercepted by its invokeMethod().

```
//This is an excerpt of GroovyInterceptable.java from Groovy source code

package groovy.lang;

public interface GroovyInterceptable extends GroovyObject {
}
```

Groovy allows metaprogramming for POJOs and POGOs. For POJOs, Groovy maintains a MetaClassRegistry class of MetaClasses, as shown in Figure 12.1. POGOs, on the other hand, have a direct reference to their MetaClass.

When you call a method, Groovy first checks whether the target object is a POJO or a POGO. Groovy's method handling is different for each of these types.

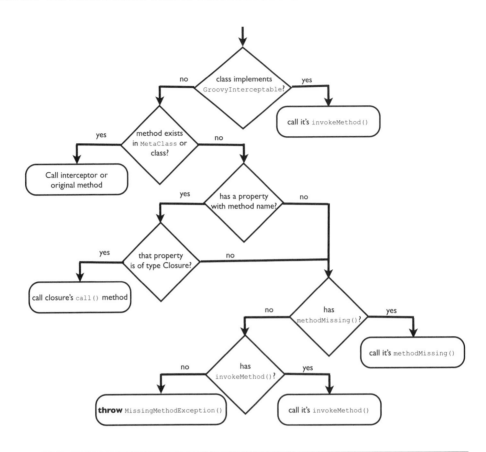

Figure 12.2: How Groovy handles method calls on a POGO

For a POJO, Groovy fetches its MetaClass from the applicationwide Meta-ClassRegistry and delegates method invocation to it. So, any interceptors or methods you've defined on its MetaClass take precedence over the original method of the POJO.

For a POGO, Groovy takes a few extra steps, as illustrated in Figure 12.2. If the object implements GroovyInterceptable, then *all* calls are routed to its invokeMethod(). Within this interceptor, you can route calls to the actual method, if you want, allowing you to do AOP-like operations.

If the POGO does not implement GroovyInterceptable, then Groovy looks for the method first in the POGO's MetaClass and then, if not found, on the POGO itself. If the POGO has no such method, Groovy looks for a property or a field with the method name. If that property or field is of type closure, Groovy invokes that in place of the method call. If Groovy finds no such property or field, it makes two last attempts. If the POGO has a method named methodMissing(), it calls it. Otherwise, it calls the POGO's invokeMethod(). If you've implemented this method on your POGO, it is used. The default implementation of invokeMethod() throws a MissingMethodException indicating the failure of the call.

Let's see in code the mechanism discussed earlier. I've created classes with different options to illustrate Groovy's method handling. Study the code, and see whether you can figure out which methods Groovy executes in each of the cases (while walking through the following code, refer to Figure 12.2, on the facing page):

`ExploringMOP/TestMethodInvocation.groovy`

```groovy
class TestMethodInvocation extends GroovyTestCase
{
  void testMethodCallonPOJO()
  {
    def val = new Integer(3)

    assertEquals "3", val.toString()
  }

  void testInterceptedMethodCallonPOJO()
  {
    def val = new Integer(3)
    Integer.metaClass.toString = {-> 'intercepted' }

    assertEquals "intercepted", val.toString()
  }

  void testInterceptableCalled()
  {
    def obj = new AnInterceptable()
    assertEquals 'intercepted', obj.existingMethod()
    assertEquals 'intercepted', obj.nonExistingMethod()
  }

  void testInterceptedExistingMethodCalled()
  {
    AGroovyObject.metaClass.existingMethod2 = {-> 'intercepted' }
    def obj = new AGroovyObject()
    assertEquals 'intercepted', obj.existingMethod2()
  }
```

```groovy
  void testUnInterceptedExistingMethodCalled()
  {
    def obj = new AGroovyObject()
    assertEquals 'existingMethod', obj.existingMethod()
  }

  void testPropertyThatIsClosureCalled()
  {
    def obj = new AGroovyObject()
    assertEquals 'closure called', obj.closureProp()
  }

  void testMethodMissingCalledOnlyForNonExistent()
  {
    def obj = new ClassWithInvokeAndMissingMethod()
    assertEquals 'existingMethod', obj.existingMethod()
    assertEquals 'missing called', obj.nonExistingMethod()
  }

  void testInvokeMethodCalledForOnlyNonExistent()
  {
    def obj = new ClassWithInvokeOnly()
    assertEquals 'existingMethod', obj.existingMethod()
    assertEquals 'invoke called', obj.nonExistingMethod()
  }

  void testMethodFailsOnNonExistent()
  {
    def obj = new TestMethodInvocation()
    shouldFail (MissingMethodException) { obj.nonExistingMethod() }
  }
}

class AnInterceptable implements GroovyInterceptable
{
  def existingMethod() {}
  def invokeMethod(String name, args) { 'intercepted' }
}

class AGroovyObject
{
  def existingMethod() { 'existingMethod' }
  def existingMethod2() { 'existingMethod2' }
  def closureProp = { 'closure called' }
}

class ClassWithInvokeAndMissingMethod
{
  def existingMethod() { 'existingMethod' }
  def invokeMethod(String name, args) { 'invoke called' }
  def methodMissing(String name, args) { 'missing called' }
}
```

```
class ClassWithInvokeOnly
{
  def existingMethod() { 'existingMethod' }
  def invokeMethod(String name, args) { 'invoke called' }
}
```

The following output confirms that all the tests pass and Groovy handles the method as discussed:

```
.........
Time: 0.047

OK (9 tests)
```

12.2 Querying Methods and Properties

You can find out at runtime if an object supports a certain behavior by querying for its methods and properties. This is especially useful for behavior you add dynamically at runtime. Groovy allows you to add behavior not only to classes but also to select instances of a class.

Use getMetaMethod() of MetaObjectProtocol[3] to get a metamethod. Use getStaticMetaMethod() if you're looking for a static method. Similarly, use getMetaProperty() and getStaticMetaProperty() for a metaproperty. To get a list of overloaded methods, use the plural form of these methods— getMetaMethods() and getStaticMetaMethods(). If you want simply to check for existence and not get the metamethod or metaproperty, use hasProperty() to check for properties and respondsTo() for methods.

MetaMethod "represents a Method on a Java object a little like Method except without using reflection to invoke the method," says the Groovy documentation. If you have the name of a method as a string, call getMetaMethod() and use the resulting MetaMethod to invoke your method, as shown here:

ExploringMOP/UsingMetaMethod.groovy

```
str = "hello"
methodName = 'toUpperCase'
// Name may come from an input instead of being hard coded

methodOfInterest = str.metaClass.getMetaMethod(methodName)

println methodOfInterest.invoke(str)
```

---

3. MetaClass extends MetaObjectProtocol.

Here's the output from the previous code:

```
HELLO
```

You don't have to know a method name at coding time. You can get it as input and invoke the method dynamically.

To find out whether an object would respond to a method call, use the respondsTo() method. It takes as parameters the instance you're querying, the name of the method you're querying for, and an optional comma-separated list of arguments intended for that method for which you're querying. It returns a list of MetaMethods for the matching methods. Let's use that in an example:

ExploringMOP/UsingMetaMethod.groovy

```
print "Does String respond to toUpperCase()? "
println String.metaClass.respondsTo(str, 'toUpperCase')? 'yes' : 'no'

print "Does String respond to compareTo(String)? "
println String.metaClass.respondsTo(str, 'compareTo', "test")? 'yes' : 'no'

print "Does String respond to toUpperCase(int)? "
println String.metaClass.respondsTo(str, 'toUpperCase', 5)? 'yes' : 'no'
```

The output from the previous code is as follows:

```
Does String respond to toUpperCase()? yes
Does String respond to compareTo(String)? yes
Does String respond to toUpperCase(int)? no
```

getMetaMethod() and respondsTo() offer a nice convenience. You can simply send the arguments for a method you're looking for to these methods. They don't insist on an array of Class of the arguments like the getMethod() method in Java reflection. Even better, if the method you're interested in does not take any parameters, don't send any arguments, not even a null. This is because the last parameter to these methods is an array of parameters and is treated optional by Groovy.

There was one more magical thing taking place in the previous code: you used Groovy's special treatment of boolean (for more information, see Section 3.5, *Groovy boolean Evaluation*, on page 43). The respondsTo() method returns a list of MetaMethods, and since you used the result in a conditional statement (the ?: operator), Groovy returned true if there were any methods and false otherwise. So, you don't have to explicitly check whether the size of the returned list is greater than zero. Groovy does that for you.

12.3 Dynamically Accessing Objects

You've looked at ways to query for methods and properties and also at ways to invoke them dynamically. There are other convenient ways to access properties and call methods in Groovy. We will look at them now using an instance of String as an example. Suppose you get the names of properties and methods as input at runtime and want to access these dynamically. Here are some ways to do that:

ExploringMOP/AccessingObject.groovy

```
def printInfo(obj)
{
  // Assume user entered these values from standard input
  usrRequestedProperty = 'bytes'
  usrRequestedMethod = 'toUpperCase'

  println obj[usrRequestedProperty]
  //or
  println obj."$usrRequestedProperty"

  println obj."$usrRequestedMethod"()
  //or
  println obj.invokeMethod(usrRequestedMethod, null)
}

printInfo('hello')
```

Here's the output from the previous code:

```
[104, 101, 108, 108, 111]
[104, 101, 108, 108, 111]
HELLO
HELLO
```

To invoke a property dynamically, you can use the index operator [] or use the dot notation followed by a GString evaluating the property name, as shown in the previous code. To invoke a method, use the dot notation or call the invokeMethod on the object, giving it the method name and list of arguments (null in this case).

To iterate over all the properties of an object, use the properties property (or the getProperties() method), as shown here:

ExploringMOP/AccessingObject.groovy

```
println "Properties of 'hello' are: "
'hello'.properties.each { println it }
```

The output is as follows:

```
Properties of 'hello' are:
empty=false
class=class java.lang.String
bytes=[B@74f2ff9b
```

In this chapter, you looked at the fundamentals for metaprogramming in Groovy. With this foundation, you're well equipped to explore MOP further, understand how Groovy works, and take advantage of the MOP concepts you'll see in the next few chapters.

Chapter 13

Intercepting Methods Using MOP

In Groovy you can implement Aspect-Oriented Programming (AOP) [Lad03] like method interception or method advice fairly easily. There are three types of advice. And, no, I'm not talking about the good advice, the bad advice, and the unsolicited advice we receive every day. I'm talking about the *before*, *after*, and *around* advice. The before advice is code or a concern you'd want to execute before a certain operation. After advice is executed after the execution of an operation. The around advice, on the other hand, is executed *instead* of the intended operation. You can use MOP to implement these advices or interceptors. You don't need any complex tools or frameworks to do that in Groovy.

There are two approaches in Groovy to intercept method calls: either let the object do it or let its MetaClass do it. If you want the object to handle it, you need to implement the GroovyInterceptable interface. This is not desirable if you're not the author of the class, if the class is a Java class, or if you want to introduce interception dynamically. The second approach is better in these cases. You'll look at both of these approaches in this chapter.[1]

13.1 Intercepting Methods Using GroovyInterceptable

If a Groovy object implements GroovyInterceptable, then its invoke-Method() is called when *any* of its methods are called—both existing methods and nonexisting methods. That is, GroovyInterceptable's invoke-Method() hijacks all calls to the object.

---

1. There's one more way to intercept methods, using categories, but I'll defer discussing that until Section 14.1, *Injecting Methods Using Categories*, on page 198.

> ### invokeMethod, GroovyInterceptable, and GroovyObject
>
> If a Groovy object implements the GroovyInterceptable inter-face, then its invokeMethod() is called for *all* its method calls. For other Groovy objects, it is called only for methods that are nonexistent at the time of call. The exception to this is if you implement invokeMethod() on its MetaClass. In that case, it is again called always for both types of methods.

If you want to perform an around advice, simply implement your logic in this method, and you're done. However, if you want to implement the before or after advice (or both), implement your before/after logic, and route the call to the actual method at the appropriate time. To route the call, use the MetaMethod for the method you can obtain from the MetaClass (see Section 12.2, *Querying Methods and Properties*, on page 185).

Suppose you want to run filters—such as validation, login verification, logging, and so on—before you run some methods of a class. You don't want to manually edit each method to call the filters because such effort is redundant, tedious, and error prone. You don't want to ask callers of your methods to invoke the filters either, because there's no guarantee they'll call. Intercepting method calls to apply the filters is a good option. It'll be seamless and automatic.

Let's look at an example[2] in which you want to run check() on a Car before any other method is executed. Here's the code that uses Groovy-Interceptable to achieve this:

InterceptingMethodsUsingMOP/InterceptingCalls.groovy

```
Line 1  class Car implements GroovyInterceptable
     -  {
     -    def check() { System.out.println "check called..." }
     -
     5    def start() { System.out.println "start called..." }
     -
     -    def drive() { System.out.println "drive called..." }
     -
```

---

2. I'll use System.out.println() instead of println() in the examples in this chapter to avoid the interception of informational print messages.

```
      def invokeMethod(String name, args)
10    {
         System.out.print("Call to $name intercepted... ")

         if (name != 'check')
         {
15          System.out.print("running filter... ")
            Car.metaClass.getMetaMethod('check').invoke(this, null)
         }

         def validMethod = Car.metaClass.getMetaMethod(name, args)
20       if (validMethod != null)
         {
            validMethod.invoke(this, args)
         }
         else
25       {
            return Car.metaClass.invokeMethod(this, name, args)
         }
      }
   }
30
   car = new Car()

   car.start()
   car.drive()
35 car.check()
   try
   {
      car.speed()
   }
40 catch(Exception ex)
   {
      println ex
   }
```

Here's the output from the previous code:

```
Call to start intercepted... running filter... check called...
start called...
Call to drive intercepted... running filter... check called...
drive called...
Call to check intercepted... check called...
Call to speed intercepted... running filter... check called...
groovy.lang.MissingMethodException:
  No signature of method: Car.speed()
  is applicable for argument types: () values: {}
```

Since Car implements GroovyInterceptable, all method calls on an instance of Car are intercepted by its invokeMethod(). In that method, if the method name is not check, you invoke the before filter, which is the check() method. Determine whether the method called is a valid existing method with the help of the MetaClass's getMetaMethod(). If the method is valid, call that method using the invoke() method of the MetaMethod, as on line number 22.

If the method is not found, simply route the request to the MetaClass, as on line number 26. This gives an opportunity for the method to be synthesized dynamically, as you'll see in Section 14.4, *Method Synthesis Using methodMissing*, on page 209. If the method does not exist, MetaClass's invokeMethod() will throw a MissingMethodException.

In this example, you created a before advice. You can easily create an after advice by placing the desired code after line number 22. If you want to implement around advice, then eliminate the code on line number 22.

13.2 Intercepting Methods Using MetaClass

You used GroovyInterceptable to intercept method calls in Section 13.1, *Intercepting Methods Using GroovyInterceptable*, on page 189. That approach is good if you're the author of the class whose methods you want to intercept. However, that approach won't work if you don't have the privileges to modify the class source code or if it is a Java class. Furthermore, you may decide at runtime to start intercepting calls based on some condition or application state. In these cases, intercept methods by implementing the invokeMethod() method on the MetaClass.

Let's rewrite the example from Section 13.1, *Intercepting Methods Using GroovyInterceptable*, on page 189, this time using the MetaClass. In this version, the Car does not implement GroovyInterceptable and does not have the invokeMethod():[3]

InterceptingMethodsUsingMOP/InterceptingCallsUsingMetaClass.groovy

```
Line 1  class Car
   -    {
   -      def check() { System.out.println "check called..." }
   -
   5      def start() { System.out.println "start called..." }
   -
   -      def drive() { System.out.println "drive called..." }
   -    }
   -
```

---

3. Even if it has invokeMethod(), the invokeMethod() you add to MetaClass takes precedence if Car does not implement GroovyInterceptable.

```
10   Car.metaClass.invokeMethod = { String name, args ->
  -    System.out.print("Call to $name intercepted... ")
  -
  -    if (name != 'check')
  -    {
15     System.out.print("running filter... ")
  -      Car.metaClass.getMetaMethod('check').invoke(delegate, null)
  -    }
  -
  -    def validMethod = Car.metaClass.getMetaMethod(name, args)
20     if (validMethod != null)
  -    {
  -      validMethod.invoke(delegate, args)
  -    }
  -    else
25     {
  -      return Car.metaClass.invokeMissingMethod(delegate, name, args)
  -    }
  -  }
  -
30
  -  car = new Car()
  -
  -  car.start()
  -  car.drive()
35  car.check()
  -  try
  -  {
  -    car.speed()
  -  }
40 catch(Exception ex)
  -  {
  -    println ex
  -  }
```

The output from the previous code is as follows:

```
Call to start intercepted... running filter... check called...
start called...
Call to drive intercepted... running filter... check called...
drive called...
Call to check intercepted... check called...
Call to speed intercepted... running filter... check called...
groovy.lang.MissingMethodException:
  No signature of method: Car.speed()
  is applicable for argument types: () values: {}
```

On line number 10, you implemented, in the form of a closure, the invokeMethod() and set it on Car's MetaClass. This method will now intercept all calls on an instance of Car. There are two differences between this version of invokeMethod() and the version you implemented on

Car in Section 13.1, *Intercepting Methods Using GroovyInterceptable*, on page 189. The first difference is the use of delegate instead of this (see line number 16, for example). The delegate within the intercepting closure refers to the target object whose methods are being intercepted. The second difference is on line number 26, where you call invokeMissing-Method() on the MetaClass instead of calling invokeMethod. Since you're already in invokeMethod(), you should not call it recursively here.

As I mentioned earlier, one nice aspect of using the MetaClass to intercept calls is you can intercept calls on POJOs as well. To see this in action, let's intercept calls to methods on an Integer and perform AOP-like advice:

InterceptingMethodsUsingMOP/InterceptInteger.groovy

```groovy
Integer.metaClass.invokeMethod = { String name, args ->
  System.out.println("Call to $name intercepted on $delegate... ")

  def validMethod = Integer.metaClass.getMetaMethod(name, args)
  if (validMethod == null)
  {
    return Integer.metaClass.invokeMissingMethod(delegate, name, args)
  }

  System.out.println("running pre-filter... ")

  result = validMethod.invoke(delegate, args) // Remove this for around-advice

  System.out.println("running post-filter... ")

  result
}

println 5.floatValue()
println 5.intValue()
try
{
  println 5.empty()
}
catch(Exception ex)
{
  println ex
}
```

The output from the previous code is as follows:

```
Call to floatValue intercepted on 5...
running pre-filter...
running post-filter...
5.0
```

```
Call to intValue intercepted on 5...
running pre-filter...
running post-filter...
5
Call to empty intercepted on 5...
groovy.lang.MissingMethodException:
  No signature of method: java.lang.Integer.empty()
  is applicable for argument types: () values: {}
```

The invokeMethod() you added on the MetaClass of Integer intercepts method calls on 5, an instance of Integer. To intercept calls on any Object and not only Integers, add the interceptor to Object's MetaClass.

If you're interested in intercepting calls only to nonexistent methods, then use methodMissing() instead of invokeMethod(). We'll discuss this in Chapter 14, *MOP Method Injection and Synthesis*, on page 197.

You can provide both invokeMethod() and methodMissing() on MetaClass. invokeMethod() takes precedence over methodMissing(). However, by calling invokeMissingMethod(), you're letting methodMissing() handle nonexisting methods.

The ability to intercept method calls using MetaClass was influenced by Grails. It was originally introduced in Grails[4] and was later moved into Groovy. Take a minute to examine the MetaClass that's giving you so much power:

InterceptingMethodsUsingMOP/ExamineMetaClass.groovy

```
println Integer.metaClass.getClass().name
```

The output from the previous code is as follows:

```
groovy.lang.ExpandoMetaClass
```

ExpandoMetaClass is an implementation of the MetaClass interface and is one of the key classes responsible for implementing dynamic behavior in Groovy. You can add methods to this class to inject behavior into your class, and you can even specialize individual objects using this class.

There is a gotcha here depending on ExpandoMetaClass. It is one among different implementations of MetaClass. By default, Groovy currently does not use ExpandoMetaClass. When you query for the metaClass, however, the default is replaced with an instance of ExpandoMetaClass.

---

4. See http://graemerocher.blogspot.com/2007/06/dynamic-groovy-groovys-equivalent-to.html.

Here's an example that shows this behavior:

InterceptingMethodsUsingMOP/MetaClassUsed.groovy

```groovy
class MyClass {}

println "MetaClass of 2 is " + 2.metaClass.getClass().name
println "MetaClass of Integer is " + Integer.metaClass.getClass().name
println "MetaClass of 2 now is " + 2.metaClass.getClass().name

obj1 = new MyClass()
println "MetaClass of obj1 is " +  obj1.metaClass.getClass().name
println "MetaClass of MyClass is " + MyClass.metaClass.getClass().name
println "MetaClass of obj1 still is " +  obj1.metaClass.getClass().name

obj2 = new MyClass()
println "MetaClass of obj2 created later is " +  obj2.metaClass.getClass().name
```

The output from the previous code is as follows:

```
MetaClass of 2 is groovy.lang.MetaClassImpl
MetaClass of Integer is groovy.lang.ExpandoMetaClass
MetaClass of 2 now is groovy.lang.ExpandoMetaClass
MetaClass of obj1 is groovy.lang.MetaClassImpl
MetaClass of MyClass is groovy.lang.ExpandoMetaClass
MetaClass of obj1 still is groovy.lang.MetaClassImpl
MetaClass of obj2 created later is groovy.lang.ExpandoMetaClass
```

To begin with, the metaclass of Integer was an instance of MetaClassImpl. When you query for the metaClass property, it is replaced with an instance of ExpandoMetaClass. For your own Groovy classes, the MetaClass used for instances created before you query for metaClass on your class is different from the instances created after you query.[5] This behavior has caused some surprises when working with metaprogramming.[6] It would be nice if Groovy consistently used ExpandoMetaClass as the default implementation. There are discussions about this change in the Groovy community.

In this chapter, you saw how to intercept methods calls to realize AOP-like method advice capabilities. You'll find this feature useful to mock methods for the sake of testing, temporarily replace problem methods, study alternate implementations for algorithms without having to modify existing code, and more. You can go further with MOP by adding methods dynamically as well. You'll explore this in the next chapter.

---

5. Groovy allows each POGO to be associated with its own instance of MetaClass. This gives you the advantage of refining specific instances, as you'll see in Chapter 14, *MOP Method Injection and Synthesis*, on the next page.

6. You can find examples in Section 14.2, *Injecting Methods Using ExpandoMetaClass*, on page 203 and in Section 14.4, *Method Synthesis Using methodMissing*, on page 209.

MOP Method Injection and Synthesis

In Groovy you can open a class at any time. That is, you can add methods to classes dynamically, allowing them to change behavior at runtime. Rather than working with a static structure and predefined set of methods, objects can be agile, flexible, and assimilate behavior based on what's going on in your application. You can add a method based on a certain input you receive, for example. The ability to modify the behavior of your classes is central to metaprogramming and Groovy's MOP.

Using Groovy's MOP, you can inject behavior in one of several ways. You can use the following:

- Categories
- ExpandoMetaClass
- GroovyInterceptable
- GroovyObject's invokeMethod( )
- GroovyObject's methodMissing( )

I separate adding behavior into two types: injection and synthesis.

I'll use the term method injection to refer to the case in which at code-writing time you know the names of methods you want to add to one more more classes. *Method injection* allows you to add behavior dynamically into classes. You can add a set of reusable methods—like utility functions—that represent a certain functionality, to any number of classes. You can inject methods either by using categories or by using ExpandoMetaClass.

On the other hand, *method synthesis* will refer to the case in which you want to dynamically figure out the behavior for methods upon invocation. Groovy's invokeMethod(), methodMissing(), and GroovyInterceptable are useful for method synthesis. For example, Grails/GORM synthesizes finder methods like findByFirstName() and findByFirstNameAndLastName() for domain objects upon invocation.

A synthesized method may not exist as a separate method until you call it. When you call a nonexistent method, Groovy can intercept the call, allow your application to implement it on the fly, let you cache that implementation for future invocation, and then invoke it—Graeme Rocher calls it the "Intercept, Cache, Invoke" pattern.

In this chapter, you'll learn about MOP facilities for method injection and method synthesis.

14.1 Injecting Methods Using Categories

Groovy categories provide a controlled way to inject methods—the effect of method injection is contained within a block of code. A category is an object that has the ability to alter your class's MetaClass. It does so within the scope of the block and the executing thread. It reverses the change when you exit the block. Categories can be nested, and you can also apply multiple categories in a single block. You will explore the behavior and use of categories using examples in this section.

Suppose you have a Social Security number in a String or StringBuffer. You want to inject a method toSSN() that will return the string in the format xxx-xx-xxxx. Let's discuss some ways to achieve this.

Say the first plan of attack is to create a class SSNStringBuilder that extends StringBuffer and write the method toSSN() in it. Unfortunately, users of StringBuffer won't have this method. It's available only on SSNStringBuilder. Also, you can't extend the *final* class String, so you don't have this method on it.

Instead, take advantage of Groovy's categories by creating a class StringUtil and adding a static method toSSN() in it. This method takes one parameter, the target object on which the method is to be injected. The method checks the size of the string and returns a string in the intended format. To use the new method, call a special method use() that takes two parameters: a category and a closure block of code within which the injected method(s) are in effect.

The code is as follows:

InjectionAndSynthesisWithMOP/UsingCategories.groovy

```groovy
class StringUtil
{
  def static toSSN(self) //write toSSN(String self) to restrict to String
  {
    if (self.size() == 9)
    {
      return "${self[0..2]}-${self[3..4]}-${self[5..8]}"
    }
  }
}

use(StringUtil)
{
  println "123456789".toSSN()
  println new StringBuffer("987654321").toSSN()
}

try
{
  println "123456789".toSSN()
}
catch(MissingMethodException ex)
{
  println ex.message
}
```

Here's the output from the previous code:

```
123-45-6789
987-65-4321
No signature of method: java.lang.String.toSSN()
  is applicable for argument types: () values: {}
```

The method you injected is available only within the *use* block. When you called toSSN() outside the block, you got a MissingMethodException.

The calls to toSSN() on instances of String and StringBuffer within the block are routed to the static method in the category StringUtil. The parameter self of toSSN() is assigned to the target instance. Since you did not define the type of the self parameter, its type defaults to Object, and toSSN() is available on any object. If you want to restrict it to only Strings and StringBuffers, you will have to create two versions of toSSN() with explicit parameter types, one with String self and the other with StringBuffer self.

Groovy categories require the injection method to be static and take at least one parameter. The first parameter (called self in this example) refers to the target of the method call. Any parameters that your injected method takes will trail. The parameters can be any legal Groovy parameters—objects and closures.

Let's take a moment to understand the magic that happened when you called use() in the previous example. Groovy routes calls to the use() method in your script to the public static Object use(Class categoryClass, Closure closure) method of the GroovyCategorySupport class. This method defines a new scope—a fresh property/method list on the stack for the target objects' MetaClass. It then examines each of the static methods in the given category class and adds its static methods with at least one parameter to the property/method list. Finally, it calls the closure attached. Any method calls from within the closure are intercepted and sent to the implementation provided by the category, if present. This is true for new methods you add and existing methods that you're intercepting. Finally, upon return from the closure, use() ends the scope created earlier, discarding the injected methods in the category.

Injected methods can take objects and closures as parameters. Here is an example to show that. Let's write another category FindUtil. Here you are providing a method called extractOnly() that will extract part of a string specified by a closure parameter to it:

InjectionAndSynthesisWithMOP/UsingCategories.groovy

```groovy
class FindUtil
{
  def static extractOnly(String self, closure)
  {
    def result = ''
    self.each {
      if (closure(it)) { result += it }
    }
    result
  }
}

use(FindUtil)
{
  println "121254123".extractOnly { it == '4' || it == '5' }
}
```

The result of the previous call is as follows:

> **Built-in Categories**
>
> Groovy comes with a couple of categories to make our lives easier. DOMCategory (see Section 9.1, *Using DOMCategory*, on page 148) allows you to treat DOM objects like JavaBeans and use Groovy path expressions (GPath) (see Section 9.1, *Using XMLParser*, on page 150). ServletCategory allows you to use Servlet API objects' attributes using the JavaBeans convention.

You can apply more than one category at the same time—to bring in multiple sets of methods. use() takes either one category or a list of categories. Here's an example to use both the categories you created earlier:

InjectionAndSynthesisWithMOP/UsingCategories.groovy
```
use(StringUtil, FindUtil)
{
  str = "123487651"
  println str.toSSN()
  println str.extractOnly { it == '8' || it == '1' }
}
```

The output from the previous code is as follows:

```
123-48-7651
181
```

Even though use() takes a List of Class instances, Groovy is quite happy to accept a comma-separated list of class names. This is because Groovy turns the name of a class, once defined, into a reference to the Class metaobject; e.g., String is equivalent to String.class, in other words, String == String.class.

When you mix multiple categories, the obvious question is about the order in which method calls get resolved when there is a method name collision. The last category in the list takes the highest precedence.

Groovy allows you to nest calls to use. That is, you can call use() from within a closure of another call to use(). An inner category takes precedence over the outer.

So far, you've seen how to inject new methods into an existing class. In Chapter 13, *Intercepting Methods Using MOP*, on page 189, you saw ways to intercept existing methods. You can use categories for that as well. Suppose you want to intercept calls to toString() and pad the response with two exclamations on each side. Here's how to do that using categories:

InjectionAndSynthesisWithMOP/UsingCategories.groovy

```groovy
class Helper
{
  def static toString(String self)
  {
    def method = self.metaClass.methods.find { it.name == 'toString' }
    '!!' + method.invoke(self, null) + '!!'
  }
}

use(Helper) {
  println 'hello'.toString()
}
```

The output from the previous code is as follows:

```
!!hello!!
```

The Helper's toString() is used to intercept calls to that method on String "hello." However, within this interceptor, you want to call the original toString(). You get access to it using the MetaClass of String.

Using categories for method interception is not as elegant as the other approaches you saw in Chapter 13, *Intercepting Methods Using MOP*, on page 189. You can't use it for filtering all method calls to an instance. You'll have to write separate methods for each method you want to intercept. Also, when you have nested categories, you can't reach into the interception of the top-level categories. Use categories for method injection, but not for method interception.

Categories provide a nice method injection protocol. Their effect is contained within the flow of control in the use block. You leave the block, and the injected methods disappear. When you receive a parameter on your methods, you can apply your own categories to that parameter. It feels like you augmented the type of the object you received. When you leave your method, you're returning the object with its class unaffected. You can implement different versions of intercepted/injected methods by using different categories.

Categories have some limitations, however. Their effect is contained within the use() block and hence limited to the executing thread. So, injected methods are restricted. Existing methods can be called from anywhere, but injected methods have to be called within the block. If you enter and exit the block multiple times, there is overhead. Each time you enter, Groovy has to examine static methods and add them to a method list in the new scope. At the end of the block, it has to clean up the scope.

If the calls are not too frequent and you want the isolation that controlled method injection categories provide, use them. If those features turn into limitations, use ExpandoMetaClass for injecting methods. We'll discuss that next.

14.2 Injecting Methods Using ExpandoMetaClass

If you want to create DSLs, you need to be able to add arbitrary methods to different classes and even hierarchies of classes. You need to inject instance methods and static methods, manipulate constructors, and convert a method to a property for the sake of fluency. You'll want these capabilities if you want to create mock objects to stand in for collaborators. In this section, you'll learn the techniques to alter and enhance the structure of a class.

You can inject methods into a class by adding methods to its MetaClass. The methods you inject are available globally. You're not restricted to a block like in categories. (I discussed ExpandoMetaClass in Section 13.2, *Intercepting Methods Using MetaClass*, on page 192.) Using ExpandoMetaClass, you can add methods, properties, constructors, and static methods, and you can even borrow methods from other classes. You can use it to inject methods into POGOs and POJOs.

Let's look at an example of using ExpandoMetaClass to inject a method called daysFromNow() into Integer. You want the statement 5.daysFrom-Now() to return the date five days from today. Here's the code:

InjectionAndSynthesisWithMOP/UsingExpandoMetaClass.groovy

```
Integer.metaClass.daysFromNow = { ->
  Calendar today = Calendar.instance
  today.add(Calendar.DAY_OF_MONTH, delegate)
  today.time
  }

println 5.daysFromNow()
```

The previous code reports the following:

```
Thu Dec 20 13:16:03 MST 2007
```

In this code, you implemented daysFromNow() using a closure and introduced that into the MetaClass of Integer. (To inject the method on any
object, add it to MetaClass of Object.) Within the closure, you need to get
access to the target object of Integer. The delegate refers to the target.
See Section 5.8, *Closure Delegation*, on page 96 and Section 8.1, *Object
Extensions*, on page 133 for discussions on delegate and closures.

If you want, drop that parentheses at the end of the method call to
make it fluent (see Section 18.2, *Fluency*, on page 275) so you can
call 5.daysFromNow. However, this needs a little trick (see Section 18.8,
The Parentheses Limitation and a Workaround, on page 281). Basically,
you need to set up a property instead of method because without the
parentheses Groovy thinks it's a property and not a method. To define
a property named daysFromNow, you have to create a method named
getDaysFromNow(), so let's do that:

InjectionAndSynthesisWithMOP/UsingExpandoMetaClass.groovy
```
Integer.metaClass.getDaysFromNow = { ->
  Calendar today = Calendar.instance
  today.add(Calendar.DAY_OF_MONTH, delegate)
  today.time
  }
```

println 5.daysFromNow

The output from the previous code is shown next. The call to the property daysFromNow is now routed to the method getDaysFromNow().

Thu Dec 20 13:16:03 MST 2007

You injected a method on Integer, but what about its cousins Short and
Long? The previous method is not available on these classes. You certainly don't want to redundantly add the method to those classes. One
idea is to store the closure in a variable and then assign it to these
classes, as shown here:

InjectionAndSynthesisWithMOP/MethodOnHierarchy.groovy
```
daysFromNow = { ->
  Calendar today = Calendar.instance
  today.add(Calendar.DAY_OF_MONTH, (int)delegate)
  today.time
  }

Integer.metaClass.daysFromNow = daysFromNow
Long.metaClass.daysFromNow = daysFromNow

println 5.daysFromNow()
println 5L.daysFromNow()
```

The output is as follows:

```
Thu Dec 20 13:26:43 MST 2007
Thu Dec 20 13:26:43 MST 2007
```

Alternately, you can provide the method in the base class Number of Integer. Let's add a method named someMethod() on Number and see whether it's available on Integer and Long:[1]

InjectionAndSynthesisWithMOP/MethodOnHierarchy.groovy

```
Integer.metaClass
Long.metaClass
// Above statements will not be needed if
// ExpandoMetaClass was the default MetaClass
// in Groovy.

Number.metaClass.someMethod = { ->
    println "someMethod called"
  }

2.someMethod()
2L.someMethod()
```

The output from the previous code, shown here, confirms that the methods are available on the derived classes:

```
someMethod called
someMethod called
```

You saw how to inject a method into a class hierarchy. You might also want to introduce methods into an interface hierarchy so the methods are available on all classes implementing that interface.

When you add a method at the interface level, the method needs to be injected into the MetaClass for each of the implementing classes. That happens in Groovy only if enableGlobally() of ExpandoMetaClass has been called already. However, be aware that turning that flag on will increase the demand on memory. You'll take a look at adding a method to an interface later in Section 18.10, *ExpandoMetaClass and DSLs*, on page 285.

You can inject static methods into a class as well. You add static methods to the static property of the MetaClass.

---

1. This is an example of the effect of ExpandoMetaClass not being the default MetaClass. For more information, see Section 13.2, *Intercepting Methods Using MetaClass*, on page 192.

Let's add a static method isEven() to Integer:

```
InjectionAndSynthesisWithMOP/UsingExpandoMetaClass.groovy
```
```
Integer.metaClass.static.isEven = { val -> val % 2 == 0 }

println "Is 2 even? " + Integer.isEven(2)
println "Is 3 even? " + Integer.isEven(3)
```

The output from the previous code is as follows:

```
Is 2 even? true
Is 3 even? false
```

You figured how to inject instance methods and static methods. The third type of method a class can have is the constructor. You can add constructors as well by defining a special property with the name constructor. Since you're adding a constructor and not replacing an existing one, you'd use the << operator.[2] Let's introduce a constructor for Integer that accepts a Calendar so the instance will hold the number of days as of that date:

```
InjectionAndSynthesisWithMOP/UsingExpandoMetaClass.groovy
```
```
Integer.metaClass.constructor << { Calendar calendar ->
    new Integer(calendar.get(Calendar.DAY_OF_YEAR))
  }

println new Integer(Calendar.instance)
```

The output from the previous code is as follows:

```
349
```

In the injected constructor you are using the existing constructor of Integer that accepts an int. You could have returned the result of call to Calendar's get() instead of creating a new instance of Integer. In that case, autoboxing will take care of creating an Integer instance. Make sure that your implementation doesn't recursively call itself, leading to a StackOverflowError.

Instead of adding a new constructor, if you want to replace (or override, though strictly speaking constructors are not overridable) a constructor, you can do that by using the = operator instead of the << operator.

---

2. Using << to override existing constructors or methods will result in an error.

InjectionAndSynthesisWithMOP/UsingExpandoMetaClass.groovy

```
Integer.metaClass.constructor = { int val ->
  println "Intercepting constructor call"
  constructor = Integer.class.getConstructor(Integer.TYPE)
  constructor.newInstance(val)
  }

println new Integer(4)
println new Integer(Calendar.instance)
```

The output from the previous code is as follows:

```
Intercepting constructor call
4
Intercepting constructor call
349
```

From within the constructor override, you can still call the original implementation using reflection. As you can see, other constructors—predefined and injected—are still intact. So, when you create an Integer using a Calendar instance, it uses the constructor injected earlier, which in turn now uses the constructor override provided previously.

ExpandoMetaClass is very flexible for injecting methods. You can use the injected methods from anywhere in your application. You invoke injected methods just like you invoke regular methods. With Expando-MetaClass, you can inject methods into POJOs and POGOs. So, you can enjoy the dynamic capabilities for all classes.

ExpandoMetaClass has some limitations, however. The injected methods are available only for calls within Groovy code. You can't use it from within compiled Java code. They can't be used with reflection from Java code either.

14.3 Injecting Methods into Specific Instances

You saw ways to inject methods into a class dynamically. You can add behavior to specific instances of a class much like how you added behavior to the class. Suppose you receive a Person and based on certain conditions or state want to perform some operations on it. You figure it would be easier to inject a set of reusable methods or utility functions on it; however, you don't want to apply those globally on all Persons. Groovy makes it fairly simple to inject instances with methods.

The MetaClass is per-instance for POGOs. If you want an instance to have a different behavior than the other objects instantiated from the same class, provide it with a specialized ExpandoMetaClass. Create an instance of ExpandoMetaClass, add the desired methods to it, initialize it (required to indicate the completion of method/property additions), and attach to the instance you desire to enhance. Here is an example of adding a method to an instance of Person:

InjectionAndSynthesisWithMOP/InjectInstance.groovy
```
class Person {}

def emc = new ExpandoMetaClass(Person)
emc.sing = { ->
  'oh baby baby...'
  }
emc.initialize()

def jack = new Person()
def paul = new Person()

jack.metaClass = emc

println jack.sing()

try
{
  paul.sing()
}
catch(ex)
{
  println ex
}
```

The previous code reports the following:

```
oh baby baby...
groovy.lang.MissingMethodException:
  No signature of method: Person.sing()
  is applicable for argument types: () values: {}
```

You injected sing() on your courageous friend jack by setting the instance of MetaClass on it. You can now invoke sing() on jack. However, if you try to call it on any other instance of Person, it will fail.

You can set the metaClass property for POGOs only. It's read-only on POJOs. Thus, instance-specific method injection is available only for Groovy objects.

14.4 Method Synthesis Using methodMissing

So far you've been able to inject specific methods into a class or an instance. In this section, you'll synthesize methods with flexible and dynamic names. You don't decide the names ahead of time. In fact, you can let the users of your class decide the names as long as they follow conventions you set. When they call a nonexistent method, you can intercept it and create an implementation on the fly. The implementation is made to measure. In other words, it is created only when they ask for it.

Method synthesis is implemented in Grails/GORM for domain classes. Suppose you have a domain class (a class that represents information persistent in a database table) Person with a number of fields (columns in the table) such as firstName, lastName, cityOfResidence, and so on. Assume other fields can be added at any time. GORM allows users of your Person class to call methods such as findByFirstName(), findByLastName(), findByFirstNameAndLastName(), or even findByFirstNameAndAge() if age is a field on Person. Your Person class will not have any of these methods precreated. Each method is synthesized at runtime on the first call. In the rest of this chapter, you'll learn how to synthesize methods in Groovy.

You can intercept calls to nonexistent methods in Groovy by implementing methodMissing(). Within this method you can implement the logic for the method dynamically. You infer the semantics based on certain conventions you define. For instance, method names that start with *find* might imply a query, method names that start with *update* may imply a save, and so on.

Let's look at an example of synthesizing methods. You are going to turn jack, a boring, all-work-no-play Person, into a multiathlete. He'll play all kinds of sports.

```
InjectionAndSynthesisWithMOP/MethodSynthesisUsingMethodMissing.groovy
class Person
{
  def work() { "working..." }

  def plays = ['Tennis', 'VolleyBall', 'BasketBall']

  def methodMissing(String name, args)
  {
    System.out.println "methodMissing called for $name"
    def methodInList = plays.find { it == name.split('play')[1]}
```

```groovy
      if (methodInList)
      {
        return "playing ${name.split('play')[1]}..."
      }
      else
      {
        throw new MissingMethodException(name, Person.class, args)
      }
    }
  }
}

jack = new Person()

println jack.work()
println jack.playTennis()
println jack.playBasketBall()
println jack.playVolleyBall()
println jack.playTennis()

try
{
  jack.playPolitics()
}
catch(Exception ex)
{
  println "Error: " + ex
}
```

The output from the previous code is as follows:

```
working...
methodMissing called for playTennis
playing Tennis...
methodMissing called for playBasketBall
playing BasketBall...
methodMissing called for playVolleyBall
playing VolleyBall...
methodMissing called for playTennis
playing Tennis...
methodMissing called for playPolitics
Error: groovy.lang.MissingMethodException:
  No signature of method: Person.playPolitics()
  is applicable for argument types: () values: {}
```

work() is the only predefined domain method on Person. The call to work()
directly went to that method. However, calls to nonexistent methods are
routed to the methodMissing() method. In methodMissing(), you accept a
call if it starts with *play* and ends with one of the names in the plays
array, and you can dynamically modify this list to add other sports
you want, giving the impression that jack is assimilating new skills. If

the method is not one you support (such as playPolitics()), you throw a MissingMethodException.

From the caller point of view, there is no difference between calling a regular method and a synthesized method.

The previous implementation is quite dynamic, but there's a catch. Repeated calls to a nonexistent method, such as playTennis(), involve the same performance hit to evaluate. You can make this efficient by injecting the method on first invocation.[3] So, you are going to synthesize the method on first call, inject it into the MetaClass (cache it), and then invoke this injected method. Here is the code for that:

InjectionAndSynthesisWithMOP/MethodSynthesisUsingMethodMissing2.groovy

```groovy
class Person
{
  def work() { "working..." }

  def plays = ['Tennis', 'VolleyBall', 'BasketBall']

  def methodMissing(String name, args)
  {
    System.out.println "methodMissing called for $name"
    def methodInList = plays.find { it == name.split('play')[1]}

    if (methodInList)
    {
      def impl = { Object[] vargs ->
          return "playing ${name.split('play')[1]}..."
        }

      Person.metaClass."$name" = impl //future calls will use this

      return impl(args)
    }
    else
    {
      throw new MissingMethodException(name, Person.class, args)
    }
  }

  static { Person.metaClass }
}

jack = new Person()
println jack.playTennis()
println jack.playTennis()
```

---

3. Again, Graeme Rocher calls it the "Intercept, Cache, Invoke" pattern.

> **methodMissing and GroovyInterceptable**
>
> Unlike invokeMethod(), which is called for all methods on objects that implement GroovyInterceptable, methodMissing() is called only for methods that are nonexistent at the time of call. If an object implements GroovyInterceptable, its invokeMethod() is called if present. Only if it forwards control to its MetaClass's invokeMethod() does methodMissing() get called.

The output from the previous code is as follows:

```
methodMissing called for playTennis
playing Tennis...
playing Tennis...
```

You can see that the methodMissing() method is called only on the first call to a supported nonexistent method. The second (and subsequent) call to the same supported method goes directly to the implementation (closure) you injected into the MetaClass. There is a caveat in this example—I placed the statement Person.metaClass in the static initializer of Person. Try commenting out that statement and running the code to see the difference in output. The reason for the difference is ExpandoMetaClass is not the default MetaClass used in Groovy. For more information, see Section 13.2, *Intercepting Methods Using MetaClass*, on page 192.

In Section 13.2, *Intercepting Methods Using MetaClass*, on page 192, you intercepted calls using GroovyInterceptable. You can mix that with methodMissing() to intercept calls to both existing methods and synthesized methods, as shown here:

InjectionAndSynthesisWithMOP/InterceptingMissingMethods.groovy

```groovy
ExpandoMetaClass.enableGlobally()

class Person implements GroovyInterceptable
{
  def work() { "working..." }
  def plays = ['Tennis', 'VolleyBall', 'BasketBall']

  def invokeMethod(String name, args)
  {
    System.out.println "intercepting call for $name"

    def method = metaClass.getMetaMethod(name, args)
```

```groovy
    if (method)
    {
      return method.invoke(this, args)
    }
    else
    {
      return metaClass.invokeMethod(this, name, args)
    }
  }

  def methodMissing(String name, args)
  {
    System.out.println "methodMissing called for $name"
    def methodInList = plays.find { it == name.split('play')[1]}

    if (methodInList)
    {
      def impl = { Object[] vargs ->
          return "playing ${name.split('play')[1]}..."
        }

      Person.metaClass."$name" = impl //future calls will use this

      return impl(args)
    }
    else
    {
      throw new MissingMethodException(name, Person.class, args)
    }
  }
}

jack = new Person()
println jack.work()
println jack.playTennis()
println jack.playTennis()
```

The output from the previous code is as follows:

```
intercepting call for work
working...
intercepting call for playTennis
methodMissing called for playTennis
playing Tennis...
intercepting call for playTennis
playing Tennis...
```

14.5 Method Synthesis Using ExpandoMetaClass

In Section 14.4, *Method Synthesis Using methodMissing*, on page 209, you saw how to synthesize methods. If you don't have the privilege to edit the class source file or if the class is not a POGO, that approach will not work. You can synthesize methods using the ExpandoMetaClass in these cases.

You already saw how to interact with MetaClass in Section 13.2, *Intercepting Methods Using MetaClass*, on page 192. Instead of providing an interceptor for a domain method, you implement the methodMissing() method on it. Let's take the Person class (and the boring jack) from Section 14.4, *Method Synthesis Using methodMissing*, on page 209, but instead we'll use ExpandoMetaClass, as shown here:

`InjectionAndSynthesisWithMOP/MethodSynthesisUsingEMC.groovy`

```groovy
ExpandoMetaClass.enableGlobally()

class Person
{
  def work() { "working..." }
}

Person.metaClass.methodMissing = { String name, args ->
  def plays = ['Tennis', 'VolleyBall', 'BasketBall']

  System.out.println "methodMissing called for $name"
  def methodInList = plays.find { it == name.split('play')[1]}

  if (methodInList)
  {
    def impl = { Object[] vargs ->
        return "playing ${name.split('play')[1]}..."
      }

    Person.metaClass."$name" = impl //future calls will use this

    return impl(args)
  }
  else
  {
    throw new MissingMethodException(name, Person.class, args)
  }
}

jack = new Person()
println jack.work()
println jack.playTennis()
println jack.playTennis()
```

```
try
{
  jack.playPolitics()
}
catch(ex)
{
  println ex
}
```

The output from the previous code is as follows:

```
working...
methodMissing called for playTennis
playing Tennis...
playing Tennis...
methodMissing called for playPolitics
groovy.lang.MissingMethodException:
  No signature of method: Person.playPolitics()
  is applicable for argument types: () values: {}
```

When you called work() on jack, Person's work() was executed directly. If you call a nonexistent method, however, it is routed to the Person's MetaClass's methodMissing().[4] You implement logic in this method similar to the solution in Section 14.4, *Method Synthesis Using methodMissing*, on page 209. Repeated calls to supported nonexistent method do not incur overhead, as you can see in the previous output for the second call to playTennis(). You cached the implementation on the first call.

In Section 13.2, *Intercepting Methods Using MetaClass*, on page 192, you intercepted calls using ExpandoMetaClass's invokeMethod(). You can mix that with methodMissing() to intercept calls to both existing methods and synthesized methods, as shown here:

InjectionAndSynthesisWithMOP/MethodSynthesisAndInterceptionUsingEMC.groovy

```
ExpandoMetaClass.enableGlobally()

class Person
{
  def work() { "working..." }
}

Person.metaClass.invokeMethod = { String name, args ->
  System.out.println "intercepting call for ${name}"

  def method = Person.metaClass.getMetaMethod(name, args)
```

---

4. methodMissing() of the MetaClass will take precedence over methodMissing() if present in your class. Methods of your class's MetaClass override the methods in your class.

```
  if (method)
  {
    return method.invoke(delegate, args)
  }
  else
  {
    return Person.metaClass.invokeMissingMethod(delegate, name, args)
  }
}

Person.metaClass.methodMissing = { String name, args ->
  def plays = ['Tennis', 'VolleyBall', 'BasketBall']

  System.out.println "methodMissing called for ${name}"
  def methodInList = plays.find { it == name.split('play')[1]}

  if (methodInList)
  {
    def impl = { Object[] vargs ->
        return "playing ${name.split('play')[1]}..."
      }

    Person.metaClass."$name" = impl //future calls will use this

    return impl(args)
  }
  else
  {
    throw new MissingMethodException(name, Person.class, args)
  }
}

jack = new Person()
println jack.work()
println jack.playTennis()
println jack.playTennis()
```

The output from the previous code is as follows:

```
intercepting call for work
working...
intercepting call for playTennis
methodMissing called for playTennis
playing Tennis...
intercepting call for playTennis
playing Tennis...
```

> ### invokeMethod vs. methodMissing
>
> invokeMethod() is a method of GroovyObject. methodMissing()
> was introduced later in Groovy and is part of the MetaClass-
> based method handling. If your objective is to handle calls to
> nonexisting methods, implement methodMissing() because this
> involves low overhead. If your objective is to intercept calls to
> both existing and nonexisting methods, use invokeMethod().

14.6 Synthesizing Methods for Specific Instances

I showed how you can inject methods into specific instances of a class
in Section 14.3, *Injecting Methods into Specific Instances*, on page 207.
You can synthesize methods dynamically as well as into specific instances by providing the instance(s) with a specialized MetaClass. Here
is an example:

InjectionAndSynthesisWithMOP/SynthesizeInstance.groovy

```
class Person {}

def emc = new ExpandoMetaClass(Person)
emc.methodMissing = { String name, args ->
  "I'm Jack of all trades... I can $name"
  }
emc.initialize()

def jack = new Person()
def paul = new Person()

jack.metaClass = emc

println jack.sing()
println jack.dance()
println jack.juggle()

try
{
  paul.sing()
}
catch(ex)
{
  println ex
}
```

The previous code reports the following:

```
I'm Jack of all trades... I can sing
I'm Jack of all trades... I can dance
I'm Jack of all trades... I can juggle
groovy.lang.MissingMethodException:
  No signature of method: Person.sing()
  is applicable for argument types: () values: {}
```

Like injecting into specific instances, synthesizing methods for specific instances is limited to Groovy objects.

In this chapter, you learned how to intercept, inject, and synthesize methods. Groovy MOP makes it easy to perform AOP-like activities. You can create code that is highly dynamic, and you can create highly reusable code with fewer lines of code. You'll put all these skills together in the next chapter.

Chapter 15

MOPping Up

You've seen how to synthesize methods, and in this chapter, you'll see how to synthesize an entire class. Rather than creating explicit classes ahead of time, you can create classes on the fly, which gives you more flexibility. Delegation is better than inheritance, yet it has been hard to implement in Java. You'll see how Groovy MOP allows method delegation with only one line of code. I'll wrap this chapter up by reviewing the different MOP techniques you've seen in the previous three chapters.

15.1 Creating Dynamic Classes with Expando

In Groovy you can create a class entirely at runtime. Suppose you're building an application that will configure devices. You don't have a clue what these devices are—you know only that devices have properties and configuration scripts. You don't have the luxury of creating an explicit class for each device at coding time. So, you'll want to synthesize classes at runtime to interact with and configure these devices. In Groovy, classes can come to life at runtime at your command.

The Groovy class that gives you the ability to synthesize classes dynamically is Expando, which got its name because it is dynamically expandable. You can assign properties and methods to it either at construction time using a Map or at any time dynamically. Let's start with an example to synthesize a class Car. I'll show two ways to create it using Expando.

MOPpingUp/UsingExpando.groovy

```
carA = new Expando()
carB = new Expando(year: 2007, miles: 0)

carA.year = 2007
carA.miles = 10

println "carA: " + carA
println "carB: " + carB
```

The output from the previous code is as follows:

```
carA: {year=2007, miles=10}
carB: {year=2007, miles=0}
```

You created carA, the first instance of Expando, without any properties or methods. You injected the year and miles later. On the other hand, you created carB, the second instance of Expando, with the year and miles initialized at construction time.

You're not restricted to properties. You can define methods as well and invoke them like you would invoke any method. Let's give that a try. Once again, you can define a method at construction time or inject later at will:

MOPpingUp/UsingExpando.groovy

```
car = new Expando(year: 2007, miles: 0, turn: { println 'turning...' })
car.drive = {
  miles += 10
  println "$miles miles driven"
}

car.drive()
car.turn()
```

The output from the previous code is as follows:

```
10 miles driven
turning...
```

Suppose you have an input file with some data for Cars, as shown here:

MOPpingUp/car.dat

```
miles, year, make
42451, 2003, Acura
24031, 2003, Chevy
14233, 2006, Honda
```

You can easily work with Car objects without explicitly creating a Car class, as in the following code. You're parsing the content of the file, first extracting the property names. Then you create instances of Expando, one for each line of data in the input file, and populate it with values for the properties. You even add a method, in the form of a closure, to compute the average miles driven per year until 2008. Once the objects are created, you can access the properties and call methods on them dynamically. You can also address the methods/properties by name, as shown in the end.

```groovy
data = new File('car.dat').readLines()

props = data[0].split(", ")

data -= data[0]

def averageMilesDrivenPerYear = { miles.toLong() / (2008 - year.toLong()) }

cars = data.collect {
  car = new Expando()
  it.split(", ").eachWithIndex { value, index ->
    car[props[index]] = value
  }

  car.ampy = averageMilesDrivenPerYear

  car
}

props.each { name -> print "$name " }
println " Avg. MPY"

ampyMethod = 'ampy'
cars.each { car ->
  for(String property : props) { print "${car[property]} " }
  println car."$ampyMethod"()
}

// You may also access the properties/methods by name
car = cars[0]
println "$car.miles $car.year $car.make ${car.ampy()}"
```

The output from the previous code is as follows:

```
miles year make  Avg. MPY
42451 2003 Acura 8490.2
24031 2003 Chevy 4806.2
14233 2006 Honda 7116.5
42451 2003 Acura 8490.2
```

Use Expando whenever you want to synthesize classes on the fly. It is lightweight and flexible. One place where you will see them shine is to create mock objects for unit testing (see Section 16.8, *Mocking Using Expando*, on page 246).

15.2 Method Delegation: Putting It All Together

You use inheritance to extend the behavior of a class. On the other hand, you use delegation to rely upon contained or aggregated objects to provide the behavior of a class. Choose inheritance if your intent is to use an object in place of another object. Choose delegation if the intent is to simply use an object. Reserve inheritance for an *is-a* or *kind-of* relationship only; you should prefer delegation over inheritance most of the time. However, it's easy to program inheritance, because it takes only one keyword, extends. But it's hard to program delegation, because you have to write all those methods that route the call to the contained objects. Groovy helps you do the right thing. By using MOP, you can easily implement delegation with a single line of code, as you'll see in this section.

In the following example, a Manager wants to delegate work to either a Worker or an Expert. You're using methodMissing() and ExpandoMeta-Class to realize this. If a method called on the instance of Manager does not exist, its methodMissing() routes it to either the Worker or the Expert, whichever respondsTo() to the method (see Section 12.2, *Querying Methods and Properties*, on page 185). If there are no takers for a method among the delegates and the Manager does not handle it, the method call fails.

MOPpingUp/Delegation.groovy

```groovy
ExpandoMetaClass.enableGlobally()

class Worker
{
  def simpleWork1(spec) { println "worker does work1 with spec $spec" }
  def simpleWork2() { println "worker does work2" }
}

class Expert
{
  def advancedWork1(spec) { println "Expert does work1 with spec $spec" }
  def advancedWork2(scope, spec)
  {
    println "Expert does work2 with scope $scope spec $spec"
  }
}
```

```
class Manager
{
  def worker = new Worker()
  def expert = new Expert()

  def schedule() { println "Scheduling ..." }

  def methodMissing(String name, args)
  {
    println "intercepting call to $name..."
    def delegateTo = null

    if(name.startsWith('simple')) { delegateTo = worker }
    if(name.startsWith('advanced')) { delegateTo = expert }

    if (delegateTo?.metaClass.respondsTo(delegateTo, name, args))
    {
      Manager.metaClass."${name}" = { Object[] varArgs ->
            return delegateTo.invokeMethod(name, *varArgs)
      }

      return delegateTo.invokeMethod(name, args)
    }

    throw new MissingMethodException(name, Manager.class, args)
  }
}

peter = new Manager()
peter.schedule()
peter.simpleWork1('fast')
peter.simpleWork1('quality')
peter.simpleWork2()
peter.simpleWork2()
peter.advancedWork1('fast')
peter.advancedWork1('quality')
peter.advancedWork2('protype', 'fast')
peter.advancedWork2('product', 'quality')
try
{
  peter.simpleWork3()
}
catch(Exception ex)
{
  println ex
}
```

The output from the previous code is as follows:

```
Scheduling ...
intercepting call to simpleWork1...
worker does work1 with spec fast
worker does work1 with spec quality
```

```
intercepting call to simpleWork2...
worker does work2
worker does work2
intercepting call to advancedWork1...
Expert does work1 with spec fast
Expert does work1 with spec quality
intercepting call to advancedWork2...
Expert does work2 with scope protype spec fast
Expert does work2 with scope product spec quality
intercepting call to simpleWork3...
groovy.lang.MissingMethodException:
  No signature of method: Manager.simpleWork3()
  is applicable for argument types: () values: {}
```

You figured out a way to delegate calls, but that's a lot of work. You
don't want to put in so much effort each time you want to delegate. You
can refactor this code for reuse. Let's first look at how the refactored
code will look like when used in the Manager class:

MOPpingUp/DelegationRefactored.groovy

```groovy
class Manager
{
  { delegateCallsTo Worker, Expert, GregorianCalendar }

  def schedule() { println "Scheduling ..." }
}
```

That is short and sweet. In the initializer block you call a yet-to-be-
implemented method named delegateCallsTo() and send the names of
classes to which you want to delegate unimplemented methods. If you
want to use delegation in another class, all it takes now is that code in
the initialization block. Let's take a look at the fancy delegateCallsTo()
method:

MOPpingUp/DelegationRefactored.groovy

```groovy
ExpandoMetaClass.enableGlobally()

Object.metaClass.delegateCallsTo = {Class... klassOfDelegates ->

  def objectOfDelegates = klassOfDelegates.collect { it.newInstance() }

  delegate.metaClass.methodMissing = { String name, args ->
      println "intercepting call to $name..."

      def delegateTo = objectOfDelegates.find {
                  it.metaClass.respondsTo(it, name, args) }
```

```
    if (delegateTo)
    {
      delegate.metaClass."${name}" = { Object[] varArgs ->
          def params = varArgs?:null
          return delegateTo.invokeMethod(name, *params)
      }

      return delegateTo.invokeMethod(name, args)
    }
    else
    {
      throw new MissingMethodException(name, delegate.getClass(), args)
    }
  }
}
```

When you call delegateCallsTo() from within your class's instance initializer, it adds a methodMissing() to the class, which is known within
this closure as delegate. It takes the Class list provided as an argument
to delegateCallsTo() and creates a list of delegates, which are the can-
didates to implement delegated methods. In methodMissing(), the call
is routed to an object among the delegates that will respond to the
method. If there are no takers, the call fails. The list of classes given to
delegateCallsTo() also represents the order of precedence, and the first
one has the highest precedence. Of course, you have to see all this in
action, so here is the code to exercise the previous example:

MOPpingUp/DelegationRefactored.groovy

```
peter = new Manager()
peter.schedule()
peter.simpleWork1('fast')
peter.simpleWork1('quality')
peter.simpleWork2()
peter.simpleWork2()
peter.advancedWork1('fast')
peter.advancedWork1('quality')
peter.advancedWork2('protype', 'fast')
peter.advancedWork2('product', 'quality')
println "Is 2008 a leap year? " + peter.isLeapYear(2008)
try
{
  peter.simpleWork3()
}
catch(Exception ex)
{
  println ex
}
```

The previous code produces the following output:

```
Scheduling ...
intercepting call to simpleWork1...
worker does work1 with spec fast
worker does work1 with spec quality
intercepting call to simpleWork2...
worker does work2
worker does work2
intercepting call to advancedWork1...
Expert does work1 with spec fast
Expert does work1 with spec quality
intercepting call to advancedWork2...
Expert does work2 with scope protype spec fast
Expert does work2 with scope product spec quality
intercepting call to isLeapYear...
Is 2008 a leap year? true
intercepting call to simpleWork3...
groovy.lang.MissingMethodException:
  No signature of method: Manager.simpleWork3()
  is applicable for argument types: () values: {}
```

You can build on this idea further to meet your needs. For instance, if you want to mix some precreated objects, you can send them as an array to the first parameter of delegateCallsTo() and have those objects used along with those created from the delegates classes. The previous example shows how you can use Groovy's MOP to implement dynamic behavior such as method delegation.

15.3 Review of MOP Techniques

You've seen a number of options to intercept, inject, and synthesize methods. In this section, you'll figure out which option is right for you.

Options for Method Interception

I discussed method interception in Chapter 13, *Intercepting Methods Using MOP*, on page 189 and in Section 14.1, *Injecting Methods Using Categories*, on page 198. You can use GroovyInterceptable, ExpandoMeta-Class, or categories.

If you have the privilege to modify the class source, you can implement GroovyInterceptable on the class you want to intercept method calls. The effort is as simple as implementing invokeMethod().

If you can't modify the class or if the class is a Java class, then you can use ExpandoMetaClass or categories. ExpandoMetaClass clearly stands out in this case because a single invokeMethod() can take care of intercepting any methods of your class. Categories, on the other hand, would require separate methods, one per intercepted method. Also, if you use categories, you're restricted by the use() block.

Options for Method Injection

I discussed method injection in Section 14.1, *Injecting Methods Using Categories*, on page 198. You can use categories or ExpandoMetaClass.

Categories compete well with ExpandoMetaClasses for method injection. If you use categories, you can control the location where methods are injected. You can easily implement different versions of method injection by using different categories. You can easily nest and mix multiple categories as well. The control offered by categories—that method injection takes effect only within the use() blocks and is limited to the executing thread—may also be considered as a restriction. If you want to use the injected methods at any location and also want to inject static method and constructors, ExpandoMetaClass is a better choice. Beware, though, that ExpandoMetaClass is not the default MetaClass in Groovy.

Using the ExpandoMetaClass, you can inject methods into specific instances of a class instead of affecting the entire class. This is available only for POGOs, however.

Options for Method Synthesis

I discussed method injection in Section 14.4, *Method Synthesis Using methodMissing*, on page 209. You can use methodMissing() on a Groovy object or ExpandoMetaClass.

If you have the privilege to modify the class source, you can implement the methodMissing() method on the class for which you want to synthesize methods. You can improve performance by injecting the method on the first call. If you need to intercept your methods at the same time, you can implement GroovyInterceptable.

If you can't modify the class or if the class is a Java class, then you can add the method methodMissing() to the class's ExpandoMetaClass. If you want to intercept method calls at the same time, implement invokeMethod() on the ExpandoMetaClass as well.

Using the ExpandoMetaClass, you can synthesize methods into specific instances of a class instead of affecting the entire class. This is available only for POGOs, however.

In this and previous three chapters, you saw the power of metaprogramming in Groovy. You can dynamically create classes, methods, and properties on the fly. You can intercept calls to existing methods and even method that don't exist. The extent to which you use metaprogramming depends on your application-specific needs. You know, however, that when your application demands metaprogramming, Groovy will allow you to implement it quickly. In the remaining chapters in this part, you'll see several examples where metaprogramming plays a vital role—when unit testing with mock objects, creating builders, and creating DSLs.

Chapter 16

Unit Testing and Mocking

However weak the checks performed by a compiler might be in a static language, you don't have even that level of support in a dynamic language.[1] That's why unit testing[2] is a necessary practice in dynamic languages. Although you can easily take advantage of dynamic capabilities and metaprogramming in these languages, you have to take the time to make sure your program is doing what you expect and not just what you typed.

There has been greater awareness of unit testing among developers in the past few years; unfortunately, though, the adoption is not sufficient. Unit testing is the software equivalent of exercising. Most developers would agree that it improves the health of their code, yet many developers offer various reasons and excuses for not doing it.

Not only is unit testing critical for programming Groovy, but unit testing is easy and fun in Groovy as well. JUnit is built into Groovy. Metaprogramming capabilities make it easy to create mock objects. Groovy also has a built-in mock library. Let's take a look at how you can use Groovy to unit test your Java and Groovy applications.

16.1 Code in This Book and Automated Unit Tests

Unit testing is not something I provide as abstract advice. I have used automated unit tests for all the code in this book because I'm working with a language that's currently evolving. Groovy features change, its

---

1. Unit testing is essential for metaprogramming. As you'll see in this chapter, fortunately, metaprogramming helps a great deal with unit testing.
2. See [Bec02], [HT03], [Rai04].

implementations change, bugs are being fixed, new features are added, and so on. I updated my installation of Groovy on my machines quite a few times as I was writing these chapters and code examples. If an update broke an example because of a feature or implementation change, I needed to know that quickly without expending too much effort. Furthermore, I refactored several examples in this book as the book evolved. Again, I needed to know quickly that things were still working as expected. The automated unit tests helped me sleep better at night, because I knew that the examples were still working as expected after a language update or my own refactoring.

Soon after writing the first few examples, I decided to take a break and figure out a way to automate the testing of all examples while keeping the examples independent and in isolated files. Some of the examples are functions, and some are stand-alone programs or scripts. Groovy's metaprogramming capabilities, along with the ExpandoMeta-Class and the ability to load and execute scripts, made it a breeze to create and execute automated unit tests.

It took me a couple of hours to figure out how to get going. Whenever I write a new example, I spend about two minutes or less to get the test written for that example. That effort and time paid off within the first few days and a few times since. So far about five examples failed as I upgraded Groovy. More important, these tests gave me assurance that the other examples are working fine and are valid.

These tests helped in at least five ways:

- It helped further my understanding of Groovy features.

- It helped raise questions in the Groovy users mailing list that helped fix a few Groovy bugs.

- It helped find and fix an inconsistency in Groovy documentation.

- It continues to help me ensure that all my examples are valid and working well with the most recent version of Groovy.

- It gave me the courage to refactor any example at will, at any time, with full confidence that my refactoring improved the code structure but did not affect its intended behavior.

16.2 Unit Testing Java and Groovy Code

When you install Groovy, you automatically get a unit testing framework built on JUnit.[3,4] You can use it to test any code on the JVM—your Java code, your Groovy code, and so on. Simply extend your test class from GroovyTestCase and implement your test methods, and you're all set to run your tests.

Let's start by writing a simple test:

UnitTestingWithGroovy/ListTest.groovy
```groovy
class ListTest extends GroovyTestCase
{
  void testListSize()
  {
    def lst = [1, 2]
    assertEquals "ArrayList size must be 2", 2, lst.size()
  }
}
```

Even though Groovy is dynamically typed, JUnit expects the return type of test methods to be void. So, you had to explicitly use void instead of def when defining the test method. Groovy's optional typing helped here. To run the previous code, simply execute it like you would execute any Groovy program. So, type the following command:

```
groovy ListTest
```

The output of executing the previous code is as follows:

```
.
Time: 0.006

OK (1 test)
```

If you're familiar with JUnit, you already understand this output—one test was executed successfully.

If you're a fan of the red-green bar, you can run your unit tests from within your IDE if it supports running tests.

---

3. Thanks to excellent Java-Groovy integration, you can use any Java-based testing framework and mock objects framework (such as EasyMock, JMock, and so on, with Groovy).
4. Groovy extends JUnit 3.8.2 but not JUnit 4. You can use JUnit 4 with a little extra effort. If you like to use JUnit 4 and Hamcrest matchers with Groovy, see http://groovy.codehaus.org/Using+JUnit+4+with+Groovy.

Unit Tests Must be FAIR

When you write unit tests, keep in mind that the tests must be FAIR, that is, fast, automated, isolated, and repeatable.

Tests must be fast. As you evolve your code and refactor, you want to quickly get feedback that the code continues to meet your expectations. If the tests are slow, your developers won't bother to run them. You want a very quick edit-and-run cycle.

Tests must be automated. Manual testing is tiring, is error prone, and will take your time away from important tasks on which you're focusing. Automated tests are like angels on your shoulder—they watch you quietly as you write code and whisper in your ears (only) if your code violates set expectations. They give you early feedback if your code begins to fall apart. You'd probably agree that you'd much rather hear from your computer that your code sucks than from your co-worker. Automated unit tests make you look good and dependable. For example, when you say you're done, you know your code works as intended.

Tests must be isolated. When you got 1,031 compilation errors, the usual problem was a missed semicolon, right? That was not helpful; there's no point in one small error cascading into several reported errors. You want a direct correlation between a creeping bug or error and a failed test case. That will help you identify and fix problems quickly rather than being overwhelmed by large failed tests. Isolation will ensure that one test does not leave behind a residual state that may affect another test. It also allows you to run the tests in any order and also to run either all, one, or a select few tests as you desire.

Tests must be repeatable. You must be able to run the tests any number of times and get deterministic predictable results. The worst kind of test is the one that fails on one run and passes on a following run with no change to any code. Threading issues, for example, may bring about some of these issues. As another example, if a test inserts data with unique column constraints into a database, then a subsequent run of the same test without cleaning up a database will fail. This will not happen, however, and the test will be repeatable if the test rolls back the transaction. The repeatability of tests is key to staying sane while you rapidly evolve your application code.

You can also call junit.swingui.TestRunner's run() method and provide it your Groovy test class name to run your tests within the Swing GUI to see those red-green bars.

You may use any of the assert methods that you're already familiar with in JUnit. Groovy adds more assert methods for your convenience: assertArrayEquals(), assertLength(), assertContains(), assertToString(), assertInspect(), assertScript(), and shouldFail(), to mention a few.

When writing unit tests, consider writing three types of tests: positive, negative, and exception. Positive tests help ensure that code is behaving as expected. You can call this the test of the happy path. You deposit $100 and check whether the balance did go up by $100. Negative tests check whether the code handles, as you expect, the failure of preconditions, invalid input, and so on. You make the deposit amount negative and see what the code does. What if the account is closed? Exception tests help determine whether the code is throwing the right exceptions and behaving as expected when exceptional situations arise. What if an automated withdrawal kicks in after an account is closed? Trust me on this one—I had a creative bank that did just that. Thinking about tests in terms of these types of tests helps you think through the logic you're implementing. You handle not only code that implements logic but also consider boundary conditions and edge cases that often get you into trouble.

You can easily implement positive tests by using the asserts provided in Groovy and JUnit. Implementing negative tests and exception tests needs a bit more work, but Groovy has a mechanism to help you, as you'll see in Section 16.3, *Testing for Exceptions*, on page 235.

Even if your main project code is in Java, consider writing your test code in Groovy. Since Groovy is lightweight, you'll find it is easier, faster, and fun to write your tests in Groovy while your main code is in Java. This is also a nice way to practice Groovy on your Java-intense projects.

Suppose you have a Java class Car, as shown below, in the src directory. Also suppose that you've compiled it into the classes directory using javac.

Car.class resides in the classes/com/agiledeveloper directory.

UnitTestingWithGroovy/src/Car.java

```java
// Java code
package com.agiledeveloper;

public class Car
{
  private int miles;
  public int getMiles() { return miles; }

  public void drive(int dist)
  {
    miles += dist;
  }
}
```

You can write a unit test for this class in Groovy, and you don't have to compile the test code to run it. Here are a few positive tests for the Car. These tests are in a file named CarTest.groovy in the test directory.

UnitTestingWithGroovy/test/CarTest.groovy

```groovy
class CarTest extends GroovyTestCase
{
  def car

  void setUp()
  {
    car = new com.agiledeveloper.Car()
  }

  void testInitialize()
  {
    assertEquals 0, car.miles
  }

  void testDrive()
  {
    car.drive(10)
    assertEquals 10, car.miles
  }
}
```

The setUp() method and the corresponding tearDown() method (not shown in the previous example) sandwich each test call. You can initialize objects in setUp() and optionally clean up or reset in tearDown(). These two methods help you avoid duplicating code and, at the same time, help isolate the tests from each other.

To run this test, type the command groovy -classpath classes test/CarTest. You should see the following output:

```
..
Time: 0.003

OK (2 tests)
```

This output shows that two tests were executed, and both, not surprisingly, passed. The first test confirmed that the Car has zero miles to begin with, and driving a certain distance increases the miles by that distance. Now, write a negative test:

```
void testDriveNegativeInput()
{
  car.drive(-10)
  assertEquals 0, car.miles
}
```

You set the parameter for drive() to the negative value -10. You decide that the Car must ignore your drive request in this case, so you expect the miles value to be unchanged. The Java code, however, does not handle this condition. It modifies the miles without checking the input parameter. When you run the previous test, you will get an error:

```
...F
Time: 0.004
There was 1 failure:
1) testDriveNegativeInput(CarTest)
   junit.framework.AssertionFailedError:
   expected:<0> but was:<-10>

...

FAILURES!!!
Tests run: 3,  Failures: 1,  Errors: 0
```

This output shows that the two positive tests passed, but the negative test failed. You can now fix the Java code to handle this case property and rerun your test. You can see that using Groovy to test your Java code is pretty straightforward and simple.

16.3 Testing for Exceptions

Let's now look at writing exception tests. One way to write them is to wrap your method in try-catch blocks. If the method throws the expected exception, that is, if you land in the catch block, all is well.

If the code does not thrown any exceptions, you'll invoke fail() to indicate the failure of the test, as shown here:

UnitTestingWithGroovy/ExpectException.groovy
```
try
{
  divide(2, 0)
  fail "Expected ArithmeticException ..."
}
catch(ArithmeticException ex)
{
  assertTrue true // Success
}
```

The previous code is Java-style JUnit testing and works with Groovy as well. However, Groovy makes it easier to write exception tests by providing a method shouldFail() that elegantly wraps up the boilerplate code. Let's use that to write an exception test:

UnitTestingWithGroovy/ExpectException.groovy
```
shouldFail { divide(2, 0) }
```

The method shouldFail() accepts a closure. It invokes the closure in a guarded try-catch block. If no exception is thrown, it raises an exception by calling the fail() method. If you're interested in catching a specific exception, you can specify that information to the shouldFail() method:

UnitTestingWithGroovy/ExpectException.groovy
```
shouldFail(ArithmeticException) { divide(2, 0) }
```

In this case, shouldFail() expects the closure to throw ArithmeticException. If the code throws ArithmeticException or something that extends it, it is happy. If some other exception is thrown or if no exception is thrown, then shouldFail() fails. You can take advantage of Groovy's flexibility with parentheses[5] and write the previous call as follows:

UnitTestingWithGroovy/ExpectException.groovy
```
shouldFail ArithmeticException, { divide(2, 0) }
```

16.4 Mocking

It's very hard, if not impossible, to unit test a piece of large code[6] that has dependencies. One advantage of unit testing is that it forces you

---

5. See Section 18.8, *The Parentheses Limitation and a Workaround*, on page 281.
6. "What's large code?" Any code you can't see entirely without scrolling down in an editor window is large—no, don't make your font size smaller now.

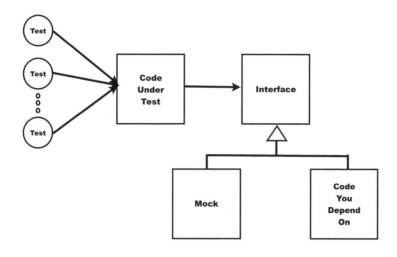

Figure 16.1: MOCKING DURING UNIT TESTING

to make the unit of code smaller. Smaller code is cohesive code. It also forces you to decouple the code from its surroundings. This means less coupling. A collateral advantage of unit testing is higher cohesion and lower coupling, which are qualities of good design. We'll discuss ways to deal with dependency in this section and ways to unit test code with dependencies in the rest of this chapter.

Coupling comes in two forms. There's code that depends on your code, and there's code that your code depends on. You need to address both types of coupling before you can unit test your code.

The code being tested has to be separated or decoupled from where it is used within an application. Suppose you have some logic in a button handler within the GUI. It's hard to unit test that logic. So, you have to separate this code, into a method, for you to unit test it.

Suppose you have logic that heavily depends on some resource. That resource may be slow to respond, expensive to use, unpredictable in behavior, or currently being developed. Thus, you have to separate that dependency from your code before you can effectively unit test your code. This is where stubs and mocks help.

Stubs vs. Mocks

In the article "Mocks Aren't Stubs," (http://martinfowler.com/articles/mocksArentStubs.html), Martin Fowler discusses the difference between stubs and mocks. A *stub* stands in for a real object. It simply reciprocates the coached expected response when called by the code being tested. The response is set up to satisfy the needs for the test to pass. A *mock* object does a lot more than a stub. It helps you ensure your code is interacting with its dependencies, the collaborators, as expected. It can keep track of the sequence and number of calls your code makes on the collaborator it stands in for. It ensures proper parameters are passed in to method calls. While stubs verify state, mocks verify behavior. When you use a mock in your test, it verifies not only the state but also the behavior of the interaction of your code with its dependencies.

Groovy provides support for creating both stubs and mocks, as you will see in Section 16.10, *Mocking Using the Groovy Mock Library*, on page 249.

The code that your code depends on is called a *collaborator*—your code collaborates with it to get its work done. The collaborator can be an object, a component, a layer, or a subsystem. It can be local, it can be kept internal to your object, it can be passed in as a parameter, or it can even be remote. Your object can't function without the collaborator. However, you need to creatively replace it for the sake of testing.

A mock stands in for the collaborator—the real object (see the sidebar on this page). It does not do any real work. It simply gives expected response to calls from your code in order to get the test working.

When running your application, you want your code to depend on the real object it needs. This is also the case when integration testing your application. However, when unit testing, you want your code to instead depend on the mock. So, you need to find a way to switch the dependency of your code from a mock to real object.

In a statically typed language like Java, you can achieve this switching by using an interface, as shown in Figure 16.1, on the previous page. There are frameworks in Java—such as EasyMock, JMock, and so on—that make mocking easier. Some of these, like JMock, even allow you to mock a class without you having to create an interface. Using a proxy-based mechanism, they intercept your call and route your request to the mock instead of the real dependent object.

Groovy's dynamic nature and metaprogramming capabilities provide a great advantage in this area. There are a few ways to create mocks in Groovy. You can use the following:

- Method overriding

- Categories

- ExpandoMetaClass

- Expando

- Map

- Groovy's mock library

We'll discuss techniques to create and use mocks in Groovy in the rest of this chapter.

16.5 Mocking by Overriding

Suppose you have a class that depends on a method that does some significant work and takes substantial time and resources, such as the following myMethod():

UnitTestingWithGroovy/com/agiledeveloper/CodeWithHeavierDependencies.groovy

```
package com.agiledeveloper

public class CodeWithHeavierDependencies
{
  public void myMethod()
  {
    def value = someAction() + 10

    println(value)
  }

  int someAction()
  {
    Thread.sleep(5000) // simulates time consuming action

    return Math.random() * 100 // Simulated result of some action
  }
}
```

You're interested in testing myMethod() (which belongs to CodeWith-HeavierDependencies). However, the method depends on someAction(), which simulates a time- and resource-consuming operation.

If you simply write a unit test for myMethod(), it will be slow. There is yet another problem—you can't assert any result from a call to myMethod() because it doesn't return anything. Instead, it prints a value to standard output. You need to figure out a way to capture what it prints and assert that. So, you have a method that is hard to test; it's slow and complicated.

One way to address these concerns is to override the offending methods. Here's how:

UnitTestingWithGroovy/TestByOverriding.groovy

```
import com.agiledeveloper.CodeWithHeavierDependencies

class TestCodeWithHeavierDependenciesUsingOverriding extends GroovyTestCase
{
  void testMyMethod()
  {
    def testObj = new CodeWithHeavierDependenciesExt()

    testObj.myMethod()

    assertEquals 35, testObj.result
  }
}

class CodeWithHeavierDependenciesExt extends CodeWithHeavierDependencies
{
  def result

  int someAction() { return 25 }

  def println(text) { result = text }
}
```

The output from the previous code is as follows:

```
.
Time: 0.015

OK (1 test)
```

In this code, you created a new class called CodeWithHeavierDependenciesExt—a mock—that extends class CodeWithHeavierDependencies. In this class, you mocked the methods someAction and println() (you took advantage of the Groovy convention to call System.out.println() simply as println() and provided a local implementation of println()—savvy?). Go ahead and run this test code and see how it succeeds. There's no delay in running the test and no messing with standard output.

You are still testing behavior, but by taking the nondeterministic behavior and making it deterministic, you're able to write an assertion against it. Find a clever way to mock out dependencies so you can focus on unit testing the behavior of your code.

In the previous example, you tested a method in a Groovy class. You can use this approach for testing Java classes as well.

Mocking by overriding your own Java methods such as someAction() is not a problem. However, unlike the Groovy code that called println(), the Java code would be calling System.out.println(). So, creating a println() in your mock derived class will not help. However, you can extend PrintStream and replace System.out. Let's take a look at a Java class that is equivalent to the previous Groovy code you tested:

UnitTestingWithGroovy/com/agiledeveloper/JavaCodeWithHeavierDependencies.java

```java
package com.agiledeveloper;

public class JavaCodeWithHeavierDependencies
{
  public int someAction()
  {
    try
    {
      Thread.sleep(5000); // simulates time consuming action
    }
    catch(InterruptedException ex) {}

    return (int) (Math.random() * 100); // Simulated result of some action
  }

  public void myMethod()
  {
    int value = someAction() + 10;

    System.out.println(value);
  }
}
```

The Groovy code to test the previous Java code is as follows:

UnitTestingWithGroovy/TestJavaByOverride.groovy

```groovy
import com.agiledeveloper.JavaCodeWithHeavierDependencies

class TestCodeWithHeavierDependenciesUsingOverriding extends GroovyTestCase
{
  void testMyMethod()
  {
    def testObj = new ExtendedJavaCode()

    def originalPrintStream = System.out
    def printMock = new PrintMock()
    System.out = printMock

    try
    {
      testObj.myMethod()
    }
    finally { System.out = originalPrintStream }

    assertEquals 35, printMock.result
  }
}

class ExtendedJavaCode extends JavaCodeWithHeavierDependencies
{
  int someAction() { return 25 }
}

class PrintMock extends PrintStream
{
  PrintMock() { super(System.out) }

  def result

  void println(int text) { result = text }
}
```

The output from the previous code is the expected result of the test passing:

```
.
Time: 0.026

OK (1 test)
```

myMethod(), the method being tested, is part of the JavaCodeWithHeavierDependencies class. You created ExtendedJavaCode to extend that class and overrode the someAction() method. You also created a class

PrintMock that extends PrintStream and assigned an instance of that to System.out. This helps intercept the call to System.out.println() and directs it to your mock implementation.

16.6 Mocking Using Categories

In Section 14.1, *Injecting Methods Using Categories*, on page 198, we discussed how categories provide controlled AOP in Groovy. In this section, you'll see how you can use it to create mocks:

UnitTestingWithGroovy/TestUsingCategories.groovy

```groovy
import com.agiledeveloper.CodeWithHeavierDependencies

class TestUsingCategories extends GroovyTestCase
{
  void testMyMethod()
  {
    def testObj = new CodeWithHeavierDependencies()

    use(MockHelper)
    {
      testObj.myMethod()

      assertEquals 35, MockHelper.result
    }
  }
}

class MockHelper
{
  def static result

  def static println(self, text) { result = text }

  def static someAction(CodeWithHeavierDependencies self) { 25 }
}
```

MockHelper has two static methods, one for each method you want to mock—someAction() and println(). Within the test, you ask the category to intercept calls to methods and substitute these two methods where appropriate by using use(MockHelper). This is much like the advice used in AOP.

The output from the previous bit of code is a reassuring pass of the test, as shown here:

```
.
Time: 0.027

OK (1 test)
```

Categories are useful only with Groovy code. It does not help to mock methods called from within compiled Java code.

The overriding approach you saw in Section 16.5, *Mocking by Overriding*, on page 239 is useful for both Java and Groovy code. However, the overriding approach can't be used if the class being tested is final. The categories approach shines in this case.

16.7 Mocking Using ExpandoMetaClass

Another way to intercept method calls in Groovy is to use the Expando-MetaClass (cf. Section 14.2, *Injecting Methods Using ExpandoMetaClass*, on page 203 and Section 14.3, *Injecting Methods into Specific Instances*, on page 207). You don't have to create a separate class as in the two approaches you've seen so far. Instead, create a closure for each method you want to mock, and set that into MetaClass for the instance being tested. Let's take a look at an example.

Create a separate instance of ExpandoMetaClass for the instance being tested. This MetaClass will carry the mock implementation of collaborator methods.

In this example, shown in the following code, you create a closure for mocking println() and set that into an instance of ExpandoMetaClass for ClassWithHeavierDependencies in line number 9. Similarly, you create a closure for mocking someAction() in line number 10. The advantage of creating an instance of ExpandoMetaClass specifically for the instance under test is that you don't globally affect the metaclass for CodeWith-HeavierDependencies. So, if you have other tests, the method you mock does not affect them (remember to keep the tests isolated from each other).

UnitTestingWithGroovy/TestUsingExpandoMetaClass.groovy

```
Line 1    import com.agiledeveloper.CodeWithHeavierDependencies

          class TestUsingExpandoMetaClass extends GroovyTestCase
          {
    5        void testMyMethod()
             {
               def result
               def emc = new ExpandoMetaClass(CodeWithHeavierDependencies)
               emc.println = { text -> result = text }
   10          emc.someAction = { -> 25 }
               emc.initialize()

               def testObj = new CodeWithHeavierDependencies()
               testObj.metaClass = emc
   15
               testObj.myMethod()

               assertEquals 35, result
             }
   20     }
```

The output from the previous code again confirms that the test passes:

```
.
Time: 0.031

OK (1 test)
```

In this example, when myMethod() calls the two methods—println() and someAction()—the ExpandoMetaClass intercepts those calls and routes them to your mock implementation. Again, this is similar to the advice on AOP.

Compared to the previous two approaches, creating the mock, setting up its expectations, and using it in the test are nicely contained within the test method in this case. There are no additional classes to create. If you have other tests, you can create the mocks necessary to satisfy those tests in a concise way.

This approach of using ExpandoMetaClass for mocking is useful only with Groovy code. It does not help to mock methods called from within precompiled Java code.

16.8 Mocking Using Expando

So far in this chapter you looked at ways to mock instance methods called from within another instance method. In the rest of this chapter, you'll look at ways to mock other objects on which your code depends.

Let's take a look at an example. Suppose the methods of a class you're interested in testing depend on a File. That'll make it hard to write a unit test. So, you need to find ways to mock this object so your unit tests on your class can be quick and automated:

UnitTestingWithGroovy/com/agiledeveloper/ClassWithDependency.groovy

```groovy
package com.agiledeveloper

public class ClassWithDependency
{
  def methodA(val, file)
  {
    file.write "The value is ${val}."
  }

  def methodB(val)
  {
    def file = new java.io.FileWriter("output.txt")
    file.write "The value is ${val}."
  }

  def methodC(val)
  {
    def file = new java.io.FileWriter("output.txt")
    file.write "The value is ${val}."
    file.close()
  }
}
```

In this code, you have three methods with different flavors of dependencies. methodA() receives an instance of what appears to be a File. The other two methods, methodB() and methodC(), instantiate an instance of FileWriter internally. The Expando class will help you with the first method only. So, consider only methodA() in this section. We'll see how to test the other two methods in Section 16.10, *Mocking Using the Groovy Mock Library*, on page 249.

methodA() writes a message to the given File object using its write() method. Your goal is to test methodA(), but without actually having to write to a physical file and then reading its contents back to assert.

You can take advantage of Groovy's dynamic typing here because methodA() does not specify the type of its parameter. So, you can send any object that can fulfill its capability, such as the write() method (see Section 4.4, *Design by Capability*, on page 68). Let's do that now. Create a class HandTossedFileMock with the write() method. You don't have to worry about all the properties and methods that the real File class has. All you care about is what the method being tested really calls. The code is as follows:

UnitTestingWithGroovy/TestUsingAHandTossedMock.groovy

```
import com.agiledeveloper.ClassWithDependency

class TestWithExpando extends GroovyTestCase
{
  void testMethodA()
  {
    def testObj = new ClassWithDependency()
    def fileMock = new HandTossedFileMock()
    testObj.methodA(1, fileMock)

    assertEquals "The value is 1.", fileMock.result
  }
}

class HandTossedFileMock
{
  def result

  def write(value) { result = value }
}
```

The output from the previous code confirms a passing test:

```
.
Time: 0.015

OK (1 test)
```

In this code, the mock implementation of write() that you created within HandTossedFileMock simply saves the parameter it receives into a result property. You're sending an instance of this mock class to methodA() instead of the real File. methodA() is quite happy to use the mock, thanks to dynamic typing.

That was not too bad; however, it would be great if you did not have to hand-toss that separate class. This is where Expando comes in (see Section 15.1, *Creating Dynamic Classes with Expando*, on page 219).

Simply tell an instance of Expando to hold a property called text and a mock implementation of the write() method. Then pass this instance to methodA(). Let's look at the code:

UnitTestingWithGroovy/TestUsingExpando.groovy

```
import com.agiledeveloper.ClassWithDependency

class TestUsingExpando extends GroovyTestCase
{
  void testMethodA()
  {
    def fileMock = new Expando(text: '', write: { text = it })

    def testObj = new ClassWithDependency()
    testObj.methodA(1, fileMock)

    assertEquals "The value is 1.", fileMock.text
  }
}
```

The output is as follows:

```
.
Time: 0.022

OK (1 test)
```

In both the previous examples, no real physical file was created when you called methodA(). The unit test runs fast, and you don't have any files to read or clean up after the test.

Expando is useful when you pass the dependent object to the method being tested. If, on the other hand, the method is creating the dependent object internally (such as the methods methodB() and methodC()), it is of no help. We'll address this in Section 16.10, *Mocking Using the Groovy Mock Library*, on the next page.

16.9 Mocking Using Map

You saw an example of using Expando as a mock object. You can also use a Map. A map, as you know, has keys and associated values. The values can be either objects or even closures. You can take advantage of this to use a Map in place of a collaborator.

Here's a rewrite of the example using Expando from Section 16.8, *Mocking Using Expando*, on page 246, this time using a Map:

UnitTestingWithGroovy/TestUsingMap.groovy

```
import com.agiledeveloper.ClassWithDependency

class TestUsingMap extends GroovyTestCase
{
  void testMethodA()
  {
    def text = ''
    def fileMock = [write : { text = it }]

    def testObj = new ClassWithDependency()
    testObj.methodA(1, fileMock)

    assertEquals "The value is 1.", text
  }
}
```

The output is as follows:

```
.
Time: 0.029

OK (1 test)
```

Just like Expando, the Map is useful when you pass the dependent object to the method being tested. It does not help if the collaborator is created internally in the method being tested. We'll address this case next.

16.10 Mocking Using the Groovy Mock Library

Groovy's mock library implemented in the groovy.mock.interceptor package is useful to mock deeper dependencies, that is, instances of collaborators/dependent objects created within the methods you're testing. StubFor and MockFor are two classes that take care of this. Let's look at them one at a time.

StubFor and MockFor are intended to intercept calls to methods like categories do (see Section 16.6, *Mocking Using Categories*, on page 243). However, unlike categories, you don't have to create separate classes for mocking. Introduce the mock methods on instances of StubFor or MockFor, and these classes take care of replacing the MetaClass for the object you're mocking.

In the sidebar on page 238, I discussed the difference between stubs and mocks. Let's start with an example using StubFor to understand the strengths and weaknesses of stubs. Then we'll take a look at the advantage mocks offer by using MockFor.

Using StubFor

Let's use Groovy's StubFor to create stubs for the File class:

UnitTestingWithGroovy/TestUsingStubFor.groovy

```
Line 1   import com.agiledeveloper.ClassWithDependency

         class TestUsingStubFor extends GroovyTestCase
    -    {
    5      void testMethodB()
    -      {
    -        def testObj = new ClassWithDependency()

    -        def fileMock = new groovy.mock.interceptor.StubFor(java.io.FileWriter)
   10        def text
    -        fileMock.demand.write { text = it.toString() }
    -        fileMock.demand.close {}

    -        fileMock.use
   15        {
    -          testObj.methodB(1)
    -        }

    -        assertEquals "The value is 1.", text
   20      }
    -    }
```

When creating an instance of StubFor, you provided the class you're interested in stubbing, in this case the java.io.FileWriter. You then created a closure for the stub implementation of the write() method. On line number 14, you called the use() method on the stub. At this time, it replaces the MetaClass of FileWriter with a ProxyMetaClass. Any call to an instance of FileWriter from within the attached closure will be routed to the stub.

Stubs and mocks, however, do not help intercept calls to constructors. So, in the previous example, the constructor of FileWriter is called, and it ends up creating a file named output.txt on the disk.

StubFor helped you test whether your method, methodB(), is creating and writing the expected content to it. However, it has one limitation. It failed to test whether the method was well behaved by closing the file. Even though you demanded the close() method on the stub, it ignored checking whether close() was actually called. The stub simply stands in for the collaborator and verifies the state. To verify behavior, you have to use a mock (see the sidebar on page 238), specifically, the MockFor class.

Using MockFor

Let's take the previous test code and make one change to it:

UnitTestingWithGroovy/TestUsingMockFor.groovy

```
//def fileMock = new groovy.mock.interceptor.StubFor(java.io.FileWriter)
def fileMock = new groovy.mock.interceptor.MockFor(java.io.FileWriter)
```

You replaced StubFor with MockFor—that's the only change. When you run the test now, it fails, as shown here:

```
.F
Time: 0.093
There was 1 failure:
1) testMethod1(TestUsingStubFor)junit.framework.AssertionFailedError:
verify[1]: expected 1..1 call(s) to 'close' but was never called.
```

Unlike the stub, the mock tells you that even though your code produced the desired result, it did not behave as expected. That is, it did not call the close() method that was set up in the expectation using demand.

methodC() does the same thing as methodB(), but it calls close(). Let's test that method using MockFor:

UnitTestingWithGroovy/TestMethodCUsingMock.groovy

```
import com.agiledeveloper.ClassWithDependency

class TestMethodCUsingMock extends GroovyTestCase
{
  void testMethodC()
  {
    def testObj = new ClassWithDependency()

    def fileMock = new groovy.mock.interceptor.MockFor(java.io.FileWriter)
    def text
    fileMock.demand.write { text = it.toString() }
    fileMock.demand.close {}

    fileMock.use
    {
      testObj.methodC(1)
    }

    assertEquals "The value is 1.", text
  }
}
```

In this case, the mock tells you that it is quite happy with the collaboration. The test passes, as shown here:

```
.
Time: 0.088

OK (1 test)
```

In the previous examples, the method under test created only one instance of the object being mocked—FileWriter. What if the method creates more than one of these objects? The mock represents all of these objects, and you have to create the demands for each of them. Let's look at an example of using two instances of FileWriter. The useFiles() method in the following code copies the given parameter to the first file and writes the size of the parameter to the second:

```groovy
class TwoFileUser
{
  def useFiles(str)
  {
    def file1 = new java.io.FileWriter("output1.txt")
    def file2 = new java.io.FileWriter("output2.txt")
    file1.write str
    file2.write str.size()
    file1.close()
    file2.close()
  }
}
```

Here's the test for that code:

UnitTestingWithGroovy/TwoFileUserTest.groovy

```groovy
class TwoFileUserTest extends GroovyTestCase
{
  void testUseFiles()
  {
    def testObj = new TwoFileUser()
    def testData = 'Multi Files'
    def fileMock = new groovy.mock.interceptor.MockFor(java.io.FileWriter)
    fileMock.demand.write() { assertEquals testData, it }
    fileMock.demand.write() { assertEquals testData.size(), it }
    fileMock.demand.close(2..2) {}

    fileMock.use
    {
      testObj.useFiles(testData)
    }
  }
}
```

The output from running the previous test is as follows:

UnitTestingWithGroovy/TwoFileUserTest.output

```
.
Time: 0.091

OK (1 test)
```

The demands you created are to be satisfied collectively by both the objects created in the method being tested. The mock is quite flexible to support more than one object. Of course, if you have a lots of objects being created, it can get hard to implement. The ability to specify multiplicity of calls, discussed next, may help in that case.

The mock keeps track of the sequence and number of calls to a method, and if the code being tested does not exactly behave like the expectation you have demanded, the mock raises an exception, failing the test.

If you have to set up expectations for multiple calls to the same method, you can do that easily. Here is an example:

```
def someWriter()
{
  def file = new FileWriter('output.txt')
  file.write("one")
  file.write("two")
  file.write(3)
  file.flush()
  file.write(file.getEncoding())
  file.close()
}
```

Suppose you care only to test the interaction between your code and the collaborator. The expectation you need to set up is for three calls to write(), followed by a call to flush(), a call to getEncoding(), then a call to write(), and finally a call to close().

You can specify the cardinality or multiplicity of a call easily using a range with demand. For example, mock.demand.write(2..4) {...} says that you expect the method write() to be called at least two times, but no more than four times. Let's write a test for the previous method to see how easy it is to express the expectations for multiple calls and the return values and also assert that the parameter values received are expected.

```groovy
void testSomeWriter()
{
  def fileMock = new groovy.mock.interceptor.MockFor(java.io.FileWriter)
  fileMock.demand.write(3..3) {} // If you want to say upto 3 times, use 0..3
  fileMock.demand.flush {}
  fileMock.demand.getEncoding { return "whatever" } // return is optional
  fileMock.demand.write { assertEquals 'whatever', it.toString() }
  fileMock.demand.close {}

  fileMock.use
  {
    testObj.someWriter()
  }
}
```

In this example, the mock asserts that write() was called three times; however, it failed to assert the parameters passed in. You can modify the code to assert for parameters, as shown here:

```groovy
def params = ['one', 'two', 3]
def index = 0
fileMock.demand.write(3..3) { assert it == params[index++] }
  // If you want to say upto 3 times, use 0..3
```

Unit testing takes quite a bit of discipline. However, the benefits outweigh the cost. Unit testing is critical in dynamic languages that offer greater flexibility.

In this chapter, I presented techniques for managing dependencies via stubs and mocks. You can use Groovy to unit test your Java code. You can use your existing unit testing and mock frameworks. You can also override methods to mock your Groovy and Java code. To unit test your Groovy code, you can use categories and ExpandoMetaClass. Both let you mock by intercepting method calls. ExpandoMetaClass give you the added advantages that you don't have to create extra classes and that your test is concise. For simple mocking of parameter objects, use Maps or Expando. If you want to set up expectations for multiple methods and mock dependencies that are internal to methods being tested, use StubFor. To test the state as well as the behavior, use MockFor.

You saw how the dynamic nature of Groovy along with its metaprogramming capability makes unit testing a breeze. As you evolve your code, refactor it, and get a better understanding of your application requirements, unit testing with Groovy can help maintain your velocity of development. It'll give you confidence that your application is continuing to meet your expectations—use it as a carabiner as you ascend through your application development complexities.

Chapter 17

Groovy Builders

Builders are internal DSLs that provide ease in working with certain types of problems. For instance, if you have a need to work with nested, hierarchical structures, such as tree structures, XML representations, or HTML representations, you'll find builders to be very useful. Basically, builders provide syntax that does not tie you closely with the underlying structure or implementation. They are facades because they don't replace the underlying implementation; instead, they provide an elegant way to work with it.

Groovy provides builders for a number of everyday tasks, including working with XML, HTML, DOM, SAX, Swing, and even Ant. In this chapter, you'll take a look at two of them—XML MarkupBuilder and Swing-Builder—to get a flavor of the builders. You'll then explore two techniques to create your own builders.

17.1 Building XML

Most of us love to hate XML. Working with XML gets harder as the document size gets larger, and also the tools and API support are not pleasant. I have this theory about XML that it's like humans. It starts out cute when it's small and gets annoying when it becomes bigger.

XML may be a fine format for machines to handle, but it's rather unwieldy to work with directly. Basically, no one really wants to work with XML, but you're often forced to do so. Groovy alleviates this a great deal by making working with XML almost fun.

Let's take a look at an example of one way to create XML documents in Groovy—using a builder:

```groovy
bldr = new groovy.xml.MarkupBuilder()

bldr.languages {
  language(name: 'C++') { author('Stroustrup')}
  language(name: 'Java') { author('Gosling')}
  language(name: 'Lisp') { author('McCarthy')}
}
```

This code uses the groovy.xml.MarkupBuilder to create an XML document. When you call arbitrary methods or properties on the builder, it kindly assumes that you're referring to either an element name or an attribute name in the resulting XML document depending on the context of the call. Here's the output from the previous code:

```
<languages>
  <language name='C++'>
    <author>Stroustrup</author>
  </language>
  <language name='Java'>
    <author>Gosling</author>
  </language>
  <language name='Lisp'>
    <author>McCarthy</author>
  </language>
</languages>
```

You called a method named languages() that does not exist on the instance of the MarkupBuilder class. Instead of rejecting you, the builder smartly assumed your call meant to define a root element of your XML document, which is a rather nice assumption.

The closure attached to that method call now provides an internal context. DSLs are context sensitive. Any nonexistent method called within that closure is assumed to be a child element name. If you pass Map parameters to the method calls (such as language(name: value)), they're treated as attributes of the elements. Any single parameter value (such as author(value)) indicates element content instead of attributes. You can study the previous code and the related output to see how the MarkupBuilder inferred the code.

In the previous example, I hard-coded the data that I wanted to go into my XML document, and also the builder wrote to the standard output.

In a real project, neither of those conditions may be usual. I want data to come from a collection that can be populated from a data source or input stream. Also, I want to write out to a Writer instead of to the standard output.

The builder can readily attach to a Writer that it can take as a constructor argument. So, let's attach a StringWriter to the builder. Let the data for the document come from a map.[1] Here's an example that takes data from a map, creates an XML document, and writes that into a String-Writer:

`UsingBuilders/BuildXML.groovy`

```
langs = ['C++' : 'Stroustrup', 'Java' : 'Gosling', 'Lisp' : 'McCarthy']

writer = new StringWriter()
bldr = new groovy.xml.MarkupBuilder(writer)

bldr.languages {
  langs.each { key, value ->
      language(name: key) {
        author (value)
    }
  }
}

println writer
```

The output from the previous code is as follows:

```
<languages>
  <language name='C++'>
    <author>Stroustrup</author>
  </language>
  <language name='Java'>
    <author>Gosling</author>
  </language>
  <language name='Lisp'>
    <author>McCarthy</author>
  </language>
</languages>
```

The MarkupBuilder is quite adequate for small to medium documents. However, if your document is large (a few megabytes), you can use StreamingMarkupBuilder, which is kinder in memory usage. Let's rewrite

---

1. The data may come from arbitrary source, for example, from a database. See Section 10.2, *Database Select*, on page 159.

the previous example using the StreamingMarkupBuilder, but to add some flavor, let's also include namespaces and XML comments:

UsingBuilders/BuildUsingStreamingBuilder.groovy

```
langs = ['C++' : 'Stroustrup', 'Java' : 'Gosling', 'Lisp' : 'McCarthy']

xmlDocument = new groovy.xml.StreamingMarkupBuilder().bind {
  mkp.xmlDeclaration()
  mkp.declareNamespace(computer: "Computer")
  languages {
    comment << "Created using StreamingMarkupBuilder"
    langs.each { key, value ->
      computer.language(name: key) {
        author (value)
      }
    }
  }
}

println xmlDocument
```

The output from the previous code is as follows:

```
<?xml version="1.0"?>
<languages xmlns:computer='Computer'>
  <!--Created using StreamingMarkupBuilder-->
    <computer:language name='C++'>
      <author>Stroustrup</author>
    </computer:language>
    <computer:language name='Java'>
      <author>Gosling</author>
    </computer:language>
    <computer:language name='Lisp'>
      <author>McCarthy</author>
    </computer:language>
</languages>
```

Using StreamingMarkupBuilder, you can declare namespaces, XML comments, and so on, using the builder support property mkp. Once you define a namespace, to associate an element with a namespace you can use the dot notation on the prefix, such as computer.language where computer is a prefix.

The builders for XML make the syntax easy and elegant. You don't have to deal with the pointy syntax of XML to create XML documents.

17.2 Building Swing

The elegance of the builders concept is not restricted to XML structure. Groovy provides a builder for creating Swing applications as well. When working with Swing, you need to perform some mundane tasks such as creating components (like buttons), registering event handlers, and so on. Typically to implement an event handler, you write an anonymous inner class and in the implementation handler methods receive parameters (such as ActionEvent) even if you don't care for them. SwingBuilder along with Groovy closures eliminates the drudgery.

You can use the nested or hierarchical structure provided by the builder to create a container (such as JFrame) and its components (such as buttons, textboxes, and so on). Initialize components by using Groovy's flexible name-value pair initialization facility. Defining an event handler is trivial. Simply provide it a closure. You're building the familiar Swing application, but you will find the code size is smaller. This helps you quickly make changes, experiment, and get feedback. You're still using the underlying Swing API, but the syntax is a lot different. You're using the Groovy idioms[2] to talk to Swing. Now, let's create a Swing application using the SwingBuilder class:

```
UsingBuilders/BuildSwing.groovy
```
```
bldr = new groovy.swing.SwingBuilder()

frame = bldr.frame(
  title: 'Swing',
  size: [50, 100],
  layout: new java.awt.FlowLayout(),
  defaultCloseOperation:javax.swing.WindowConstants.EXIT_ON_CLOSE
) {
  lbl = label(text: 'test')
  btn = button(text: 'Click me', actionPerformed: {
    btn.text = 'Clicked'
    lbl.text = "Groovy!"
    } )
}

frame.show()
```

The output from the previous code is shown in Figure 17.1, on the next page.

---

2. See my blog about languages and idioms at http://tinyurl.com/2kpsm4.

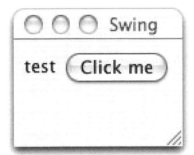 

Figure 17.1: A LITTLE SWING APPLICATION CREATED USING SWINGBUILDER

You initialized an instance of JFrame and assigned its title, size, and layout, and you also set the default close operation, all in one simple statement. This is equivalent to five separate statements in Java. Also, registering the event handler was as simple as providing a closure to the actionPerformed property of button (for JButton). This eliminated the effort in Java to create an anonymous inner class and implement the action-Performed() method with the ActionEvent parameter. Sure, there was a lot of syntax sugar, but the elegance and reduced code size makes it easier to work with the Swing API.

You looked at SwingBuilder, which is a facade that brings Groovy elegance and ease to building Swing applications. Similarly, SwingXBuilder (see http://groovy.codehaus.org/SwingXBuilder) is a facade for the SwingX UI library (for the SwingLabs extensions to the Swing library, see http://swingx.dev.java.net). If you use JIDE (https://jide-oss.dev.java.net/), you can use the JideBuilder (http://groovy.codehaus.org/JideBuilder) in Groovy. Groovy's GraphicsBuilder (http://groovy.codehaus.org/GraphicsBuilder) provides a Groovy way of building JavaFX-type Java2D Graphics.

17.3 Custom Builder Using Metaprogramming

As I discussed earlier, builders provide you with a way to create an internal DSL for specialized complex tasks that use nested or hierarchical structure or format. When working with a specialized task in your application, explore to see whether a builder exists that can solve the problem. If you don't find any builders, you can create your own.

You can create a custom builder in two ways. You can take up the entire effort on your shoulders by using the metaprogramming capabilities of Groovy, as you'll see in this section. Alternately, you can use the Builder-Support (Section 17.4, *Using BuilderSupport*, on page 263) or Factory-BuilderSupport (Section 17.5, *Using FactoryBuilderSupport*, on page 267) already provided in Groovy.

You'll create a builder that builds a to-do list. Here's the code that's using the builder you will create:

UsingBuilders/UsingTodoBuilder.groovy

```
bldr = new TodoBuilder()

bldr.build {
  Prepare_Vacation (start: '02/15', end: '02/22') {
    Reserve_Flight (on: '01/01', status: 'done')
    Reserve_Hotel(on: '01/02')
    Reserve_Car(on: '01/02')
  }
  Buy_New_Mac {
    Install_QuickSilver
    Install_TextMate
    Install_Groovy {
      Run_all_tests
    }
  }
}
```

The output of running the previous code (once you create the ToDo-Builder) is as follows:

```
To-Do:
 - Prepare Vacation [start: 02/15 end: 02/22]
   x Reserve Flight [on: 01/01]
   - Reserve Hotel [on: 01/02]
   - Reserve Car [on: 01/02]
 - Buy New Mac
   - Install QuickSilver
   - Install TextMate
   - Install Groovy
     - Run all tests
```

Completed tasks are marked with a x. Nesting of tasks is shown by indentation, and task parameters such as start date are shown next to their names.

In the previous DSL for the to-do list, you have created item names such as "Reserve Car" using an underscore instead of space so you can fit them as method names in Groovy. The only known method is build().

The rest—methods and properties—are handled using methodMissing()
and propertyMissing(), as shown next.

The result is mostly standard straightforward Groovy code with a good
use of metaprogramming. When a nonexistent method or property is
called, you assume it's an item. You check whether a closure is attached
by testing the last parameter in args, obtained using the index -1. You
then set the delegate of the presented closure to the builder and invoke
the closure to traverse down the nested tasks.

UsingBuilders/TodoBuilder.groovy

```groovy
class TodoBuilder
{
  def level = 0
  def result = new StringWriter()

  def build(closure)
  {
    result << "To-Do:\n"
    closure.delegate = this
    closure()
    println result
  }

  def methodMissing(String name, args)
  {
    handle(name, args)
  }

  def propertyMissing(String name)
  {
    Object[] emptyArray = []
    handle(name, emptyArray)
  }

  def handle(String name, args)
  {
    level++

    level.times { result << " "}
    result << placeXifStatusDone(args)
    result << name.replaceAll("_", " ")
    result << printParameters(args)
    result << "\n"

    if (args.length > 0 && args[-1] instanceof Closure)
    {
      def theClosure = args[-1]
      theClosure.delegate = this
      theClosure()
    }
```

```
    level--
  }

  def placeXifStatusDone(args)
  {
    args.length > 0 && args[0] instanceof Map &&
      args[0]['status'] == 'done' ? "x "`: "- "
  }

  def printParameters(args)
  {
    def values = ""
    if (args.length > 0 && args[0] instanceof Map)
    {
      values += " ["
      def count = 0
      args[0].each { key, value ->
        if (key == 'status') return
        count++
        values += (count > 1 ? " " : "")
        values += "${key}: ${value}"
      }
      values += "]"
    }

    values
  }
}
```

Building your own custom builder as shown earlier is not difficult. Do not hesitate to follow these steps. For very complex cases with deeper nesting and extensive use of Map and regular parameters, BuilderSupport, which you will see next, may help.

17.4 Using BuilderSupport

You saw how to create a custom builder using methodMissing() and propertyMissing(). If you're creating more than one builder, chances are you'd refactor some of the method recognition code into a common base class. That has been done for you already. The class BuilderSupport provides convenience methods that recognize the node structure. Instead of writing the logic to deal with the structure, you simply listen to calls as Groovy traverses the structure and takes appropriate action. Extending the abstract class BuilderSupport feels like working with SAX.[3]

---

3. Simple API for XML (SAX) is a popular event-driven parser for XML. It triggers events on a handler your provide as it parses and recognizes elements and attributes in a document.

Let's look at how to use the builder before figuring out how to implement it, in the spirit of finding out what it does before realizing how it does it:

```
UsingBuilders/UsingTodoBuilderWithSupport.groovy
```

```
bldr = new TodoBuilderWithSupport()

bldr.build {
  Prepare_Vacation (start: '02/15', end: '02/22') {
    Reserve_Flight (on: '01/01', status: 'done')
    Reserve_Hotel(on: '01/02')
    Reserve_Car(on: '01/02')
  }
  Buy_New_Mac {
    Install_QuickSilver
    Install_TextMate
    Install_Groovy {
      Run_all_tests
    }
  }
}
```

The output of running the previous code (once you create the ToDo-BuilderWithSupport) is as follows:

```
To-Do:
 - Prepare Vacation [start: 02/15 end: 02/22]
 x Reserve Flight [on: 01/01]
 - Reserve Hotel [on: 01/02]
 - Reserve Car [on: 01/02]
 - Buy New Mac
  - Install QuickSilver
  - Install TextMate
  - Install Groovy
   - Run all tests
```

BuilderSupport expects you to implement two specific set of methods: set-Parent() and overloaded versions of createNode(). Optionally you can implement other methods such as nodeCompleted(). Remember the different options you have in calling a method; you can call a method with no parameters (foo()), call it with some value (foo(6)), call it with a map (foo(name:'Brad', age: 12)), or call it with a map and a value (foo(name:'Brad', age:12, 6)). BuilderSupport provides four versions of createNode(), one for each of the previous options. The appropriate method is called when you invoke methods on an instance of the builder. The setParent() is called to let you (the author of the builder) know the parent of the current node being processed. Whatever you return from createNode() is considered to be a node, and the builder support sends that as a parameter to nodeCompleted().

The BuilderSupport does not handle missing properties like it handles methods. However, you can still use the propertyMissing() method to handle those cases.

The code for the TodoBuilderWithSupport that extends the BuilderSupport is shown next. The format for the to-do list chosen supports only method calls with no parameters (and properties) and method calls that accept a Map. So in the versions of createNode() that accept an Object parameter, you throw an exception to indicate an invalid format. In the other two versions of that method, and in the propertyMissing() method, you keep track of the level of nesting by incrementing the level variable. You decrement level in the nodeCompleted() method since that's called when you leave a nesting level. In the createNode() methods, you return the name of the node created so you can compare that in nodeCompleted() to find when you exit the topmost node build. If your need is more complex, alternately you can return an instance of your own custom class that represents different nodes. Also, if you need to perform some other operations when a node is created—such as attaching the child nodes to their parent—setParent() is a good place. This method receives the instances of node for the parent and the child—the node object returned by createNode() when those nodes were created. The rest of the code for the TodoBuilderWithSupport is processing the nodes found and creating the desired output.

Play with it to see which methods get called in which order. You can insert a few println statements in these methods to get an understanding of the sequence.

UsingBuilders/TodoBuilderWithSupport.groovy

```groovy
class TodoBuilderWithSupport extends BuilderSupport
{
  int level = 0
  def result = new StringWriter()

  void setParent(parent, child) {}

  def createNode(name)
  {
    if (name == 'build')
    {
      result << "To-Do:\n"
      return 'buildnode'
    }
    else
    {
      return handle(name, [:])
    }
  }
}
```

```groovy
def createNode(name, Object value)
{
  throw new Exception("Invalid format")
}

def createNode(name, Map attribute)
{
  handle(name, attribute)
}

def createNode(name, Map attribute, Object value)
{
  throw new Exception("Invalid format")
}

def propertyMissing(String name)
{
  handle(name, [:])
  level--
}

void nodeCompleted(parent, node)
{
  level--
  if (node == 'buildnode')
  {
    println result
  }
}

def handle(String name, attributes)
{
  level++
  level.times { result << " "}
  result << placeXifStatusDone(attributes)
  result << name.replaceAll("_", " ")
  result << printParameters(attributes)
  result << "\n"
  name
}

def placeXifStatusDone(attributes)
{
    attributes['status'] == 'done' ? "x " : "- "
}

def printParameters(attributes)
{
  def values = ""
  if(attributes.size() > 0)
  {
```

```
      values += "  ["
      def count = 0
      attributes.each { key, value ->
        if (key == 'status') return
        count++
        values += (count > 1 ? " " : "")
        values += "${key}: ${value}"
      }
      values += "]"
    }

    values
  }
}
```

17.5 Using FactoryBuilderSupport

You'll use FactoryBuilderSupport if you're working with well-defined node names such as button, checkbox, label, and so on, in the SwingBuilder. The BuilderSupport you saw in Section 17.4, *Using BuilderSupport*, on page 263 is good for working with hierarchical structures. However, it's not convenient to deal with different types of nodes. Suppose you have to work with twenty different types of nodes. Your implementation of createNode() will get complicated. Based on the name, you'll create different nodes, which leads to a messy switch statement. Chances are you'll quickly lean toward an abstract factory ([GHJV95]) approach to create these nodes. That's what FactoryBuilderSupport does. Based on the node name, it delegates the node creation to different factories. All you have to do is map the names to the factories.

FactoryBuilderSupport was inspired by the SwingBuilder, and in Groovy 1.5, SwingBuilder was modified to extend FactoryBuilderSupport instead of BuilderSupport. Let's take a look at an example of implementing and using a builder that extends FactoryBuilderSupport.

Let's create a builder named RobotBuilder that can create and program a robot. As a first step, think about how you will use it:

UsingBuilders/UsingFactoryBuilderSupport.groovy

```
def bldr = new RobotBuilder()

def robot = bldr.robot('iRobot') {
    forward(dist: 20)
    left(rotation: 90)
    forward(speed: 10, duration: 5)
}

robot.go()
```

You'd like RobotBuilder to take that code and produce this output:

```
Robot iRobot operating...
move distance... 20
turn left... 90 degrees
move distance... 50
```

Now, let's look at the builder. RobotBuilder extends FactoryBuilderSupport. In its instance initializer, you map the node names robot, forward, and left to the corresponding factories using FactoryBuilderSupport's register-Factory() method. That's all you have in RobotBuilder. All the hard work of traversing the hierarchy of nodes and calling the appropriate factory is done by the FactoryBuilderSupport. The factories and nodes, which you'll see soon, take care of the rest of the details:

UsingBuilders/UsingFactoryBuilderSupport.groovy

```
class RobotBuilder extends FactoryBuilderSupport
{
  {
    registerFactory('robot', new RobotFactory())
    registerFactory('forward', new ForwardMoveFactory())
    registerFactory('left', new LeftTurnFactory())
  };
}
```

Classes Robot, ForwardMove, and LeftTurn, shown next, represent the nodes robot, forward, and left, respectively.

UsingBuilders/UsingFactoryBuilderSupport.groovy

```
class Robot
{
  String name
  def movements = []

  void go()
  {
    println "Robot $name operating..."
    movements.each { movement -> println movement }
  }
}

class ForwardMove
{
  def dist
  String toString() { "move distance... $dist"}
}

class LeftTurn
{
  def rotation
  String toString() { "turn left... $rotation degrees"}
}
```

The Robot has a name property and an ArrayList of movements. Its go() method traverses each movement and prints the details. The other two classes, ForwardMove and LeftTurn, have one property each. Even though the class ForwardMove has only one property named dist, in the code shown at the beginning of this section you've assigned properties speed and duration for the left node. The factory will take care of working with these properties as you'll see soon.

Let's look at the factories. FactoryBuilderSupport relies upon the Factory interface. This interface provides methods to control the creation of a node, handles setting the node's properties, sets the parent and child relationships between nodes, and determines whether the node is a leaf node. A default implementation of Factory called AbstractFactory is already provided in Groovy, as shown here:

```
// Excerpt of AbstractFactory.java - part of Groovy
public abstract class AbstractFactory implements Factory
{
    public boolean isLeaf() { return false; }

    public boolean onHandleNodeAttributes(FactoryBuilderSupport builder,
            Object node, Map attributes ) { return true; }

    public void onNodeCompleted(FactoryBuilderSupport builder,
            Object parent, Object node ) { }

    public void setParent(FactoryBuilderSupport builder,
            Object parent, Object child ) { }

    public void setChild(FactoryBuilderSupport builder,
            Object parent, Object child ) { }
}
```

The default implementation of isLeaf() returns false to indicate that the node can have a closure with subnodes. The onHandleNodeAttributes() is a good place for any special handling of properties, like the duration and speed of the left node. Within this method, you'll remove from attributes any property that you have processed. If you return true, as in the default implementation, FactoryBuilderSupport will populate any remaining properties found in attributes into the node instance. The method onNodeCompleted() is called when the processing of the node is completed, and you can perform any final operations at the end of node creation you like. setParent() is called on the child node's factory so you can set up any parent-child relationship. Similarly, setChild() is called on the parent node's factory. The only method from Factory that's missing in AbstractFactory is the newInstance() method that is responsible for instantiating the actual node.

In this example, you need a factory for Robot, ForwardMove, and LeftTurn. The classes RobotFactory, ForwardMoveFactory, and LeftTurnFactory are as follows:

UsingBuilders/UsingFactoryBuilderSupport.groovy

```groovy
class RobotFactory extends AbstractFactory
{
  def newInstance(FactoryBuilderSupport builder, name, value, Map attributes )
  {
      new Robot(name: value)
  }

  void setChild(FactoryBuilderSupport builder, Object parent, Object child)
  {
    parent.movements << child
  }
}

class ForwardMoveFactory extends AbstractFactory
{
  boolean isLeaf() { true }

  def newInstance(FactoryBuilderSupport builder, name, value, Map attributes )
  {
    new ForwardMove()
  }

  boolean onHandleNodeAttributes(FactoryBuilderSupport builder,
              Object node, Map attributes) {
    if (attributes.speed && attributes.duration)
    {
        node.dist = attributes.speed * attributes.duration
        attributes.remove('speed')
        attributes.remove('duration')
    }

    true
  }
}

class LeftTurnFactory extends AbstractFactory
{
  boolean isLeaf() { true }

  def newInstance(FactoryBuilderSupport builder, name, value, Map attributes)
  {
    new LeftTurn()
  }
}
```

In each factory's newInstance() method, you instantiate the appropriate node. In the RobotFactory's setChild(), you add the movement node to Robot's list of movements. Since forward and left are leaf nodes, in their factory's isLeaf() method you return true. You support the special properties of the forward node in the ForwardMoveFactory's onHandleNodeAttributes().

Let's take a minute to see the benefit of the isLeaf() methods. In the following example, you provide a closure to the forward node:

UsingBuilders/UsingFactoryBuilderSupport.groovy

```
def robotBldr = new RobotBuilder()
robotBldr.robot('bRobot') {
  forward(dist: 20) { }
}
```

The FactoryBuilderSupport class realizes that the forward node can't have nested levels and so rejects it, as shown here:

```
java.lang.RuntimeException: 'forward' doesn't support nesting.
```

The implementation of a builder to deal with multiple well-defined nodes is a lot cleaner with FactoryBuilderSupport than with BuilderSupport. FactoryBuilderSupport provides other convenience methods to intercept the life cycle of node creation, so you can take more control of the node traversal, if you want. For example, you can use the preInstantiate() method to perform actions before the factory creates a node, or you can perform actions after a node is completed by overriding postNodeCompletion(). If you have a need to perform other tasks while building, you can use convenience methods like getCurrentNode() and getParentNode() of FactoryBuilderSupport to easily work with the hierarchical structure you're creating. Refer to http://groovy.codehaus.org/FactoryBuilderSupportas well as http://groovy.codehaus.org/api/groovy/util/FactoryBuilderSupport.htmlfor more details on the builder and its API.

In this chapter, you saw how to use Groovy's builders. Builders provide you with a DSL syntax to perform mundane tasks such as creating an XML or HTML document. You can use one of the builders provided or create your own custom builder, as you saw in this chapter. And if you create a useful builder, consider contributing it to the community.

Chapter 18

Creating DSLs in Groovy

Domain-specific languages (DSLs) are "targeted at a particular type of problem."[1] Their syntax is focused on the intended domain or problem. You don't use them for general-purpose programming like you use Java, Groovy, or C++, because DSLs have a very limited scope and capability.

A DSL is small, simple,[2] expressive, and focused on a problem area or domain. DSLs have two characteristics: they're context-driven and fluent.

DSLs have been around for a long time. Chances are you've worked with them in applications with special keyword input files used to communicate with external applications. Ant is an example of a DSL. Gant (see Appendix A, on page 287 for reference) is also an example of a DSL. Specifically, it's a wrapper around Ant that uses Groovy instead of XML to specify build tasks.

The dynamic nature of Groovy and its metaprogramming capabilities makes it attractive for building DSLs. In this chapter, you'll learn about DSLs and how to use Groovy to build them.

18.1 Context

Context is one of the characteristics of a DSL. As humans, we rely heavily on context when we communicate. We're efficient, and context provides for continuity in our conversations. The other day I heard my

---

1. See the reference to Marin Fowler's discussions on DSLs in Appendix A, on page 287.
2. However, it may not be simple to design, though.

friend Neal holler, "Venti latte with two extra shots!" He's using the Star-
bucks DSL. Nowhere did he mention the word "coffee," but he sure got a
very good one, at a high price. That's context-driven. I heard my friend
Scott respond to a question, "Place a $ in a GString." I have no doubt
he was teaching how to create a printable expression in Groovy[3]—that
again is context-driven.

Let's look at Java code to order pizza. This code lacks context. The
reference joesPizza is used repeatedly:

CreatingDSLs/OrderPizza.java

```java
//Java code
package com.agiledeveloper;

public class OrderPizza
{
  public static void main(String[] args)
  {
    PizzaShop joesPizza = new PizzaShop();
    joesPizza.setSize(Size.LARGE);
    joesPizza.setCrust(Crust.THIN);
    joesPizza.setTopping("Olives", "Onions", "Bell Pepper");
    joesPizza.setAddress("101 Main St., ...");
    int time = joesPizza.setCard(CardType.VISA, "1234-1234-1234-1234");
    System.out.printf("Pizza will arrive in %d minutes\n", time);
  }
}
```

The same code written in Groovy is less cluttered, thanks to the iden-
tity() method (see Section 8.1, *Object Extensions*, on page 133):

CreatingDSLs/OrderPizza.groovy

```groovy
import com.agiledeveloper.*

PizzaShop joesPizza = new PizzaShop()
joesPizza.identity {
    setSize(Size.LARGE)
    setCrust(Crust.THIN)
    setTopping("Olives", "Onions", "Bell Pepper")
    setAddress("101 Main St., ...")
    int time = setCard(CardType.VISA, "1234-1234-1234-1234")
    printf("Pizza will arrive in %d minutes\n", time)
}
```

---

3. See Section 6.1, *Literals and Expressions*, on page 101.

Since parentheses are almost optional in Groovy (see Section 18.8, *The Parentheses Limitation and a Workaround*, on page 281) and typing is also optional, you can make the previous code a tad lighter:

CreatingDSLs/OrderPizza2.groovy

```
import com.agiledeveloper.*

PizzaShop joesPizza = new PizzaShop()
joesPizza.identity {
    setSize Size.LARGE
    setCrust Crust.THIN
    setTopping "Olives", "Onions", "Bell Pepper"
    setAddress "101 Main St., ..."
    time = setCard(CardType.VISA, "1234-1234-1234-1234")
    printf "Pizza will arrive in %d minutes\n", time
}
```

Context makes things terse (in a good way), less cluttered, and effective.

18.2 Fluency

Fluency is another characteristic of a DSL. It helps make code readable and flow naturally. It's not easy to design for fluency, but you should do it so it's easier on your users. We'll now discuss some examples of fluency and explore a few ways to write loops in Groovy:

CreatingDSLs/FluentLoops.groovy

```
// Traditional Looping
for(int i = 0; i < 10; i++)
{
  println(i);
}

// Groovy ways
for(i in 0..9) { println i }

0.upto(9) { println it }

10.times { println it }
```

All the previous loops produce the same result. Groovy provides fluency for looping, among other things. Fluency is not restricted to Groovy. EasyMock (which inspired the Groovy mock library) exhibits fluency in setting up the mock expectations in Java:

```
expect(alarm.raise()).andReturn(true);
expect(alarm.raise()).andThrow(new InvalidStateException());
```

The previous code indicates that the alarm mock should return true on the first call and throw an exception on the second.

You can find another good example of a DSL in Grails/GORM. For example, you can specify data constraints on an object's properties using the following syntax:

```
class State
{
        String twoLetterCode

        static constraints = {
                twoLetterCode unique: true, blank: false, size: 2..2
        }
}
```

Grails smartly recognizes this fluent and expressive syntax for expressing the constraints and generates the validation logic both for the front end and for the back end.

Groovy builders (see Chapter 17, *Groovy Builders*, on page 255) are good examples of DSLs. They're fluent and built on context.

18.3 Types of DSLs

When designing a DSL, you have to decide between two types—external and internal.

An external DSL defines a new language. You have the flexibility to choose the syntax. You then parse the commands in your new language to take actions. When I took my first job, the company asked me to maintain a DSL that needed extensive use of lex and yacc.[4] The parsing was a lot of "fun." You can use languages such as C++ and Java that do heavyweight lifting for you with the support of extensive parsing capabilities and libraries. For example, you can use ANTLR to build DSLs ([Par07]).

An internal DSL, also called an *embedded DSL*, defines a new language as well but within the syntactical confines of another languages. You don't use any parsers, but you have to construe the syntax by tactfully mapping to constructs such as methods and properties in the underlying language. The users of your internal DSL might not realize they're

---

4. I first thought they asked me to do it because I was good. I later understood they don't ask a new employee to do stuff because they're good but because no one else wants to do it!

using syntax of a broader language. However, creating the internal DSL takes significant design effort and clever tricks to make the underlying language work for you.

I mentioned Ant and Gant earlier. Ant, which uses XML, is an example of an external DSL. Gant, on the other hand, uses Groovy to solve the same problem and is an example of an internal DSL.

18.4 Designing Internal DSLs

Dynamic languages are better suited to designing and implementing internal DSLs. They have good metaprogramming capabilities and flexible syntax, and you can easily load and execute code fragments.

Not all dynamic languages are created equal, however.

I find it very easy to create DSLs in Ruby, for example. It is dynamically typed, parentheses are optional, the symbol (:) can be used instead of double quoting strings, and so on. The elegance of Ruby heavily favors creating internal DSLs.

Creating internal DSLs in Python can be a bit of a challenge. The significant whitespace can be a hindrance.

Groovy's dynamic typing and metaprogramming capabilities help a great deal. However, it's picky about parentheses and does not have the elegant symbol that Ruby does. You will have to work around some of these restrictions, as you'll see later.

It takes significant time, patience, and effort to design an internal DSL. So, be creative, tactfully work around issues, and be willing to compromise at places to succeed in your design efforts.

18.5 Groovy and DSLs

Groovy has a number of key capabilities to help create internal DSLs, including the following:

- Dynamic and optional typing (Section 4.5, *Optional Typing*, on page 74).
- The flexibility to load scripts dynamically, manipulate, and execute (Section 11.6, *Using Groovy Scripts from Groovy*, on page 171).

- Groovy classes are open, thanks to categories and ExpandoMeta-Class (see Chapter 14, *MOP Method Injection and Synthesis*, on page 197).
- Closures provide a nice context for execution (Chapter 5, *Using Closures*, on page 81).
- Operator overloading helps freely define operators (Section 3.6, *Operator Overloading*, on page 44).
- Builder support (Chapter 17, *Groovy Builders*, on page 255).
- Flexible parentheses.[5]

In the rest of this chapter, you'll look at examples of creating DSLs in Groovy using these capabilities.

18.6 Closures and DSLs

The identity() method helps delegate calls within a closure, giving you a context of execution. You can take advantage of this approach to create your own methods with context and fluency.

Let's revisit the pizza-ordering example. Say you want to create a syntax that flows naturally. You don't want to create an instance of PizzaShop because that is more of an implementation detail. You want the context to be implicit. Let's take a look at the following code (wait until the next section to see how you can make this more fluent and context-driven):

CreatingDSLs/ClosureHelp.groovy

```
time = getPizza {
  setSize Size.LARGE
  setCrust Crust.THIN
  setTopping "Olives", "Onions", "Bell Pepper"
  setAddress "101 Main St., ..."
  setCard(CardType.VISA, "1234-1234-1234-1234")
}

printf "Pizza will arrive in %d minutes\n", time
```

The getPizza() method accepts a closure within which you call methods to order pizza using the instance methods of a PizzaShop class. However, the instance of that class is implicit. The delegate (see Section 5.8,

---

5. This is useful and annoying at the same time. Groovy requires no parentheses for calling methods that take parameters but insists on having them for methods with no parameters. See Section 18.8, *The Parentheses Limitation and a Workaround*, on page 281 for a simple trick to work around this annoyance.

Closure Delegation, on page 96) takes care of routing the methods to the implicit instance, as you can see in the implementation of the following getPizza() method:

```
CreatingDSLs/ClosureHelp.groovy

def getPizza(closure)
{
  PizzaShop pizzaShop = new PizzaShop()
  closure.delegate = pizzaShop
  closure()
}
```

The output from executing the call to the getPizza() code is as follows:

```
Pizza will arrive in 25 minutes
```

Wait a second, how did you get the time value printed in the output? Because the last statement in getPizza() was a call to the closure, whatever it returned, getPizza() returned. The last statement within the closure is setCard(), so its result was returned to the caller. This DSL imposes ordering: the setCard() must be the last method called to order pizza. You can work on improving the interface so the ordering is more obvious. Also, you can replace calls to set methods like setSize Size.LARGE with assignment statements like size = Size.LARGE, if you want.

18.7 Method Interception and DSLs

You can implement the DSL for ordering pizza without really using a PizzaShop class. You can do that by purely intercepting method calls. Let's first start with the code to order pizza (stored in a file named orderPizza.dsl):

```
CreatingDSLs/orderPizza.dsl

size large
crust thin
topping Olives, Onions, Bell_Pepper
address "101 Main St., ..."
card visa, '1234-1234-1234-1234'
```

It hardly looks like code. It looks more like a data file. However, that's pure Groovy code, and you're going to execute it.[6] But before that, you have to perform a few tricks, er, I mean design your DSL.

---

6. Everything you see in that file, except the strings in double quotes, are either method names or variable names.

Let's create a file named GroovyPizzaDSL.groovy and in it define the variables large, thin, and visa (other variables like small, thick, masterCard can be defined at will). Now define a method acceptOrder() that will call into a closure that will eventually execute your DSL. Also implement the methodMissing() method that will be called for any method that does not exist (pretty much all methods called in your DSL file orderPizza.dsl).

CreatingDSLs/GroovyPizzaDSL.groovy

```groovy
def large = 'large'
def thin = 'thin'
def visa = 'Visa'
def Olives = 'Olives'
def Onions = 'Onions'
def Bell_Pepper = 'Bell Pepper'

orderInfo = [:]

def methodMissing(String name, args)
{
  orderInfo[name] = args
}

def acceptOrder(closure)
{
  closure.delegate = this
  closure()
  println "Validation and processing performed here for order received:"
  orderInfo.each { key, value ->
    println "${key} -> ${value.join(', ')}"
    }
}
```

You have to figure out a way to put these two files together and execute. You can do that quite easily (see Section 11.6, *Using Groovy Scripts from Groovy*, on page 171), as shown next. Invoke GroovyShell, load the previous two scripts, form into a cohesive script, and evaluate.

CreatingDSLs/GroovyPizzaOrderProcess.groovy

```groovy
def dslDef = new File('GroovyPizzaDSL.groovy').text
def dsl = new File('orderPizza.dsl').text

def script = """
${dslDef}
acceptOrder {
  ${dsl}
}
"""

new GroovyShell().evaluate(script)
```

The output from the previous code is as follows:

```
Validation and processing performed here for order received:
size -> large
crust -> thin
topping -> Olives, Onions, Bell Pepper
address -> 101 Main St., ...
card -> Visa, 1234-1234-1234-1234
```

As you can see, designing and executing a DSL in Groovy (as in order-pizza.dsl) is pretty easy if you know how to exploit its MOP capabilities.

18.8 The Parentheses Limitation and a Workaround

Let's leave the pizza example behind and move on to look at a simple register. This section will show how to create a DSL for a simple register, the device that lets you total amounts. Here is the first attempt to create that:

CreatingDSLs/Total.groovy

```groovy
value = 0
def clear() { value = 0 }
def add(number) { value += number }
def total() { println "Total is $value" }

clear()
add 2
add 5
add 7
total()
```

The output from the previous code is as follows:

```
Total is 14
```

In this code, you wrote total() and clear() instead of total and clear, respectively. Let's drop the parentheses and try to call total:

CreatingDSLs/Total.groovy

```groovy
try
{
  total
}
catch(Exception ex)
{
  println ex
}
```

Executing the previous code gives the following result:

```
org.codehaus.groovy.runtime.metaclass.MissingPropertyExceptionNoStack:
  No such property: total for class: Total
```

Groovy thinks that the call to total refers to a (nonexistent) property. Working with a language to design a DSL is like playing with a 2-year-old: you don't fight with the kid when he gets cranky; you go along a little bit. So, in this case, tell Groovy that it's OK and work with it. Simply create the properties it wants:

```
value = 0
def getClear() { value = 0 }
def add(number) { value += number }
def getTotal() { println "Total is $value" }
```

You wrote properties with the names total and clear by writing the methods getTotal() and getClear(). Now, Groovy is quite happy (like the kid) to play with us, and you can call these properties without parentheses:

```
clear
add 2
add 5
add 7
total
clear
total
```

The output from the previous code is as follows:

```
Total is 14
Total is 0
```

18.9 Categories and DSLs

Categories allow you to intercept method calls in a controlled fashion.[7] You can put that to use in creating a DSL. Let's figure out ways to implement the following fluent call: 2.days.ago.at(4.30).

2 is an instance of Integer, and you know that days is not a property on it. You'll inject that, using categories, as a property (the getDays() method). The days is just noise. It provides connectivity in the sentence "two days ago at 4.30." You can implement the method getDays() that accepts Integer and returns the received instance. In the getAgo() method (for the ago property), accept an instance of Integer, and return so many

---

7. See Section 14.1, *Injecting Methods Using Categories*, on page 198.

days before the current date using the operations on the Calendar class. Finally, in the at() method, set the time on that date to the time given, and return an instance of Date. All this can be used within the use() block, as shown in the following code:[8]

CreatingDSLs/DSLUsingCategory.groovy

```groovy
class DateUtil
{
  static int getDays(Integer self) { self }

  static Calendar getAgo(Integer self)
  {
    def date = Calendar.instance
    date.add(Calendar.DAY_OF_MONTH, -self)
    date
  }

  static Date at(Calendar self, Double time)
  {
    def hour = (int)(time.doubleValue())
    def minute = (int)(Math.round((time.doubleValue() - hour) * 100))
    self.set(Calendar.HOUR_OF_DAY, hour)
    self.set(Calendar.MINUTE, minute)
    self.set(Calendar.SECOND, 0)
    self.time
  }
}

use(DateUtil)
{
  println 2.days.ago.at(4.30)
}
```

The output from the previous code is as follows:

```
Thu Jan 31 04:30:00 MST 2008
```

A final concern with the DSL syntax created here is that you used 2.days.ago.at(4.30). It's more natural to use 4:30 instead of 4.30, so it would be nice to instead use 2.days.ago.at(4:30). Groovy allows you to accept a Map as a parameter to methods.

---

8. I'm not performing error checking on the time you provide, so you can send 4.70 if you'd like instead of 5:10; it's an undocumented feature. Also, you may want to clone the instance of Calendar given to you and modify the clone to avoid any side effects in other places where you may use these methods.

By defining the parameter of the method ago() as Map instead of Double, you can achieve that, as shown here:

CreatingDSLs/DSLUsingCategory2.groovy

```groovy
class DateUtil
{
  static int getDays(Integer self) { self }

  static Calendar getAgo(Integer self)
  {
    def date = Calendar.instance
    date.add(Calendar.DAY_OF_MONTH, -self)
    date
  }

  static Date at(Calendar self, Map time)
  {
    def hour = 0
    def minute = 0
    time.each {key, value -> hour = key.toInteger()
      minute = value.toInteger()
      }
    self.set(Calendar.HOUR_OF_DAY, hour)
    self.set(Calendar.MINUTE, minute)
    self.set(Calendar.SECOND, 0)
    self.time
  }
}

use(DateUtil)
{
  println 2.days.ago.at(4:30)
}
```

The output from the previous code is as follows:

```
Thu Jan 31 04:30:00 MST 2008
```

The only restriction in this approach using categories is that you can use the DSL only within the use() blocks. This may not be such a severe restriction. It might actually be good because the method injection is controlled. Once you leave the block of code, the methods injected are forgotten, which might be desirable. In Section 18.10, *ExpandoMeta-Class and DSLs*, on the next page, you will see how to implement the same syntax using ExpandoMetaClass.

18.10 ExpandoMetaClass and DSLs

Categories take effect only within the use blocks, and their effect is fairly limited in scope. If you want the method injection to be effective throughout your application, you can use the ExpandoMetaClass instead of categories. Let's use ExpandoMetaClass to implement the DSL syntax you saw in the previous section:

CreatingDSLs/DSLUsingExpandoMetaClass.groovy

```
Integer.metaClass.getDays = { ->
  delegate
}

Integer.metaClass.getAgo = { ->
    def date = Calendar.instance
    date.add(Calendar.DAY_OF_MONTH, -delegate)
    date
  }

Calendar.metaClass.at = { Map time ->
    def hour = 0
    def minute = 0
    time.each {key, value -> hour = key.toInteger()
      minute = value.toInteger()
      }
    delegate.set(Calendar.HOUR_OF_DAY, hour)
    delegate.set(Calendar.MINUTE, minute)
    delegate.set(Calendar.SECOND, 0)
    delegate.time
}

try
{
  println 2.days.ago.at(4:30)
}
catch(Exception ex)
{
  println ex
}
```

If you try to run this code, you will get an exception:

```
groovy.lang.MissingMethodException:
  No signature of method: java.util.GregorianCalendar.at()
  is applicable for argument types: (java.util.LinkedHashMap) values: {[4:30]}
```

The reason for this exception is that the method was added to the interface Calendar, and by default ExpandoMetaClass does not provide that to inheriting/implementing classes. One solution is to add the at() method to the class GregorianCalendar. However, that would be wrong in principle since you're not supposed to know the details of the implementation while working at the level of interfaces. You can fix this problem by adding one line of code before any other code is executed. Put the following at the top of the code and rerun the code: ExpandoMetaClass.enableGlobally() (see Section 14.2, *Injecting Methods Using ExpandoMetaClass*, on page 203). The output from the previous code after this change is as follows:

```
Fri Nov 23 04:30:00 MST 2007
```

As you learned in this chapter, creating an internal DSL in Groovy is fairly easy. The dynamic nature and optional typing allows you to create a fluent interface. Closures help you create context. Groovy's categories and ExpandoMetaClass are helpful to inject, intercept, and synthesize method calls and properties. Finally, Groovy's ability to load and execute arbitrary scripts comes in handy to execute the DSLs.

Appendix A

Web Resources

Groovy Home . . . . http://groovy.codehaus.org
Home of the Groovy project for documentation and downloads.

Groovy Download Page . . . . http://groovy.codehaus.org/Download
Direct link to the Groovy download page for latest released version and previous
versions.

Groovy Daily Build . . . . http://build.canoo.com/groovy
Place to download current builds of Groovy project, if you like to stay on the
bleeding edge.

Groovy API Javadoc . . . . http://groovy.codehaus.org/api
Javadoc for the Groovy API.

The GDK . . . . http://groovy.codehaus.org/groovy-jdk
List of the methods that are part of the Groovy JDK—Groovy extensions to the
JDK.

Markmail for Groovy Mailing List . . . . http://groovy.markmail.org
Convenient place to search for any topics discussed in the Groovy users mailing
list.

Groovy Mailing Lists . . . . http://groovy.codehaus.org/Mailing+Lists
List and details of Groovy mailing lists.

A Bit of Groovy History . . . . . http://glaforge.free.fr/weblog/index.php?itemid=99
A blog by Guillaume Laforge on Groovy history.

MetaClass and Method Interception. . .
. . . http:
//graemerocher.blogspot.com/2007/06/dynamic-groovy-groovys-equivalent-to.html
A blog by Graeme Rocher on Groovy's metaprogramming capabilities and open
classes.

Gant Home . . . . http://gant.codehaus.org
A site for Gant, which is like Ant but uses Groovy instead of XML.

Groovy Scriptom API . . . . .http://groovy.codehaus.org/COM+Scripting
Groovy API that allows you to interact with Windows ActiveX and COM.

Groovy Closures Definition . . .
. . . http://groovy.codehaus.org/Closures+-+Formal+Definition
Discussions and definition of Groovy closures.

Some Differences Between Java and Groovy . . .
. . . http://groovy.codehaus.org/Differences+from+Java
List and details of some differences between Java and Groovy.

Eclipse Plug-in for Groovy . . . . .http://groovy.codehaus.org/Eclipse+Plugin
Plug-in for Groovy development on the Eclipse IDE.

IntelliJ IDEA . . . . http://www.jetbrains.com/idea
Popular Java IDE with exceptional Groovy support.

TextMate . . . . .http://macromates.com
TextMate, a popular editor on the Mac.

TextMate Groovy Bundle . . .
. . . http://docs.codehaus.org/display/GROOVY/TextMate
Groovy bundle for TextMate, a popular editor on the Mac.

Tweaking the Groovy Bundle for TextMate Editor . . .
. . . http://tinyurl.com/ywotsj
Venkat's blog on a tweak to Groovy bundle for the easy/quick display of output.

Using Notepad2 . . . . http://tinyurl.com/yqfucf
A blog entry showing how to use Notepad2 to edit and run Groovy on Windows.

E Text Editor . . . . http://www.e-texteditor.com
TextMate-like editor for Windows.

FactoryBuilderSupport . . . . .http://groovy.codehaus.org/FactoryBuilderSupport
Groovy's FactoryBuilderSupport class, which is the new base class for SwingBuilder.

API for FactoryBuilderSupport . . .
. . . http://groovy.codehaus.org/api/groovy/util/FactoryBuilderSupport.html
API for the FactoryBuilderSupport class, which is the new base class for Swing-Builder.

Groovy String Support . . .
. . . http://groovy.codehaus.org/groovy-jdk/java/lang/String.html
Extensions and support for Strings in Groovy.

Groovy Looping . . . . http://groovy.codehaus.org/Looping
Shows different ways to loop in Groovy.

Groovy Collections Support...

. . . http://groovy.codehaus.org/groovy-jdk/java/util/Collection.html

Extensions and features Groovy has added to collections.

Groovy's Support for Map...

. . . http://groovy.codehaus.org/groovy-jdk/java/util/Map.html

Extensions and features Groovy has added to Java's Map.

SwingX UI . . . . http://swingx.dev.java.net

SwingX UI Library—SwingLabs extensions to Swing.

SwingXBuilder . . . . http://groovy.codehaus.org/SwingXBuilder

Details about the SwingXBuilder—Groovy's support for building SwingX UI applications.

JIDE . . . . https://jide-oss.dev.java.net

JIDE Swing component library.

Builder for JIDE . . . . http://groovy.codehaus.org/JideBuilder

JideBuilder for using JIDE in Groovy.

GraphicsBuilder . . . . http://groovy.codehaus.org/GraphicsBuilder

GraphicsBuilder for building JavaFX-type Java2D graphics.

Groovy's Support for java.math Classes...

. . . http://groovy.codehaus.org/Groovy+Math

Groovy support of java.math classes to provide better accuracy.

State of IDE Support for Groovy . . . . http://groovy.codehaus.org/IDE+Support

Different IDEs that support Groovy development and their current state.

Groovy Operator Overloading...

. . . http://groovy.codehaus.org/Operator+Overloading

Groovy operator overloads and their method mapping.

Runtime vs. Compile Time/Static vs. Dynamic...

. . . http://groovy.codehaus.org/Runtime+vs+Compile+time,+Static+vs+Dynamic

Discussions and rationale for Groovy's support of dynamic typing.

Using JUnit 4 with Groovy...

. . . http://groovy.codehaus.org/Using+JUnit+4+with+Groovy

Steps to use JUnit 4.0 with Groovy.

JRuby Home . . . . http://jruby.codehaus.org

Home of the JRuby project for documentation and downloads.

Grails Home . . . . http://grails.org/

Home of the Grails project for documentation and downloads.

Getting Started with Grails . . . . http://www.infoq.com/minibooks/grails

Jason Rudolph's book on working with Grails.

Sun/Java Scripting Project Home . . . . https://scripting.dev.java.net
Details about scripting languages and JSR 223: Scripting for the Java Platform.

Java Download . . . . http://java.sun.com/javase/downloads/index.jsp
Download page for Java and JDK.

Why Getter and Setter Methods Are Evil. . .
. . . http://www.javaworld.com/javaworld/jw-09-2003/jw-0905-toolbox.html
An article by Allen Holub.

Why Copying an Object Is a Terrible Thing to Do. . .
. . . http://www.agiledeveloper.com/articles/cloning072002.htm
An article that addresses issues with object copying in Java.

Xerces XML Parser . . . . http://xerces.apache.org/xerces-j
Popular Java-based XML parser.

Higher-Order Function . . . . http://c2.com/cgi/wiki?HigherOrderFunction
Discussions on higher-order functions.

Duck Typing . . . . http://c2.com/cgi/wiki?DuckTyping
What's duck typing?

Why Scripting Languages Matter http://www.oreillynet.com/pub/wlg/3190
Tim O'Reilly discussing the nature of applications and the role played by scripting languages.

Technical Debt . . . . http://martinfowler.com/bliki/TechnicalDebt.html
Martin Fowler discussing the term *technical debt*.

Mocks Aren't Stubs . . . . http://martinfowler.com/articles/mocksArentStubs.html
Martin Fowler discussing the similarities and difference between mocks and stubs.

Good, Bad, and Ugly of Java Generics. . .
. . . http://www.agiledeveloper.com/articles/GenericsInJavaPartI.pdf
An article discussing the good, bad, and the ugliness of Java Generics.

Languages and Idioms http://tinyurl.com/2kpsm4
A blog entry discussing languages and idioms.

Experience with GSQL http://tinyurl.com/327dmm
A blog entry about experiences using GSQL.

Crash of the Mars Orbiter. . .
. . . http://www.cnn.com/TECH/space/9909/30/mars.metric.02
CNN coverage of the crash of the Mars Orbiter.

Clip from *Raiders of the Lost Ark*. . .
. . . http://www.youtube.com/watch?v=m5TcfywPj0E
Sword fight scene from the movie *Raiders of the Lost Ark*.

Pragmatic Programmer .... http://pragprog.com
Web site of the publisher of this book.

No Fluff Just Stuff .... http:www.nofluffjuststuff.com
A popular traveling Java conference.

Appendix B

Bibliography

[Bec96]   Kent Beck. *Smalltalk Best Practice Patterns*. Prentice Hall, Englewood Cliffs, NJ, 1996.

[Bec02]   Kent Beck. *Test Driven Development: By Example*. Addison-Wesley, Reading, MA, 2002.

[ES90]   Margaret A. Ellis and Bjarne Stroustrup. *The Annotated C++ Reference Manual*. Addison-Wesley Longman, Boston, MA, 1990.

[Fea04]   Michael Feathers. *Working Effectively with Legacy Code*. Prentice Hall, Englewood Cliffs, NJ, 2004.

[Fri97]   Jeffrey E. F. Friedl. *Mastering Regular Expressions*. O'Reilly & Associates, Inc, Sebastopol, CA, 1997.

[GHJV95]   Erich Gamma, Richard Helm, Ralph Johnson, and John Vlissides. *Design Patterns: Elements of Reusable Object-Oriented Software*. Addison-Wesley, Reading, MA, 1995.

[Gra07]   James Edward Gray II. *TextMate: Power Editing for the Mac*. The Pragmatic Programmers, LLC, Raleigh, NC, and Dallas, TX, 2007.

[HT03]   Andrew Hunt and David Thomas. *Pragmatic Unit Testing In Java with JUnit*. The Pragmatic Programmers, LLC, Raleigh, NC, and Dallas, TX, 2003.

[Knu97]   Donald Ervin Knuth. *The Art of Computer Programming: Fundamental Algorithms*, volume 1. Addison Wesley Longman, Reading, MA, third edition, 1997.

[Lad03]   Ramnivas Laddad. *AspectJ in Action: Practical Aspect-Oriented Programming*. Manning Publications Co., 2003.

[Mey97]   Bertrand Meyer. *Object-Oriented Software Construction*. Prentice Hall, Englewood Cliffs, NJ, second edition, 1997.

[Par07]   Terence Parr. *The Definitive ANTLR Reference: Building Domain-Specific Languages*. The Pragmatic Programmers, LLC, Raleigh, NC, and Dallas, TX, 2007.

[Rai04]   J. B. Rainsberger. *JUnit Recipes : Practical Methods for Programmer Testing*. Manning Publications Co., Greenwich, CT, 2004.

[Roc06]   Graeme Rocher. *The Definitive Guide to Grails*. Apress, Berkeley, CA, 2006.

[Rud07]   Jason Rudolph. *Getting Started with Grails*. InfoQ, 2007.

[Seb04]   Robert W. Sebesta. *Concepts of Programming Languages*. Addison-Wesley, Reading, MA, 2004.

[SH07]   Justin Gehtland Stuart Halloway. *Rails for Java Developers*. The Pragmatic Programmers, LLC, Raleigh, NC, and Dallas, TX, 2007.

[Tat06]   Bruce Tate. *From Java to Ruby: Things Every Manager Should Know*. The Pragmatic Programmers, LLC, Raleigh, NC, and Dallas, TX, 2006.

[TH05]   David Thomas and David Heinemeier Hansson. *Agile Web Development with Rails*. The Pragmatic Programmers, LLC, Raleigh, NC, and Dallas, TX, 2005.

Index

Groovy and More...

Groovy Recipes

See how to speed up nearly every aspect of the development process using *Groovy Recipes*. Groovy makes mundane file management tasks like copying and renaming files trivial. Reading and writing XML has never been easier with XmlParsers and XmlBuilders. Breathe new life into Arrays, Maps, and Lists with a number of convenience methods. Learn all about Grails, and go beyond beyond HTML into the world of Web Services: REST, JSON, Atom, Podcasting, and much much more.

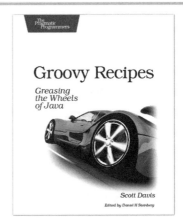

Groovy Recipes: Greasing the Wheels of Java
Scott Davis
(264 pages) ISBN: 978-0-9787392-9-4. $34.95
http://pragprog.com/titles/sdgrvr

Prototype and script.aculo.us

Tired of getting swamped in the nitty-gritty of cross-browser, Web 2.0–grade JavaScript? Get back in the game with Prototype and script.aculo.us, two extremely popular JavaScript libraries that make it a walk in the park. Be it Ajax, drag and drop, autocompletion, advanced visual effects, or many other great features, all you need is write one or two lines of script that look so good they could almost pass for Ruby code!

Prototype and script.aculo.us: You never knew JavaScript could do this!
Christophe Porteneuve
(330 pages) ISBN: 1-934356-01-8. $34.95
http://pragprog.com/titles/cppsu

The Pragmatic Bookshelf

The Pragmatic Bookshelf features books written by developers for developers. The titles continue the well-known Pragmatic Programmer style and continue to garner awards and rave reviews. As development gets more and more difficult, the Pragmatic Programmers will be there with more titles and products to help you stay on top of your game.

Visit Us Online

Programming Groovy's Home Page
http://pragprog.com/titles/vslg
Source code from this book, errata, and other resources. Come give us feedback, too!

Register for Updates
http://pragprog.com/updates
Be notified when updates and new books become available.

Join the Community
http://pragprog.com/community
Read our weblogs, join our online discussions, participate in our mailing list, interact with our wiki, and benefit from the experience of other Pragmatic Programmers.

New and Noteworthy
http://pragprog.com/news
Check out the latest pragmatic developments in the news.

Save on the PDF

Save on the PDF version of this book. Owning the paper version of this book entitles you to purchase the PDF version at a terrific discount. The PDF is great for carrying around on your laptop. It's hyperlinked, has color, and is fully searchable.

Buy it now at pragprog.com/coupon.

Contact Us

Phone Orders:	1-800-699-PROG (+1 919 847 3884)
Online Orders:	www.pragprog.com/catalog
Customer Service:	orders@pragprog.com
Non-English Versions:	translations@pragprog.com
Pragmatic Teaching:	academic@pragprog.com
Author Proposals:	proposals@pragprog.com